REGNUM STUDIES IN MISSION

Trinity in Dialogue with Muslims

Series Preface

Regnum Studies in Mission are born from the lived experience of Christians and Christian communities in mission, especially but not solely in the fast growing churches among the poor of the world. These churches have more to tell than stories of growth. They are making significant impacts on their cultures in the cause of Christ. They are producing 'cultural products' which express the reality of Christian faith, hope and love in their societies.

Regnum Studies in Mission are the fruit often of rigorous research to the highest international standards and always of authentic Christian engagement in the transformation of people and societies. And these are for the world. The formation of Christian theology, missiology and practice in the twenty-first century will depend to a great extent on the active participation of growing churches contributing biblical and culturally appropriate expressions of Christian practice to inform World Christianity.

Series Editors

REGNUM STUDIES IN MISSION

Trinity in Dialogue with Muslims

Mark Beaumont

First published 2024 by Regnum Books International

Regnum is an imprint of the Oxford Centre for Mission Studies
St. Philip and St. James Church
Woodstock Road
Oxford, OX2 6HR, UK
www.regnumbooks.net

British Library Cataloguing in Publication Data
A catalogue record for this book is available from the British Library

ISBN: 979-8-8898-3895-1
eBook ISBN: 979-8-8898-3896-8

Typeset by Words by Design

Cover photo by Alexander Grey on unsplash.com

Distributed by Fortress Press in the US, Canada, India, and Brazil

Contents

Dedication

To Kyoko,
who reflects the Trinity in her encouragement of the writing of this book.

Foreword
The Trinity: A Foundation or Stumbling Block?

by Ayman Ibrahim

As a Christian growing up in Egypt, I was surrounded by Muslims who cherished their religious traditions and adhered to Islam's core teachings. Most of my neighbours, friends, and classmates were Muslims and, for the most part, we all lived in harmony with sporadic tensions. Still, in the 1970s and 1980s, Coptic Christians were often criticized publicly for their beliefs, especially their commitment to the doctrine of the Trinity – the belief in a Triune God, one divine being and three persons. In those days, Muslim preachers were often willing and able to voice their criticism of this crucial Christian doctrine through TV and radio programs, while Christians were not allowed to present their case. The Muslim criticism of the Trinity varied, but it often took a direction between two extremes. On the one hand, many Muslims, in their attempt to advance Islam's religious superiority, pointed to the doctrine of the Trinity with mockery, highlighting it as illogical and implausible – a twisted and corrupt religious belief, precisely as compared to the Islamic doctrine of *tawḥīd*, the divine unicity, unitarianism, or strict monotheism. On the other hand, other Muslims openly and clearly charged Coptic Christians of polytheism, accusing them with the greatest sin of all, the *shirk* (associating partners with the deity). This public charge against a major Christian doctrine often left the Copts in a defensive position, and, at times, created situations of harassment and discrimination.

Still, the Copts, when given a chance, were ready to articulate and willing to defend their beliefs in the Trinity, sometimes relying on metaphorical analogies, logical methods, or even Qur'ānic references, among other means. In any church sermon, public lecture, or written tract, it was most important for Copts to begin by emphasizing the well-known Trinitarian formula found in Matthew 28:19, *bism al-Āb wa-l-Ibn wa-l-Rūḥ al-qudus* (In the name of the Father, and of the Son, and of the Holy Spirit), but they always ensured to conclude it with *ilāhun wāḥidun* (One God) to convey to their immediate context the clear Christian belief in one divine being. After all, Christians have largely treated the doctrine as primarily God's revelation of himself, not as a simple intellectual argument to preserve.

To be sure, that which the Copts practiced in the last few decades of the previous century was not a unique creation. Today's Copts have been building on a marvellous history of creative and developing Christian presentations of their unique understanding of God – as Triune – to their Muslim neighbours. While this history has indeed begun from the earliest days of Christian-Muslim interactions in the seventh century, it chiefly stemmed as a response to the Qur'ān's open rejection of the Trinity and chastisement of those who believe in it. This rejection propelled Christians to respond. As arguably the earliest and holiest Muslim source, Islam's scripture is clear about rejecting any hint of plurality within the deity. It warns against those who make God a third of three gods, and labels them as to have *kafarū* (unbelieved) (Q 5:73). A verse earlier, the Qur'ān denies that Christ is in any way a part of the Divine, insisting that those who say that "God is the Christ" have clearly *kafarū* (unbelieved) (Q 5:72). The deployment of the term *kafarū* is a uniquely Muslim scriptural tool that establishes a stigma against anyone who embraces any form of plurality within the deity. More importantly, the rejection of the Trinity is further emphasized, a few verses later, when the Qur'ān makes Jesus himself condemn it, denying that he has ever taught his followers that he and his mother were gods apart from God (Q 5:116–117). While undoubtedly these assertions deviate significantly from the Christian teaching on the Trinity, these verses, and the like, served as a kernel for a strong Muslim tradition that grew rapidly in the conquered lands. The tradition expanded and flourished through numerous exegetical writings (Ar. *tafsīr*), largely produced under the ᶜAbbāsids and resulting in a developing Christian-Muslim discourse around the Trinity. The result is a long history of religious Christian-Muslim interaction until our day. Here is one reason why we should all be thrilled, as we welcome Mark Beaumont's newest work, *Trinity in Dialogue with Muslims*.

Beaumont surveys both medieval and modern Christian expositions of the Trinity for Muslims. He highlights arguments of Christian thinkers from various denominational backgrounds, and pinpoints specific creative theological turns, particularly in how Christians devised new explanations. Not only does he examine their presentations and compare their varying articulations of the doctrine to their Muslim neighbours, but he also highlights how Muslims responded to Christian arguments. By covering classical interactions and modern debates, as well as surveying apologetic and polemic texts, Beaumont brings the vivid Christian-Muslim interactions over the Trinity to light in one remarkable volume. This is a huge service for academics and students of Christian-Muslim relations.

This study of the history of Christian-Muslim dialogues on the Trinity emphasizes at least three points.

First, it demonstrates how theological particularities have been important for both faiths throughout centuries. While many modern discussions may prefer a notion that Christians and Muslims *simply* worship the same God, it is clear that the two communities have largely understood his character and attributes in crucially different ways. In times when religious discourses may tend to dilute the differences to emphasize the similarities, this survey highlights the unquestionable complexity of the beliefs cherished by the respective communities. Second, this survey suggests that the Christian explanations of the Trinity to their Muslim counterparts not only grew in number and sophistication over time, but were also adjusted and articulated in response to the sectarian, social, and political contexts within which they emerged. Arguably, the same can be said about the evolving nature of the Muslim charges against the major

Christian doctrine. It appears that both the Muslim arguments and the Christian responses were products of their time. Not only was Islam, as a new emerging faith, largely being shaped while engaging existing religious communities, but its very emergence forced Christians to consider and articulate their major doctrine in new ways. Religious polemics and apologetics do not emerge in vacuum; both reflect and represent socio-political necessities and religious requirements of their times. Third, this survey additionally explains how both traditions have largely utilized similar arguments for centuries, albeit with some logical adjustments, theological twists, and rational turns. It also highlights that rarely was it the case that Christian-Muslim conversations have actually led to convincing results to any party. It is plausible to deduce that the doctrine of the Trinity has always been a strong foundation for Christians and a stumbling block for Muslims. Indeed, this has been the case for centuries and it does not seem to change anytime soon.

Ayman S. Ibrahim, Ph.D.
Bill and Connie Jenkins Professor of Islamic Studies
Director, Jenkins Center for the Christian Understanding of Islam
The Southern Baptist Theological Seminary
Louisville, Kentucky

Introduction

This history of Christian attempts to present the Trinity to Muslims follows my earlier study, *Christology in Dialogue with Muslims*, published in 2005.[1] While the earlier work concentrated on two particular eras of dialogue on Jesus, this new work covers a much broader timescale, but is still in two parts. Part One deals with the beginning of Christian communication with Muslims after the Arab armies took over the Middle East in the seventh century up to the thirteenth century. Part Two studies the writing of mainly Western Christians who began to take dialogue with Muslims seriously from the nineteenth century until today. Such a survey of Christian presentations of the Trinity for Muslims has not been published so far. The only existing book-length study of Christian writing on the Trinity within an Islamic context is by the Lebanese Christian Rachid Haddad.[2] While Haddad's analysis of the Arabic terminology used by Middle Eastern Christians is profound, he does not look at Muslim reactions to these writers. A feature that this new book shares with my earlier study of Jesus is the comparison of Christian writing with Muslim written responses. Thus, the reader can view the nature of the debate between Christians and Muslims on the Trinity in each period.

Part One begins with John of Damascus in the mid-eighth century, who wrote a summary of Eastern Christian writing on the Trinity and then a polemical treatment of the Muslim denial of the Trinity, in which he charges Muslims with cutting out the Word and Spirit of God from His nature, despite the fact that the Qur'ān holds that the Word and Spirit of God were given to Jesus at his conception in Q4:171. Many other Middle Eastern Christians followed John's interpretation of Q4:171, right up to the thirteenth century. John's appeal to Q4:171 was used by the early ninth-century Christian theologian ʿAmmār al-Baṣrī, to argue that God has two essential attributes: speech and life. Muslims had begun to debate among themselves in the eighth century whether God's attributes spoken about in the Qur'ān were essential to Him or were simply metaphors for His transcendent majesty that were not possible to describe. The latter view was predominant at first and ʿAmmār al-Baṣrī sought to argue that God did have certain attributes that truly described His nature, and that the Trinity is supported by the essential attributes of speech and life, which are the Word and the Spirit. In this he was relying on the ancient tradition of Eastern Christianity from Irenaeus that God had two hands: the Word and the Spirit. ʿAmmār al-Baṣrī's argument was followed by several Christian writers up to the

[1] See Mark Beaumont, *Christology in Dialogue with Muslims: A Critical Analysis of Christian Presentations of Christ for Muslims from the Ninth and Twentieth Centuries* (Oxford: Regnum, 2005).

[2] See Rachid Haddad, *La Trinité Divine Chez les Théologiens Arabes 750–1050* (Paris: Beauchesne, 1985).

thirteenth century. After Muslim sentiment shifted from the late ninth century towards the Ashʿarī doctrine that God has seven essential attributes, the eleventh-century Christian theologian Ibn al-Ṭayyib argued that these seven essential attributes can be subsumed under just three essential attributes: God's self-existent nature, along with his speech and life.

In this era of Muslim rule in the Middle East, Christians also presented analogies for the Trinity from aspects of the created world in an attempt to defend the notion that oneness can co-exist with multiplicity from Muslim critique that Christians were in denial of the pure oneness of God. Popular analogies were found in the sun that is a disc and has rays as well as heat but is one sun, and a human being who is a combination of body, soul and spirit but is one human being, and three individual humans who together share one common human nature. Some writers developed distinctive analogies. The early tenth-century Christian philosophical theologian Yaḥya ibn ʿAdī spoke of God having three essential attributes: intellect (*ʿaql*), the intelligent one (*ʿāqil*), and intellection (*maʿqūl*), and says that the Father who is the cause of the Son and the Spirit is the intellect (*ʿaql*), the Son is the one who is intelligent (*ʿāqil*) in the sense that he thinks, and the Spirit is the intellection (*maʿqūl*) in the sense that he is the thought. This psychological analogy was adopted by several Christian writers. When Muslims reacted by stating that nothing from creation can be compared with the Creator, Christians pointed out that the Qurʾān contains many descriptions of God from aspects of creation, such as his hands and eyes.

Part Two considers the presentations of the Trinity for Muslims made in the modern era. Christian missionaries from the West felt the need to answer the Muslim rejection of the Trinity. They were not attracted to the earlier Eastern Christian argument concerning essential attributes of God supporting the Trinity, but they did rely on analogies from creation to argue for a Triune Creator. Some of these analogies were new. The nineteenth-century German Lutheran Karl Pfander repeats the early use of the analogies from fire and the human being. Heat, light and combustion are different from one another, yet when combined form only one fire. A human consists of body, soul and spirit, yet he is not three men, and his body, soul and spirit do not conflict with the oneness of his personality. He then adds a new analogy from the discoveries of modern science that a single ray of sunlight consists of the three primary colours, red, green and blue, yet its unity is not destroyed by this plurality. The twentieth-century English Anglican David Brown uses the early analogy of the human being as threefold. A man is neither simply his body, nor his mind, nor his spirit, but a unity of these three exceedingly complex elements, which are normally integrated together so that he lives and acts as a single person. He adds the analogy of a family of one man, one woman and so many children, who are in a living relationship with each other. They depend on one another physically, emotionally, intellectually and spiritually, and so are united together. This analogy supports Brown's social view of the Trinity. A solitary God would have had no activity beyond the contemplation of Himself, but a Triune God is active in the love expressed by the three centres of personal consciousness within the divine being.

Western theologians in the second half of the twentieth century began to take other religions seriously as dialogue partners. Some began to relate to Islam. A Catholic example is the Swiss theologian Hans Küng, who argues that modern Christians should leave aside the fixed Greek tradition of the credal formulations in favour of a return to the more fluid, dynamic language found in the apostolic writings of Paul and John. He believes that greater freedom for modern Christians to adopt that New Testament language will make communication with Muslims more possible with a much simpler conception of the Trinity. An Anglican example is the English theologian Keith Ward, who has engaged in a profound dialogue with Muslim thought. He believes that the Eastern Christian social Trinity of three centres of consciousness is likely to make dialogue with Muslims even more difficult for Christians. He prefers to assert the unity of God by describing the Father, Son and Holy Spirit as aspects of the work of the one God in relation to the creation. He believes that the reformed Protestant Karl Barth and the Catholic Jesuit Karl Rahner are both right to speak of the revelation of the one God in three modes of activity. Muslims, he argues, are much more likely to understand this formulation of the Trinity to represent the oneness of God than the concept of three persons in relation.

Finally, there are theologians living within Muslim majority nations who have written about the Trinity with Muslims in mind. The Egyptian Coptic priest Ibrahim Luqa is largely tied to the great tradition of Eastern Christian theology and repeats for a twentieth-century Egyptian audience the arguments of the earlier period concerning the essential attributes of God being speech and life and the appeal to analogies. Luqa refers to the analogy of fire. Burning, heat and light are one fire. Just as fire is one substance in three properties, so God is one substance in three properties. He also uses Yaḥya ibn ʿAdī's analogy of the human mind to point out that the intelligence (*ʿaql*), the one who thinks (*ʿāqil*) and the meaning of thought (*maʿqūl*) are one in God.

Imad Shehadeh, a Jordanian Evangelical theologian, has written the most detailed presentation of the Trinity in the twenty-first century with a Muslim readership in the background. He prefers the social theory of the Trinity in line with the tradition of Eastern Christianity and offers the analogy of loving relationships between three human beings. Just as the love exchanged between two human beings extends beyond the two to become a shared love between three, so the exchanged love between the Father, Son and Holy Spirit completes their relationship as one God. This reciprocal love is then poured out on human beings. He declares his wonder at the way the mutual indwelling of the persons of the Trinity extends to believers, such that the Father, Son and Holy Spirit dwell within believers, and believers are in the Father and the Son. Shehadah commends the richness of the three members of the Trinity interacting with each other for the sake of humanity over against the blandness of the Muslim conception of a totally transcendent God who does not interact with humans.

Muslims have continued in the modern era to restate older arguments against the Trinity as being a perversion of the pure oneness of God, but there is an awareness that, for Christians, faith in the Trinity is not a peripheral doctrine that might be moved aside in favour of a unitarian understanding of the nature of God.

PART ONE

DIALOGUE ON THE TRINITY IN THE ERA OF MUSLIM RULE IN THE MIDDLE EAST

The Islamic faith in the oneness of God arises from the teaching of the Qurʾān, which twice criticises those who confess the Trinity. Q5:72–73 calls on Christians to give up adding gods to the one true God.

> They are unbelievers who say that God is Christ, son of Mary. Christ said "Children of Israel, worship God, my Lord and your Lord". Whoever associates another with God, God will keep out of the garden, and the fire will be his destiny … They are unbelievers who say that God is one third of a Trinity. There is no God but One.

The accusation of polytheism is heard here clearly. The contention with the Christians is over the status of Christ, with the text charging Christians with making a second god alongside God. While the concept of the Trinity is mentioned, there is no reference to the third member of the Trinity here. The second passage in which the Trinity is challenged is Q4:171.

> People of the Book, do not exaggerate in your religion. Only speak the truth about God. Christ Jesus, son of Mary, was the messenger of God, and His word which He cast on Mary, and a spirit from Him. Believe in God and His messengers and do not say "Trinity"; give it up for your own good. Surely God is One God. Far be it for Him to have a son.

In this context, the Qurʾān provides another reason for Christians to refrain from speaking of the divine status of Christ and thus the Trinity. The problem is Christians believing that God had a son, which is something unacceptable to God. Q72:3 demonstrates why this should be the case. "Our Lord has neither taken a wife nor a son". Thus, sonship is understood as related to family life created by God but which must not be attributed to Him, as some humans do who associate other deities with Him. Again, the third member of the Trinity is not brought out, though there is a reference to "spirit" from God in Christ. There is a third text in the Qurʾān relevant to the accusation that Christians have added deities to the one God. In Q5:116–7, God interrogates Jesus about his teaching.

> Jesus, son of Mary, did you say to people, "take me and my mother as gods alongside God"'. Jesus replies, "I did not say what I did not have the right to say … I only told them what you commanded me to say: worship God, my Lord and your Lord."

According to this dialogue, the original Jesus brought the message of submission to God alone to those of his time, but the implication is obvious that Christians deviated from this pristine teaching by adulterating it with veneration of Jesus himself along with his mother. Another consequence of this text is that the Trinity referred to in the other texts could be Father, Son and Mary. This is exactly what was deduced by Fakhr al-Dīn al-Rāzī (d. 1209) in the most detailed discussion of this text by any of the classical commentators on the Qur᾿ān. He believes that Christians made up the story that Jesus taught his disciples to worship him along with his mother as a means of giving legitimacy to miracles they performed in the name of Jesus and his mother.[1] In his interpretation of Q4:171 al-Rāzī argues that Christians developed a belief that the attributes of God indwelt Jesus and Mary and that this is condemned in the Qur᾿ān when Christians are warned not to speak of three when God is one. He thinks that Christians began with devotion to Jesus and Mary and grew to attribute divinity to them.[2] So the nameless third member of the Trinity in the two texts referring to the Trinity can be identified as Mary, the mother of Jesus.

The arrival of Muslim rulers who were insistent on the unity of God among Christians who testified to the unity of God in His Triune nature introduced a considerable challenge to those Christians who were in the ascendency throughout the Middle East. Now they were on the defensive, needing to stem the movement of members of their own community to Islam, which would eventually lead to Muslims becoming the majority. In the period of gradual transfer from majority to minority status, Christian theologians attempted both to make their faith in the Trinity intelligible to Muslim intellectuals with whom they debated and to give reasons to Christians for holding firm to their faith. If the Qur᾿ān rejected the Trinity, then it is clear how difficult the task would be for Christians who encountered such views. They would need to defend their belief in God as one essence (*ousia*) in three persons (*hypostases*) which was shared by all three main denominations of the church in the Middle Eastern territories under Muslim rule. They may have been divided over their understanding of the union of the divine and human in Christ, but they were united in their faith in the Triune God. The upholders of the Chalcedonian definition that Jesus was perfect God and perfect man were called Melkites by their rivals, since they were loyal to the Byzantine emperor, the *Malik* in the Syriac language. The followers of Nestorius who had been exiled to Persia by the Emperor Zeno after 474 for refusing to confess that Mary was the Godbearer were called Nestorians by their rivals. The third group believed that Jesus had only one divine nature over against the other two groups, who held that Jesus was both divine and human. They were called Jacobites by their rivals, since they were formed by Jacob Baradaeus after the condemnation of miaphysite Christology by the Emperor Justinian in 536.

The earliest testimony to Christian reaction to Islamic rejection of the Trinity comes from the eighth century. John of Damascus (d.c. 750) provides the first known written Christian response to the Qur᾿ānic condemnation of the Trinity. John wrote in Greek for a Christian readership, though he may have engaged in oral debate with Muslims in Arabic. However, in the next generation, an

[1] Fakhr al-Dīn al-Rāzī, *The Large Commentary on the Qur᾿ān (Al-Tafsīr al-Kabīr)*, (Beirut: 1978) on Q5:116–117.
[2] Al-Rāzī, *The Large Commentary*, on Q4:171.

anonymous 'Apology for the Trinity' was written in Arabic with the evident aim of presenting a Christian view of the Trinity to Muslims using insights from John's work. In 781, the Muslim Caliph al-Mahdī summoned Timothy I, the Patriarch of the Nestorian Church of the East in Baghdad, to a two-day session of answering questions about the Christian faith. This encounter was recorded by Timothy in Syriac to edify his own flock, and this was translated into Arabic probably in the last decade of the century to make available to enquiring Muslims an accurate account of Christianity. The Trinity was one of several topics raised by the Caliph, and though the written debate may be a stylised version of events, there is no reason to doubt that the questions were just the sort to be put to Christians by Muslims.[3]

The groundwork of the eighth-century responses to the Qurʾānic attack on the Trinity was built on by three early ninth-century apologists, Abū Qurra (d.c. 830), Abū Rāʾiṭa (d.c. 835) and ʿAmmār al-Baṣrī (d.c. 860), who all attempted to defend and explain the Trinity in Arabic for a Muslim audience that was increasingly involved in debate with Christian intellectuals. The fact that Abū Qurra and ʿAmmār al-Baṣrī were both honoured by leading Muslim thinkers by a written response to their teaching suggests that these Christian apologists were making an impact on their intended readership. ʿĪsā ibn Sabīh al-Murdār (d. 840) wrote a refutation entitled *Against Abū Qurra the Christian* (*Kitāb ʿalā Abī Qurra al-Naṣrānī*) and Abū al-Hudhayl al- ʿAllāf (d.c. 840) wrote a "refutation of ʿAmmār the Christian in his reply to the Christians", according to the *Fihrist* of Ibn al-Nadīm.[4] Unfortunately, neither of these Muslim refutations is extant, but there are two ninth-century Muslim responses to the Trinity that provide the earliest written Muslim reactions to Christian defence of the Trinity for a Muslim audience. These are the 'Refutation of the Christians' ('Al-radd ʿalā al-Naṣārā') by al-Qāsim ibn Ibrāhīm al-Rassī (d. 860) and the 'Refutation of the Three Christian Sects' ('Al-radd ʿalā al-thalātha firaq min al-Naṣārā') by Abū ʿĪsā Muḥammad ibn Hārūn al-Warrāq (d.c. 860). The latter is an exhaustive description and painstaking demolition of the Trinity from a logical point of view, based on the presupposition of the oneness of God.

---

[3] For an earlier version of this chapter see Mark Beaumont, 'Speaking of the Triune God: Christian Defence of the Trinity in the Early Islamic Period', *Transformation* 29 (2012), pp. 111–27.

[4] See Bayard Dodge (trans.), *The Fihrist of al-Nadīm: A Tenth-Century Survey of Muslim Culture, vol 1* (New York: Columbia University Press, 1970), pp. 388 and 394.

1. Christian Presentations of the Trinity in the Early Period of Muslim Rule

John of Damascus (d.c. 750)

In the third decade of the eighth century John of Damascus wrote a three-volume work entitled *The Fount of Knowledge* (*Pege Gnoseos*) during his retirement from serving the Muslim Caliph in Damascus. The second volume, *Heresies* (*De Haeresibus*), critiques one hundred heresies concluding with "The Heresy of the Ishmaelites". The third volume, *On the Orthodox Faith* (*De Fide Orthodoxa*), expounds in a systematic way John's view of orthodox beliefs. According to Norman Russell, John wrote *On the Orthodox Faith* for a monastic audience around the time that he joined a monastic community near Jerusalem.[1] John defines the Trinity in the already established Greek patristic way. "We know and confess that God is one, that is to say, one substance (*ousia*), and that he is acknowledged in three hypostases and exists as such, by which I mean as Father and Son and Holy Spirit."[2] He admits that it is not possible to fully comprehend the manner of God's nature. "What the essence of God is, or how it is in all things, or how God is generated by, or proceeds from God, it is impossible for us to say."[3] Yet it is possible to know that God is rational in his essential being.

> The one God possesses rationality, and this rationality will not be lacking in subsistence (*ouk anhypostaton*), nor will it begin to be or cease to be. For there was no time when God was without rationality. And he always possesses his own Word begotten from him, not like our own speech, which lacks subsistence and is lost in the air, but as something subsistent, living, perfect, not going away out of him but always remaining within him, for where is there that is outside him?[4]

John is remarkably sure of this aspect of God's character which arises from his confidence in the revelation of the unbegotten Word in Jesus Christ. In addition, John is sure that the Spirit of God rests in the Word and reveals God through him.

> Moreover, it is necessary that the Word should also have a spirit. For even our speech is not devoid of breath. When we learned about the Spirit of God that witnesses together with the Word and manifests his activity, we did not consider it a breath lacking in hypostasis – for the grandeur of the divine nature would thus be reduced to something humble, if the Spirit that is in it were to be conceived as resembling our own breath – but an essential power, contemplated as it is in itself

---

[1] John of Damascus, *On the Orthodox Faith*, Norman Russell (trans.), (New York: St Vladimir's Seminary Press, 2022), p. 36.

[2] John of Damascus, *On the Orthodox Faith*, p. 61.

[3] John of Damascus, *On the Orthodox Faith*, p. 62.

[4] John of Damascus, *On the Orthodox Faith*, p. 68.

> in its own individuating hypostasis, proceeding from the Father and resting in the Word and making him manifest.[5]

In other words, the Spirit of God is not merely a fleeting breath that momentarily influences the Word of God but is much more an aspect of God's essential nature. Both the Word and the Spirit have an eternal identity within the nature of God. Neither of them is in any way temporary or a secondary feature of God.

> Neither can the Spirit be separated from God, in whom it is, or from the Word, with whom it bears witness, nor can it be poured out into non-existence, but existing hypostatically like the Word, it is alive, capable of choosing, self-moving, active, always desiring the good, by its will possessing the power that corresponds to every purpose, and having neither beginning nor end. For never has the Father been without Word, or the Word without Spirit.[6]

John goes on to recognise that the doctrine of the Trinity was taught explicitly by Jesus Christ. "We believe in Father, Son, and Holy Spirit, in whom we have also been baptized; for it is thus that the Lord commanded the apostles to baptize, 'baptizing them,' he said, 'in the name of the Father and of the Son and of the Holy Spirit'."[7]

He then defines the relationships between the three members of the Trinity. The Father is defined as unbegotten. "We believe in one Father, the principle and cause of all things, not begotten of anyone, who alone exists as uncaused and unbegotten."[8] The Son is defined as begotten of the Father who is "Father of his one and single only-begotten Son, our Lord and God and Savior Jesus Christ."[9] John goes on to affirm that the generation of the Son never had a beginning in time. "With regard to the Son's generation, it is impious to say that there was an interval of time or that the existence of the Son came into being after the Father."[10] The Spirit is defined as proceeding from the Father who is the "originator of the all-holy Spirit".[11]

From one perspective "the three hypostases of the holy Godhead are the same as each other (for they are consubstantial [*homoousios*] and uncreated)".[12] But from another perspective they are not the same.

> For only the Father is unbegotten (for his being is not from another hypostasis), only the Son is begotten (for he is begotten from the substance of the Father without beginning and outside of time), and only the Holy Spirit proceeds from the substance of the Father, not begotten but brought forth by procession.[13]

---

[5] John of Damascus, *On the Orthodox Faith*, p. 69.
[6] John of Damascus, *On the Orthodox Faith*, p. 70.
[7] John of Damascus, *On the Orthodox Faith*, p. 71.
[8] John of Damascus, *On the Orthodox Faith*, p. 72.
[9] John of Damascus, *On the Orthodox Faith*, p. 72.
[10] John of Damascus, *On the Orthodox Faith*, p. 72.
[11] John of Damascus, *On the Orthodox Faith*, p. 72.
[12] John of Damascus, *On the Orthodox Faith*, p. 76.
[13] John of Damascus, *On the Orthodox Faith*, p. 76.

John states that all this is revealed in "What the divine Scripture teaches".[14] Yet he immediately issues a caveat that the difference between being begotten and proceeding have not been revealed. "We have been taught that there is a difference between generation and procession, but what the manner of the difference is we have in no way been informed."[15]

John then points out that the three are indeed one.

> We say that the three hypostases are in one another in order to exclude our introducing a plurality and community of gods. By the three hypostases we acknowledge the absence of composition and confusion; by the consubstantiality (*homoousios*) and mutual indwelling of the hypostases … we acknowledge the absence of division and the fact that they are one God. For God and his Word and his Spirit are in reality one God.[16]

This is the reason why Christians do not confess three gods. The plurality does not cancel out the unity but rather reinforces the complex nature of God revealed in Scripture as Father, Son and Holy Spirit.

> Therefore neither do we call the Father, the Son, and the Holy Spirit three gods, but rather one God, the Holy Trinity, in whom the Son and the Spirit are referred to one cause, not merged or fused together … so that they coinhere in each other and they interpenetrate each other (*perichoresin echein*).[17]

Norman Russell notes,

> This is the first time John uses the expression *perichoresis* adopted from Gregory of Nazianzus [ep. 101.31], who used it to express the way the two natures of Christ interpenetrate each other. John applies this to the way the three hypostases of the Trinity interpenetrate each other.[18]

There are limits to the interpenetration of the three hypostases. The Father is not from the Son or the Spirit. The Son is from the Father. The Spirit is from the Father. But the Spirit is not from the Son.

> One needs to know that we deny that the Father is from anyone; we call him the Father of the Son. And we deny that the Son is either a cause or a father; we say that he is from the Father and the Son of the Father. We say that the Holy Spirit is from the Father and also call him the Spirit of the Father. But although we do not say that the Spirit is from the Son, we call him the Spirit of the Son (for the divine Apostle says: "Anyone who does not have the Spirit of Christ" Romans 8.9) and we confess that he is manifested and communicated to us through the Son (for "he breathed on them" and said to his disciples: "Receive the Holy Spirit" John 20.22) … But we do not say that the Son is from the Spirit.[19]

This final caution shows the difference between the Eastern understanding of the relationship between the Son and the Spirit and the Western conviction from Augustine (c. 430) onwards that the very Scripture passages John quotes

---

[14] John of Damascus, *On the Orthodox Faith*, p. 76.
[15] John of Damascus, *On the Orthodox Faith*, p. 78.
[16] John of Damascus, *On the Orthodox Faith*, pp. 79–80.
[17] John of Damascus, *On the Orthodox Faith*, p. 81.
[18] John of Damascus, *On the Orthodox Faith*, p. 81.
[19] John of Damascus, *On the Orthodox Faith*, p. 83.

demonstrate that the Spirit is from the Son as well as from the Father. Augustine argues,

> Nor can we say that the Holy Spirit does not also proceed from the Son, for then the statement that he is the Spirit of the Father and of the Son is meaningless. Nor can I see what else the Son meant when he breathed on the face of his disciples and said, "Receive the Holy Spirit" ... This was a demonstration, by a fitting symbol, that the Holy Spirit proceeds not only from the Father but from the Son.[20]

The Greek tradition believed that the Spirit was caused by the Father but not by the Son and can only be said to be passed on by the Son by means of the authorisation of the Father.

In "The Heresy of the Ishmaelites" John attempts to defend the Trinity against Muslim attack not by quoting the carefully worked out definitions of the Trinity already studied, but by referring to Q4:171 as support for a Trinitarian faith. Thus, while John sees Islam as the most recent of the heresies that he is condemning in the list of one hundred, he is quite prepared to find reflections of true belief within the scriptures of the Muslims, just as he finds truth within other heresies, such as those of the Christian Nestorians or Miaphysites, who held the same orthodox view of the Trinity as John but failed to believe in the process of the Incarnation correctly, as John's Chalcedonian church did. John reports that Muslims accuse Christians of associating Christ with God in an unacceptable way because Christians say that "Christ is the Son of God and God".[21] John suggests that Christians should quote the Muslim belief that "Christ is the Word and Spirit of God" and say, "If the Word is in God it is obvious that he is God as well".[22] But if Muslims deny that the Word and Spirit are in God then they can be accused of cutting off these attributes of God from Him. "Thus trying to avoid making associates to God, you have mutilated him."[23] John is making the assumption here that the hypostases of Christ the Word and the Holy Spirit are actually meant in Q4:171, "Christ Jesus, son of Mary, was the messenger of God, and His word which He cast on Mary, and a spirit from Him". This is quite remarkable in a piece of polemical writing that more or less ridicules the contents of Muslim scriptures as a collection of absurd stories. John seems to be condemning the one he calls the false prophet of Islam for developing a largely deviant message on the basis of a few kernels of truth, and to be taking it as his task to separate the wheat from the chaff for the sake of his fellow Christians. In the process, John is advocating that Christians rely, not on an appeal to their own scriptures, nor on the exposition of their own doctrinal beliefs, but on grounds acceptable to Muslims. This apologetic procedure would be followed by others, in particular by the author of an anonymous apology for Christianity which incorporates the language of Q4:171 quite directly.

---

[20] Augustine, 'On the Trinity', 4.29, in Henry Bettenson (trans.), *The Later Christian Fathers* (Oxford: Oxford University Press, 1970), p. 227.

[21] John of Damascus, 'The Heresy of the Ishmaelites', Daniel J. Sahas (trans.), in *John of Damascus on Islam* (Leiden: Brill, 1972), pp. 132–141 (p. 137).

[22] John of Damascus, 'The Heresy of the Ishmaelites', p. 137.

[23] John of Damascus, 'The Heresy of the Ishmaelites', p. 137.

An Anonymous Apology for Christianity (c. 750)

This apology, not in Greek but in Arabic, comes from the same Chalcedonian community as John and shows signs of common assumptions about the Qurʾān containing some testimony to the truth.[24] The writer says at the end of the treatise that "if this religion was not truly from God, it would not have stood firm nor stood erect for seven hundred and forty-six years", so it appears to have been composed in the middle of the eighth century, around the same time as John's work.[25] There is a detailed presentation of the Trinity using language taken from the Qurʾān, which suggests that the unknown writer is attempting to set out Christian belief for a Muslim reader, with the parallel purpose of showing fellow Christians a way to communicate their faith to Muslims. The fact that it is composed in Arabic demonstrates that the language of the Muslim rulers was becoming used in some Christian communities, for example in Palestinian monasteries.[26] After a lengthy prayer, the writer addresses a Muslim reader by declaring "We do not distinguish God from His Word and His Spirit. We do not worship another god alongside God in His Word and His Spirit."[27] The first sentence echoes the argument of John of Damascus that Christians do not mutilate the Triune God by separating His Word and Spirit from Him. The second sentence alludes to Q5:72–73, which alleges that Christians worship gods alongside the one true God and refashions the phraseology to include Christ the Word and the Holy Spirit in the definition of the one true God. Such language would not have been necessary in a treatise written before the challenge of Islam. The author points to the way God speaks in the plural as "We" in the creation story in Genesis and concludes, "We do not say three gods ... But we do say that

---

[24] The Arabic text (Sinai 154) is edited and translated into English by Margaret D. Gibson as *A Treatise on the Triune Nature of God* (London: Cambridge University Press, 1899). See the English translation of the treatise by Mark N. Swanson, 'An Apology for the Christian Faith' in Samuel Noble and Alexander Treiger (eds), *The Orthodox Church in the Arab World* (DeKalb, IL: Northern Illinois University Press, 2014), pp. 40–59.

[25] Samir K. Samir discovered this statement on one of the pages of the manuscript not included in the printed version by Gibson, who said that she was unable to photograph "a few pages from the end". Samir believes that this dates the writing to just before 750. See Samir K. Samir, 'The Earliest Arab Apology for Christianity (c. 750)' in Samir K. Samir and Jorgen S. Nielsen (eds), *Christian Arabic Apologetics During the Abbasid Period (750–1258)*, (Leiden: Brill, 1994), pp. 57–116 (p. 61). Mark Swanson calculates the date not from the birth of Christ, but from the beginning of the church, and suggests 788. See Mark Swanson, 'Some Considerations for the Dating of *fī tatlīt allāh al-wāhid* (Sinai Ar. 154) and *al-gāmiʿ wugūh al-īmān* (London, British Library op. 4950)', *Parole de L'Orient* 18 (1993), pp. 118–41 (p. 140). However, Sidney Griffith argues that Palestinian scribes were more likely to compute the date from the beginning of the year of the Incarnation, thus placing the composition around 755. See Sidney H. Griffith, *The Church in the Shadow of the Mosque* (Princeton: Princeton University Press, 2008), p. 54.

[26] See Sidney H. Griffith, 'The Monks of Palestine and the Growth of Christian Literature in Arabic', *The Muslim World* 78 (1988), pp. 1–28.

[27] Margaret D. Gibson (ed. and trans.), *A Treatise on the Triune Nature of God* (London: Cambridge University Press, 1899), p. 75.

God and His Word and His Spirit is One God and One Creator".[28] Obviously here is a rebuttal of Q5:73, "They are unbelievers who say that God is one third of a Trinity", and Q4:171, "Believe in God and His messengers and do not say 'Trinity'". The language of the Qurʾān sets the tone of the presentation, which seeks to supply to a Muslim reader correct information concerning Christian belief in God as Triune.

The author proceeds to list seven analogies for the Trinity to indicate the validity of conceiving God as one in three. First: the disc, rays and heat of the sun do not imply three suns. "We do not say three suns."[29] Second: the eye, the pupil and the light in the eye are not three eyes. Third: the soul, the body and the spirit are not three human beings. Fourth: the root, the branches and the fruit of a tree are not three trees. Fifth: the source, the river and the lake are the same water. Sixth: the human mind, the word that comes from the mind and the spirit that resides in the mind are all of one human being. Seventh: the mouth, the tongue and the word that is spoken all come from one person. "All these demonstrate our faith in the Father, the Son and the Holy Spirit ... and people should believe this."[30] However, he recognises that "We do not perceive anything of the power and greatness of God ... by analogies ... but by faith".[31] He quotes the Qurʾān from Q4:171 and Q16:102 to back up his faith in the Trinity and challenge his Muslim reader to accept this truth. "Believe in God and His Word; and also in His Holy Spirit; surely the Holy Spirit has brought down from your Lord mercy and guidance ... You find in the Qurʾān that God and His Word and His Spirit is One God and One Lord. You have said that you believe in God and His Word and His Spirit, so do not reproach us, you people, for believing in God and His Word and His Spirit."[32]

The methodology of this unknown Christian apologist is similar to that of John of Damascus in terms of referring to the teaching of the Qurʾān concerning the Word and Spirit of God and arguing that these cannot be separated from Him. He goes beyond John in quoting Q16:102 in which the Holy Spirit is mentioned as bringing guidance from God in order to stress that the Qurʾān speaks of the third member of the Trinity in his activity of bringing revelation to humanity. There is a more thorough application of Qurʾānic terminology in this apology, which may be explained by the author's decision to write in Arabic rather than Greek, with the consequent desire to utilise as much of the Qurʾān as was suitable to convey Christian meaning. The striking difference between this work and that of John is the absence of polemic found in the latter. Whereas John ridiculed much of the teaching of Islam as absurd, this writer never mocks his reader but appeals to one who "knows the truth and opens his breast to believe in God and His Scriptures".[33] Thus, the tone of this apology is respectful even when the writer challenges his Muslim reader to desist from quoting Qurʾānic texts that

---

[28] Gibson, *A Treatise*, p. 76.
[29] Gibson, *A Treatise*, p. 76.
[30] Gibson, *A Treatise*, p. 76.
[31] Gibson, *A Treatise*, p. 76.
[32] Gibson, *A Treatise*, pp. 77–78.
[33] Gibson, *A Treatise*, p. 75.

attack the Trinity. Muslims should not reproach Christians because the latter do not believe in three gods, and Muslims should listen carefully to Christians when they explain their belief in God and His Word and His Spirit. There need not be alienation and controversy between Christians and Muslims if they search their scriptures in a careful way. This is an optimistic approach that depends on the good will of both sides. However, the gulf between the teaching of the Christian and Muslim scriptures was usually too great for this kind of dialogue, as can be seen in the encounter of Timothy I, the Patriarch of the East Syrian (Nestorian) church and the Muslim Caliph al-Mahdī in 781.

Dialogue between the Caliph al-Mahdī and Timothy I, Patriarch of the East Syrian (Nestorian) Church (781)

Caliph al-Mahdī summoned Timothy I for an audience with him in Baghdad shortly after Timothy became Patriarch of the East Syrian church in 780.[34] A report of the debate was produced in Syriac and subsequently translated into Arabic but may not conform to the actual conversation in every detail. Nevertheless, it is hardly likely that Timothy would have dared to misrepresent the speech of the Caliph, so the questions posed by him in the report are likely to be those he asked in the debate, which are mainly concerned with Timothy's understanding of the Trinity, the Incarnation, the Scriptures, and the status of the Prophet Muḥammad.[35] The opening question of al-Mahdī is a reference to Q72:3, "Our Lord has neither taken a wife nor a son", as he asks Timothy, "How can someone like you, knowledgeable and wise, say that the most high God took a wife and had a son?"[36] Timothy simply denies the allegation. Here is evidence from the late eighth century for a Muslim interpretation of the Trinity as God, Mary and Jesus and the need for Christians to be able to explain their conception of the Trinity, not on Muslim assumptions of what Christians believed, but rather on what they held to be true. After discussion of the Incarnation, al-Mahdī asks, "Do you believe in three gods?" Timothy replies that Christians believe in "three hypostases (*aqānīm*) ... The Father, the Son and the Holy Spirit, which are together one God, one nature, and one essence (*jawhar*)".[37] Timothy holds that this was clearly taught by Jesus in the gospel and is also proved from studying

---

[34] Timothy describes his two-day audience with the Caliph in a letter to the priest Sargis in 782/3. See epistle 59 in *Les Lettres du Patriarche Nestorien Timothée I*, Raphaël J. Bidawid (ed. and trans.), (Rome: Testi e Studi, 1956), pp. 42–43.

[35] The Syriac version is edited and translated into English by Alphonse Mingana as 'The Apology of Timothy the Patriarch before the Caliph Mahdi', *Woodbrooke Studies* II (1928), pp. 1–162. The Arabic version is edited by Louis Cheikho in *Al-Machriq* 19 (1921), pp. 359–74 and 408–18 and reproduced with a French translation by Hans Putman in *L'Église sous Timothée I: 780–832* (Beirut: Dar el-Machreq, 1975), appendix, pp. 7–51. Putman believes that the Arabic version is a summary of the longer Syriac one made in 794–795.

[36] Putman (trans.), 'Dialogue Between the Caliph al-Mahdī and Timothy I, Patriarch of the East Syrian (Nestorian) Church' in *L'Église sous Timothée I: 780–832* (Beirut: Dar el-Machreq, 1975), appendix, p. 7.

[37] Putman, *Dialogue*, p. 13.

created things. Just as the Caliph is one person in his mind and spirit, and these cannot be separated from him, so it is with God and his Word and Spirit. The sun with its rays and heat are one inseparable sun. We do not say that a person who speaks is without life or spirit so "if someone says that God exists without Word and Spirit then he blasphemes".[38]

Timothy uses similar analogies for the Trinity as the writer of the 'Anonymous Apology' to make the same point that the Word and Spirit cannot be separated from God. These were obviously common to Christians from the different denominations. However, Timothy embarks on a much more profound explanation of the Trinity than his immediate predecessors and the language of one essence (*ousia*) in three persons (*hypostases*) is translated into Arabic as one *jawhar* in three *aqānīm*. The latter term is a transliteration of the Syriac "*qenômê*" with which Timothy was familiar, but the former is a newly coined Arabic word for the Syriac "*ousia*", itself a transliteration of the Greek.[39]

Timothy provides a series of proofs from the Bible for the Trinitarian nature of God, but these do not appear to make much of an impression on the Caliph, who asks, "How are the Son and Spirit not the same, since you say that God is simple and not composite?"[40] Timothy replies by making a distinction between the essence and the hypostases. With respect to the essence (*jawhar*) there is no distinction between them, but with respect to their own particular characteristics as hypostases (*aqānīm*), one of them is begotten (*yūlad*) and the other is not begotten but proceeds (*yanbathiq*).[41] The Father is the origin of the Son and the Spirit. From eternity the Son is begotten and the Holy Spirit emanates (*yuṣdir*), and the begetting and the emanating are without bodily separation or by means of bodily members. This is because God is not composite or embodied. Timothy offers an analogy from human nature to explain this. "From the human soul (*nafs*) the spoken word is born and love emanates without separation or by means of members. Yet love is distinguished from word and word from love." While the method of begetting and emanating is not clear, the basic idea is possible and is found in nature. Just as smell and taste emanate from an apple, but do not come from a part of the apple but from the whole fruit, and just as the smell is not the taste, so the Son is begotten from the Father and the Spirit emanates from Him. "The eternal comes from the eternal and the uncreated emanates from the uncreated."[42]

Just like the author of the 'Anonymous Apology', Timothy uses Biblical proofs and analogies for the Trinity, but develops fresh points of comparison, such as the human perception of an apple, which is rather obscure as an analogy of the Trinity. Better is the human soul that is the source of word and love but is indivisible, since this picture is closer to the relationships within the Trinity that

---

[38] Putman, *Dialogue*, pp. 13–14.
[39] See Sidney H. Griffith, 'The Concept of *Al-Uqnūm* in ʿAmmār al-Baṣrī's Apology for the Doctrine of the Trinity', in Samir K. Samir (ed.), *Actes du Premier Congrès International d'Études Arabes Chrétiennes* (Rome: Pontificum Institutum Studiorum Orientalium, 1982), pp. 169–90 (p. 179).
[40] Putman, *Dialogue*, p. 16.
[41] Putman, *Dialogue*, p. 16.
[42] Putman, *Dialogue*, p. 17.

can be characterised as the Father as source, the Son as Word and the Holy Spirit as love between them. Nevertheless, the Caliph is unmoved by such an analogy and draws the following conclusion about the inseparability of the hypostases: "If the hypostases (*aqānīm*) are not separated or divided one from another, then the Father and the Holy Spirit became human along with the Word."[43] Timothy seeks to assure al-Mahdī that the functions of the three hypostases are different, while they maintain their inseparability of nature. He offers further analogies to secure the argument. The word of the Caliph written on parchment is not immediately connected to his soul or mind but cannot be separated from them. The spoken word is generated from the soul and mind and heard by means of the activity of the air but cannot be divided from the soul and mind. People talk not about hearing the soul or mind but about hearing the word of someone.[44] At this point the questions move to the status of Jesus Christ, so there is no recorded reaction to these pictures and the discussion of the Trinity comes to an end.

Timothy's detailed defence of the Trinity is one step removed from the 'Anonymous Apology' and two steps from John of Damascus' contribution to dialogue. Here, Timothy explains how the members of the Trinity function separately without being separated in essence in the attempt to meet the logical scrutiny of the Caliph, who reflects the attention now being given by Muslim intellectuals to Christian teaching. The earlier apologetic stressed how to communicate the Trinity to Muslims, but Timothy is required by leading Muslim thinkers to defend the Trinity against logical criticism that takes apart the notion of a Triune God. This latter apologetic activity was to become central in the succeeding generations of Christian apologists.

Theodore Abū Qurra (d.c. 830)

Abū Qurra's defence of the Trinity is entitled 'A Treatise by Theodore, Bishop of Harran, establishing that Christians do not believe in three gods when they say that the Father is God, the Son is God, and the Holy Spirit is God; and that the Father, the Son and the Holy Spirit are one God even though each of them is complete in himself.'[45] This Chalcedonian theologian calls the intended Muslim reader "the one who negates Christian teaching"[46] and spends the first half of the treatise arguing for the place of reason in defence of faith before giving Biblical proofs of the Trinity. The second half is a set of arguments to demonstrate that it is not unreasonable to believe that God is both One and Triune. The negators of Christian teaching object to the Trinity because their "reason is confused by the Christian claims that the Father, the Son and the Holy Spirit are three hypostases (*aqānīm*) in one God (*ilah wāḥid*), and that each of the hypostases is perfect God

---

[43] Putman, *Dialogue*, p. 18.
[44] Putman, *Dialogue*, p. 18.
[45] Abū Qurra, 'Treatise on the Trinity', in Constantin Bacha (ed.), *Les Oeuvres Arabes de Théodore Aboucara* (Beyrouth: Maṭbaʿat al-Fawāʾid, 1904), pp. 23–47 (p. 23). See also the English translation of the Treatise in J. Lamoreaux, *Theodore Abu Qurrah* (Provo, Utah: Brigham Young University Press, 2005), pp. 175–93.
[46] Abū Qurra, 'Treatise on the Trinity', p. 23.

in himself".[47] For the negators, reason dictates that either none of the hypostases is a god or each of them is a god. Abū Qurra begins his attempt to persuade his Muslim audience that God is three in one by expounding Biblical evidence for this belief. For example, he sees appearances of angelic messengers in Genesis 16:7-13, 22:12, 23:11-13, 48:15-6, and Exodus 3:2-6 as indications of the functioning of the Trinity.[48] Rational people should be convinced by these textual proofs that the Father is God, the Son is God and the Holy Spirit is God, but that God is always one, yet since reason sometimes is overcome by feeling it is also necessary to develop rational arguments for the Trinity.[49]

He uses the human names Peter, Paul and John as an analogy for the hypostases (*aqānīm*), since these names refer to persons (*wujūh*), and the human nature (*ṭabīʿa*) shared by these three names as an analogy for the divine nature shared by the hypostases. Abū Qurra has supplied *wajh*/*wujūh* as a translation of the Greek term *prosōpon* (person), which was a synonym for *hypostasis* in Greek theology, as Rachid Haddad has pointed out.[50] There are "three persons (*wujūh*), one God … because the term 'person' (*wajh*) is attributed to the Father, the Son and the Holy Spirit".[51] But he recognises that the analogy of three men must not lead to the supposition that the Father, Son and Holy Spirit are separated or differentiated, since they would then be three divine beings rather than one divine being.[52]

He refers to the divine nature in various ways. The three persons (*wujūh*) share the same non-physical nature (*laṭafa*).[53] Therefore, each of the persons shares the same essence (*dhāt*).[54] The three persons share the same oneness of divinity (*wāḥidiyya al-lāhūt*).[55] Najib Awad has argued that Abū Qurra uses the term *wajh*,

> to explain to Muslims the uniqueness of the person of the Father (as well as that of the Son and the Spirit) that makes him alone Father (as it makes the Son alone "Son" and the "Spirit" alone "Holy Spirit") in the Trinity, without this *wajh* conveying the sense of a separate nature or an additional deity.[56]

Three further analogies are presented to support the three persons sharing one divinity. If there are three lamps in a house, they each give light but the light is one and indivisible. When three speakers recite the same poem simultaneously, the hearer hears one poem. Three pieces of gold are just one kind of gold, not three kinds. Yet the oneness of God is "purer and higher" than the oneness in

[47] Abū Qurra, 'Treatise on the Trinity', p. 27.
[48] Abū Qurra, 'Treatise on the Trinity', pp. 29–31.
[49] Abū Qurra, 'Treatise on the Trinity', p. 33.
[50] See Haddad, *La Trinité Divine*, p. 172.
[51] Abū Qurra, 'Treatise on the Trinity', p. 34.
[52] Abū Qurra, 'Treatise on the Trinity', p. 35.
[53] Abū Qurra, 'Treatise on the Trinity', p. 38.
[54] Abū Qurra, 'Treatise on the Trinity', p. 39.
[55] Abū Qurra, 'Treatise on the Trinity', p. 37.
[56] Najib George Awad, *Orthodoxy in Arabic Terms: A Study of Theodore Abu Qurrah's Theology in its Islamic Context* (Berlin: De Gruyter, 2015), p. 234.

any of these analogies.[57] Finally, the three persons share the same nature (*ṭabī ʿa*).[58]

If it is asked whether the world was created by one or three, then the reply should be that all three, the Father, the Son and the Holy Spirit, were involved in creating the world, but that the action of creating is the action of the divine nature which they share. Abū Qurra poses his own question to his Muslim reader, "Do you say that God has word or not?" If he replies "no" then God is dumb, but if he replies "yes" then the Word has to be both perfect man and perfect God as Christians believe.[59] Here is Abū Qurra's version of the argument used by John of Damascus and the writer of the Anonymous Apology based on Q4:171, in which Word and Spirit from God are attributed to Christ. However, in this form the argument relates to the debate among Muslims about whether the Qur ʾān was eternal or created. Seppo Rissanen thinks that Abū Qurra posed difficulties for both sides in the debate. The Mu ʿtazila denied the eternity of the Qur ʾān and thus denied the eternity of the word. The Traditionists held to the eternity of the Qur ʾān but would not accept the personification of God's Word.[60] Certainly, Abū Qurra is attempting to use the background language of God's Word being cast into Mary to give validity to the functioning of the Trinity. Thus, his presentation of the reasonableness of the Trinity, which begins with textual proofs from the Bible, ends with a textual proof from the Qur ʾān. In between, he offers a series of analogies to encourage his Muslim audience to give thoughtful consideration to the Triune nature of God. The truly rational people will conclude that God is three in one. Such an appeal to rationality is taken up by the Muslim polemicist Abū ʿĪsā al-Warrāq later in the ninth century and is applied with devastating consequences to the work of Abū Qurra.

Ḥabīb Ibn Khidma Abū Rā ʾiṭa (d.c. 835)

The West Syrian Jacobite miaphysite theologian, Abū Rā ʾiṭa, was a contemporary of Abū Qurra with whom he claimed to have debated face to face.[61] Their theological disagreement lay in the interpretation of the union of divinity and humanity in the incarnate Christ, but they were in agreement over the Trinitarian formula, "One essence in three hypostases". However, their presentations of the Trinity show differences in Arabic terminology and apologetic strategy. Abū Rā ʾiṭa writes his letter on the Trinity to an unnamed recipient who may have asked for guidance in answering Muslim questions about Christian beliefs from someone who had experience of debate with Muslim

[57] Abū Qurra, 'Treatise on the Trinity', pp. 36–37.

[58] Abū Qurra, 'Treatise on the Trinity', pp. 39 and 44.

[59] Abū Qurra, 'Treatise on the Trinity', p. 44.

[60] See Seppo Rissanen, *Theological Encounter of Oriental Christians With Islam During Early Abbasid Rule* (Åbo: Åbo Akademi University Press, 1993), p. 142.

[61] Abū Rā ʾiṭa begins his 'Reply to the Melkites on the Union (of the Divine and Human in Christ)' with a reference to a debate between himself and Abū Qurra that he wishes to follow up in writing. See Georg Graf (ed.), *Die Schriften des Jacobiten Ḥabīb Ibn Ḫidma Abū Rā ʾiṭa*, CSCO 130 (Louvain: L. Durbecq, 1951), pp. 65–72 (p. 65).

intellectuals.[62] The fact that Abū Rāʾiṭa discusses concepts that derive from Aristotle in the letter shows both that he was writing to a Christian who would have appreciated a philosophical approach to theology and that he was familiar with engaging with Muslims on philosophical grounds. Sidney Griffith mentions that some Muslims who were keen on gathering the fruits of the Greek philosophers translated into Arabic by Christians in Baghdad rejected the Trinity "on the grounds of Greek logic", as in the case of Abū Yūsuf al-Kindī (d. 873).[63]

Abū Rāʾiṭa says he will try to answer the claim of "the People of the South" that, since God is one, we Christians are wrong to teach the threeness (*tathlīth*) of God along with his oneness (*tawḥid*).[64] He proposes that "the People of Truth" agree with "the People of the South" that God is one but asks them what kind of oneness they mean. Do they mean one as genus (*jins*), one as species (*nauʿ*) or one as number (*ʿadad*)?[65] These are distinctions drawn from Aristotle's *Metaphysics* that Abū Rāʾiṭa clearly thinks will be decisive for his argument with Muslim opponents.[66] Sandra Keating argues that among Christian apologists "he is one of the first to build his argument using principles of logic and elements drawn from Greek thought".[67] This is probably true for writing in Arabic, but Timothy I wrote an apology in Syriac in which he debates with a Muslim "Aristotelian" a generation before this, in which "Aristotle is the principal source of his thought".[68] Christian philosophical theologians such as Timothy and Abū Rāʾiṭa were in the habit of engaging with philosophical Muslims using a common intellectual language inherited from Greek thought.

If "genus" is meant, then God encompasses various species, which is not possible for the creator of all species. If "number" is meant, then God is subject to division, since the number "one" is a species of number which is included in the perfection of number, and this contradicts the belief that God is perfect without being divided into parts. If "species" is meant, then God is comprised of different beings and this is unacceptable.[69] In other words, the Muslim should be driven to admitting that no Aristotelian concept of oneness is adequate to describe God, and as a result, no description of God's oneness can be given by a Muslim that does not undermine His perfection. The Christian should come to the rescue by stating that "We describe Him as 'one' perfect in essence (*jawhar*)

---

[62] Abū Rāʾiṭa, 'The First Letter on the Holy Trinity', Sandra T. Keating (ed. and trans.), in *Defending the 'People of Truth' in the Early Islamic Period: The Christian Apologies of Abū Rāʾiṭa* (Leiden: Brill, 2006), pp. 164–215 (pp.166–67).

[63] See Sidney H. Griffith, 'Ḥabīb ibn Ḫidmah Abū Rāʾiṭah, a Christian *mutakallim* of the First Abbasid Century', *Oriens Christianus* 64 (1980), pp. 161–201 (p. 175) and Augustin Périer, 'Un Traité de Yahya ben ʿAdi, Defense du Dogme de la Trinité Contre les Objections d'al-Kindi', *ROC* 22 (1920–1922), pp. 3–21.

[64] Abū Rāʾiṭa, 'The First Letter on the Holy Trinity', pp. 168–69.

[65] Abū Rāʾiṭa, 'The First Letter on the Holy Trinity', pp. 170–73.

[66] See Aristotle, *Metaphysics* 5.6, in Hugh Tredennick (trans.), *Metaphysics, Books I–IX, vol. 17*, (London: Heinemann, 1933).

[67] Keating, *Defending the 'People of Truth'*, p. 157.

[68] See HPJ. Cheikho, *Dialectique du Langage sur Dieu: Lettre de Timothée I (728–823) à Serge* (Rome: Pontificum Institutum Studiorum Orientalium, 1983), p. 60.

[69] Abū Rāʾiṭa, 'The First Letter on the Holy Trinity', pp. 172–76.

and not in number, because He is in number 'three' in the hypostases (*aqānīm*)". This is a perfect description of God because, first, it upholds His complete difference from His creation in His essence so that nothing can be compared with Him; and, second, it upholds His encompassing all of the species of number, even and odd, in His hypostases.[70]

A second reliance on Aristotle comes in Abū Rāʾiṭa's discussion of the attributes of God, such as "living", "knowing", "hearing" and "seeing", which Muslims presume that Christians believe in too.[71] He asks the Muslim, "Are they single, absolute names or predicative names?" Single or absolute names are not predicated of anything, such as "earth" or "fire", whereas predicated names are related to something else, such as "knower" and "knowledge", because the knower knows through knowledge, a differentiation that derives from Aristotle's *Categories*.[72] If a Muslim understands "living" and "knowing" as acquired by God as predicates of action, then he must describe God as Creator only after He created. But if he thinks of them as belonging to God eternally, then he must describe God as eternally creating. These were the very issues debated among philosophically inclined Muslims of the late eighth and early ninth centuries, the *Mutakallimūn*, who distinguished between "attributes of the essence" (*sifāt al-dhāt*) and "attributes of action" (*sifāt al-fiʿl*).[73] Abū Rāʾiṭa goes on to argue that life and knowledge must be eternal in God because there cannot be a time when God does not have life and knowledge. They cannot be parts of God's nature but must be perfect entities that can be distinguished but are also united with one another in Him.[74] "We describe Him by continuity in essence (*jawhar*), and by dissimilarity in the individuals (*ashkhās*) or hypostases (*aqānīm*)."

If Muslims object that God cannot be divided up in this way, then let them think about three lamps in one house that each give the same light, or Moses and Aaron, who are distinct individuals yet share a common humanity.[75] Just as Adam is the begetter of Abel, Abel is the begotten and Eve is the one who proceeds from Adam and is neither begetter nor begotten, but all three share the same humanity, so the Father is the begetter of the Son, the Son is begotten of the Father, and the Holy Spirit proceeds from the Father, but all three share the same essence (*jawhar*). If a Muslim says that this really means three individual gods, then he should be told, "It is only permitted to describe Adam and Abel and Eve as three human beings on account of the difference which exists between them. It is absolutely not possible that a difference like this exists in these three hypostases."[76] He refers to the analogies of the soul, the mind and speech, and the sun, its light and heat used by the 'Anonymous Apology' and Abū Qurra to support the continuity and differentiation of the essence and hypostases.

---

[70] Abū Rāʾiṭa, 'The First Letter on the Holy Trinity', pp. 174–77.
[71] Abū Rāʾiṭa, 'The First Letter on the Holy Trinity', pp. 176–77.
[72] See Aristotle, *Categories 1–7*, in Harold P. Cooke and Hugh Tredennick (eds and trans), *The Categories, vol. 1*, (London: Heinemann, 1983).
[73] See Griffith, 'Ḥabīb ibn Ḫidmah Abū Rāʾiṭah', p. 182.
[74] Abū Rāʾiṭa, 'The First Letter on the Holy Trinity', pp. 182–85.
[75] Abū Rāʾiṭa, 'The First Letter on the Holy Trinity', pp. 184–87.
[76] Abū Rāʾiṭa, 'The First Letter on the Holy Trinity', pp. 188–89.

If the Muslim asks why there are only three hypostases and not ten or twelve, then the answer should be that "God possesses knowledge and spirit, and the knowledge of God and His spirit are permanent and perpetual, not ceasing. For it is not permitted in a description of God for Him in His eternity to be without knowledge and spirit."[77] Abū Rāʾiṭa, in contradistinction to all of his above predecessors, does not refer to Word and Spirit here. Sidney Griffith is probably right to suggest that he is avoiding the anti-Trinitarian context of Q4:171 and keeping closely to the terms of debate concerning the attributes of God among the Muslim *mutakallimūn*, but the argument is basically the same as that of John of Damascus. Yet the presentation of God with two attributes of knowledge and spirit tends to suggest that there is one divine essence with two hypostases, so Abū Rāʾiṭa, in common with each of the writers surveyed above, fails to distinguish carefully enough between the divine essence and the hypostasis of fatherhood.

Towards the end of his letter, Abū Rāʾiṭa appeals to the way God speaks in the first-person plural in the Bible and the Qurʾān, whether in Genesis 1:26, "Let us make a human being in our image and likeness", or in many places in the Qurʾān, "We said", or "We created". This must mean that the hypostases were involved in the activities described. He gives further analogies of plurality from the Bible and concedes that, although Muslims accuse Christians of altering their scriptures, they cannot prove the allegation. This is an obvious difference in methodology from Abū Qurra, who began his presentation of the Trinity with Biblical testimony, ignoring the charge of textual corruption.

Finally, Abū Rāʾiṭa deals with the concept of causation within the Trinity, which a Muslim may raise to argue that, since the Father is the cause of the Son and the Spirit, He must be more worthy of praise and worship. He refers once more to the analogy of the sun, its light and its heat, and Adam and Eve, to point out that the Son and the Spirit are not less than the Father from whom they originate, but the Son and the Spirit are "two perfect beings (*dhātān*) from one perfect being (*dhāt*)". However, he previously uses (*jawhar*) to refer to the essence of God rather than (*dhāt*), and Rachid Haddad believes that the latter term oscillates between two different senses here,[78] between meaning the essence of God (*jawhar*) and meaning the three individuals (*ashkhās*), the three hypostases (*aqānīm*). This confusion of terms could easily lead a Muslim to ask why the Son and the Spirit are not two perfect essences (*jawharain*) from one perfect essence (*jawhar*). Indeed, the charge of incoherent terminology would be made by Abū ʿĪsā al-Warrāq as symptomatic of confused thinking among the Christian theologians.

ʿAmmār al-Baṣrī (d.c. 860)

ʿAmmār al-Baṣrī wrote two defences of the Trinity: a longer one as part of a 'Book of Questions and Answers', and a shorter one as a section in his 'Book of the Proof'. Since Abū al-Hudhayl al-ʿAllāf (d.c. 840) wrote a "refutation of

[77] Abū Rāʾiṭa, 'The First Letter on the Holy Trinity', pp. 196–97.
[78] See Haddad, *La Trinité Divine*, p. 166.

ʿAmmār the Christian in his reply to the Christians" it is probable, as Sidney Griffith argues, that ʿAmmār was attempting to answer this leading Muʿtazilī thinker.[79] The longer presentation is a series of answers to nine questions posed by a Muslim about the Trinity, and these may well be the kind of questions raised by Abū al-Hudhayl al-ʿAllāf in his lost refutation of ʿAmmār. The shorter presentation comes in an apology for key Christian beliefs and practices and is designed as a manual of advice for Christians. The nine questions will be used as the basic structure of the analysis given here.

The first question is "Since the Creator is one, how can one be three and three one?"[80] The answer is that there is one eternal essence (*jawhar*) in three essential properties (*khawāṣṣ jawhariyāt*) that are not differentiated or separated. The Creator lives and speaks, so "life" and "speech" can be attributed to Him. "The principal essence (*jawhar al-ʿayn*) has the attributions of His life and His speech; His speech is the source of His wisdom and His life is the source of His spirit."[81] A second question concerns the outcome of these attributions to the Creator, which appear to establish His existence first, then His life second and His wisdom third, and so He is counted as three, divided and partitioned. ʿAmmār replies that God is not embodied, so He cannot be divided or partitioned. "The One who created the world by His word and spirit is necessarily one in His essence (*jawhar*), one in His nature (*ṭabāʿ*), and no separation or partition occur in Him."[82] If the opponents suggest that God's attributes such as "hearing", "seeing", "almighty", "merciful", "generous", and "kind", mean that Christians cannot limit God to threeness, then they need to distinguish between God's names (*asmāʾ*) and His attributes (*ṣifāt*). The names refer to actions of God, whereas the attributes refer to properties essential to Him. Only "life" and "speech" are essential properties in God. "Life and speech are properties (*khawāṣṣ*) in the structure of the essence (*jawhar*), and in the quality of the essence (*dhāt*), and the nature (*ṭabāʿ*)."[83]

ʿAmmār is faced with the same difficulty as previous apologists for the Trinity in his selection of two attributes, in this case life and speech, giving the impression of a divine essence having two essential properties. There is a clear gap between this opening argument and the accepted Trinitarian formula of one essence in three hypostases. But ʿAmmār has chosen to begin on ground familiar to Muslim intellectuals who were attempting to determine whether the names of

---

[79] See Sidney H. Griffith, 'The Concept of *Al-Uqnūm* in ʿAmmār al-Baṣrī's Apology for the Doctrine of the Trinity', pp. 180–81 and 'ʿAmmār al-Baṣrī's *Kitāb al-Burhān:* Christian Kalām in the First Abbasid Century', *Le Museon* 96 (1983), pp. 145–81 (pp. 169–72).

[80] ʿAmmār al-Baṣrī, 'Book of Questions and Answers', in Michel Hayek (ed.), *ʿAmmār al-Baṣrī: Apologie et Controverses* (Beyrouth: Dar el-Machreq, 1977), pp. 93–265 (p. 148). See the English translation of the 'Book of Questions and Answers' by Mark Beaumont in *ʿAmmār al-Baṣrī's Arabic Apologetics: The Book of the Proof Concerning the Course of the Divine Economy and the Book of Questions and Answers* (Piscataway, NJ: Gorgias Press, 2022), pp. 121–304.

[81] ʿAmmār al-Baṣrī, 'Book of Questions and Answers', p. 149.

[82] ʿAmmār al-Baṣrī, 'Book of Questions and Answers', p. 154.

[83] ʿAmmār al-Baṣrī, 'Book of Questions and Answers', pp. 156–57.

God referred to actions of God. Abū al-Hudhayl al-ʿAllāf is reported to have denied that the names did refer to actions of God. While it is acceptable for created human beings to be described as performing an act of knowing by virtue of which they can be said to be knowing, it is necessary to interpret "God is knowing" as "there is an act of knowing that is God" and "there is an object that he knows".[84] Abū al-Hudhayl was concerned to defend God's unity (*tawḥīd*) by denying that there is an entity called "knowledge" that can be identified in God. ʿAmmār is tackling this reticence head on in his argument by isolating life and speech as inherent qualities in God which are distinct from actions that are not.

The third question logically follows from the previous discussion. Why does God need His speech and His Spirit but not hearing and sight? The answer is that His speech and His Spirit are not equivalent to His hearing and His sight. ʿAmmār appeals to Biblical testimony despite the opinion of his opponent that "we and our enemies the Jews agreed together to publish this falsified book which was corrupted (*taḥrīf*) to make it agree with our religions".[85] The plural language of Genesis 1:26, 3:22, and 11:7, "let us", has to be interpreted alongside the singular language of Deuteronomy 6:4, "the Lord your God is one". The solution is found in regarding the plural "we" as the expression of one essence (*jawhar*) who creates by His Word and Spirit but not by His hearing and His sight.[86]

Question four: "Why do you call these three properties three individuals (*ashkhās*) yet you lead the hearers of your teaching to believe that you reject three gods?" ʿAmmār replies that he does not call them individuals (*ashkhās*), since that term applies only to beings with physical bodies. He calls them by the Syriac term "*aqānīm*". In order to explain the meaning of this term he appeals to the categories of Aristotle: essence (*jawhar*), power (*quwa*) and accident (*ʿarḍ*), and then he adds hypostasis (*qunūm*) to them. The essence and the hypostasis are alike in that they exist without depending on anything else, whereas power and accident depend on something else for their existence.[87]

The fifth question relates more exactly to the Trinitarian formula. "Why do you call the three hypostases Father, Son and Holy Spirit?" The basic reason is that the Apostles report Jesus as commanding baptism in the name of the Father, Son and Holy Spirit in Matthew 28:19. John also speaks of the Son as the Word of God in the opening of his gospel and later in John 14:17 declares that the Holy Spirit proceeds from the Father. The Apostles declare that "The eternal living one who speaks is Father, who has His eternal Word, and His eternal life the Holy Spirit."[88] If the opponent objects to the names "father" and "son" as implying procreation in physical terms, then he should be told that there is no physical relationship between properties of God's essence. In the Torah, God

---

[84] See Richard M. Frank, *Beings and Their Attributes: The Teaching of the Basrian School of the Muʿtazila in the Classical Period* (Albany NY: State University of New York Press, 1978), p 12.

[85] ʿAmmār al-Baṣrī, 'Book of Questions and Answers', pp. 159–60.

[86] ʿAmmār al-Baṣrī, 'Book of Questions and Answers', p. 161.

[87] ʿAmmār al-Baṣrī, 'Book of Questions and Answers', pp. 161–63.

[88] ʿAmmār al-Baṣrī, 'Book of Questions and Answers', pp. 164–65.

calls Himself "king", "Lord", and "wise", when human beings are also called by these names, but God's names do not have the same meaning as the human names.[89]

Question six asks how this interpretation based on analogy (*qiyās*) can be certain and avoid doubt. The answer is that all descriptions of God derive from Scripture, and reason depends on that which is revealed there.[90]

Question seven returns to the divine status of the members of the Trinity. "If you claim that Father, Son and Holy Spirit are each perfect God then either you believe in three gods or three parts of one perfect god." ʿAmmār answers that the three distinct members of the Trinity share the same perfect essence (*jawhar kāmil*), just as Abraham, Isaac and Jacob share the same human nature but are distinct persons. There are not three perfect essences, or three perfect gods, but "each of them in his property (*khāṣṣa*) is perfect God".[91]

The eighth question insists that if the three hypostases are perfect God, then they must be three perfect gods. This would be true, says ʿAmmār, if the essence (*jawhar*) is equivalent to the property (*khāṣṣa*), but this is not the case. Just as three flames from a fire share the same perfect essence and yet are not called three fires, and three drops of water are not called three waters, so Father, Son and Holy Spirit who share the same perfect divinity are not called three gods.

The final question is missing in the manuscript but the answer is concerned to argue that each of the three properties shares the same essential attributes (*ṣifāt dhātiya*), so there is no essential distinction between their functions.

In his 'Book of the Proof Concerning the Course of the Divine Economy', ʿAmmār repeats much of the argument in the 'Book of Questions and Answers'. However, he answers a question not found in the earlier writing. It concerns the concept "hypostases" employed by Christians. The Muslim asks, "How can you call the Word and the Spirit hypostases (*qunūm*) in God, but you do not call the word of the soul and its life hypostases, nor the heat of the fire and its light, nor of the sun and its heat?"[92] ʿAmmār explains that hypostases are perfect and do not depend on anything, unlike the life and speech of the human soul that depend on the Creator for their existence, so using the term "hypostasis" for the life and speech of the human soul would be inappropriate. He argues,

> We did not give you these comparisons of created things with the Creator to imply that created things are perfect like the Creator, with the intention that just as you would call the three realities (*maʿānī*) by which the Creator is known "hypostases" because of their perfections, so you would also call the three realities (*maʿānī*) by which the created substances are known "hypostases". If this were the case, then what would be the superiority of the Creator over created things, if everything that you find in the Creator you necessarily relate to created things?[93]

---

[89] ʿAmmār al-Baṣrī, 'Book of Questions and Answers', pp. 166–68.
[90] ʿAmmār al-Baṣrī, 'Book of Questions and Answers', p. 169.
[91] ʿAmmār al-Baṣrī, 'Book of Questions and Answers', pp. 170–71.
[92] ʿAmmār al-Baṣrī, 'Book of the Proof Concerning the Course of the Divine Economy', in Hayek, *ʿAmmār al-Baṣrī*, pp. 19–90 (p. 50).
[93] ʿAmmār al-Baṣrī, 'Book of the Proof', p. 50.

ʿAmmār uses the Arabic term "*maʿānī*", meaning "realities", to explain the Syriac term "*qunūm*", meaning "hypostases", employed by the Muslim questioner. In the 'Book of Questions and Answers', ʿAmmār uses the Arabic term "*khawāṣṣ*", meaning "properties", to explain the meaning of "hypostases". In between the writing of the two books, ʿAmmār has decided to drop "*khawāṣṣ*" in favour of "*maʿānī*" as a way of explaining the meaning of "hypostases". Perhaps he felt that the concept "properties" conveyed the wrong sense to a Muslim audience, who might have understood the hypostases to be merely aspects of the character of God. The concept "realities" might have conveyed the sense of dynamic forces that have a life of their own, so that Muslims could more clearly understand that the life of God is His Spirit at work in creation and the speech of God is His Word incarnate in Jesus. Sara Husseini has argued that this change of terms from the earlier to the later work may be because ʿAmmār changed his approach from the 'Book of Questions and Answers', where he was answering questions that Muslims asked Christians to enable Christian leaders to defend their faith, to a more polemical approach in the 'Book of the Proof' designed to demonstrate weaknesses in Muslim arguments.[94]

ʿAmmār shares with his predecessors a common approach to presenting the Biblical basis of the Trinity and analogies for the Trinity based on the sun and human nature. He shares with Abū Rāʾiṭa an appeal to Aristotelian categories to argue that life and speech are eternal properties of God in contradistinction to actions of God, such as seeing and hearing. Clearly, these two theologians were willing to enter into the debate among Muslim intellectuals of the early ninth century concerning the status of the attributes of God that had developed upon the presuppositions of Greek philosophy. While ʿAmmār's Muslim debating opponent is known to have been Abū al-Hudhayl al-ʿAllāf, the details of his arguments are lost.

In her analysis of the Trinitarian defences of Abū Qurra, Abū Rāʾiṭa and ʿAmmār al-Baṣrī, Sara Husseini has shown that ʿAmmār "displays the deepest engagement with Islamic thought of the three authors". He is the only one to "really attack a Muʿtazilī conception of the nature of God".[95]

---

[94] Sara L. Husseini, *Early Christian–Muslim Debate on the Unity of God: Three Christian Scholars and their Engagement with Islamic Thought* (Leiden: Brill, 2014), p. 138.

[95] Husseini, *Early Christian–Muslim Debate*, p. 200.

2. Christian Presentations of the Trinity for Muslims in the Medieval Period

The early attempts by Christians to communicate their belief in the Trinity to Muslims were followed by a series of writers who depended on them in defending the oneness of God in his Triune reality. By the middle of the ninth century, it was clear that Muslims came to regard Christians as suspect monotheists and the defence of Christian monotheism is at the heart of Christian apologetic writing. The Arabic writers surveyed come from the three main denominations in the Middle East: the Chalcedonian Melkites, the East Syrian Diophysites and the West Syrian Miaphysites. Melkite bishop Peter of Bayt Raʾs, towards the end of the ninth century, continues the tradition of John of Damascus and ʿAmmār al-Baṣrī in utilising Q4:171 to support the Word and Spirit as being essential to God. The West Syrian Yaḥya ibn ʿAdī in the early tenth century develops several different analogies for the Trinity that make him stand out from his predecessors. He believed that analogies from the created world would demonstrate the possibility of oneness being defined as capable of multiplicity. Two eleventh-century Church of the East theologians show divergent paths in arguing for the Trinity. Ibn al-Ṭayyib relies on two of Yaḥya ibn ʿAdī's analogies but also follows ʿAmmār al-Baṣrī's presentation of the hypostases as properties rather than persons. Iliyyā, the East Syrian Bishop of Nisibis, attempts to demonstrate to a Muslim vizier that Christians are monotheists even while believing in the Trinity. He challenges the new Sunni conviction that God has seven essential attributes by arguing that these attributes are reducible to three. He appreciates the Muslim difficulty with the Christian assertion that God is a substance, since Muslims define that concept as being an aspect of the created world which is inappropriate to describe the transcendent Creator and suggests a term for God from the Syriac language *kiyān*, which means "self-existent". The final theologian in this period is Paul of Antioch, who was bishop of the Melkite church in Sidon in the early thirteenth century. He sums up the tradition of Middle Eastern theology in dialogue with Muslims by repeating John of Damascus' argument that Q4:171 supports the Trinity. He is reliant on ʿAmmār al-Baṣrī's argument that the Word and Spirit are essential attributes of God, and he agrees with Iliyyā of Nisibis that the word "substance" applied to God continues to cause problems for Muslims, but he does not adopt the Syriac term proposed by Iliyyā. He has his own way of defending the concept "substance" by arguing that there are substances in the created world that do not have accidents, so God can be named a substance that has no accidents.

Peter of Bayt Ra᾿s (Late Ninth Century)

Peter was the Melkite bishop of Bayt Ra᾿s (Capitolias) in the Transjordanian region when he wrote his 'Book of the Proof' ('Kitāb al Burhān') in the late ninth century. He attempts to provide an apologetic defence of the Trinity and the Incarnation for his Melkite flock as they struggle to be accepted by the Muslim culture now dominant in their milieu. As Mark Swanson argues, "While the author does not bring Islamic teachings, practice and history explicitly into his arguments, they are clearly in the background."[1]

He begins his treatment of the Trinity by depending on John of Damascus' *On the Orthodox Faith*, demonstrating the significance John's work held for Melkite Chalcedonian Christians throughout the Middle East. Having argued at the outset of his treatise that there has to be a creator of the world, and that the belief of those who hold to two creators, one the creator of good and the other the creator of evil, is unacceptable, Peter quotes from the Old Testament to show that Christians believe in one creator of everything. He appeals to the *Shema* in Deuteronomy 5:6-7, "Hear O Israel, your Lord God is one".[2] He wants to align himself with Muslims who hold unswervingly to the oneness of God in order to ensure that they do not place Christians in the camp of the dualists. At the end of his critique of the dualists he states, "Those who speak of two heads and two gods are refuted by the books of God whose contents demonstrate the oneness of God (*tawḥīd Allah*)."[3] Peter's attention to dualism shows how pervasive in his area was the Zoroastrian teaching that was held by the majority of the population. He repeats the approach of ʿAmmār al-Baṣrī, who opened his defence of the oneness of God by refuting dualists.[4]

He begins his argument for the Christian conception of God by establishing that the Word of God exists eternally within Him. He states, "It is necessary for the one who believes in God to know that God is perfect and is never without His Word, and that His Word exists eternally, has no end or beginning and never ceases to exist."[5] He goes on to argue that God has speech just as humans do, unlike animals who lack this capacity, yet His speech is eternal, unlike human speech. And just as human speech comes from the mind and is not identical to the mind, yet is evidence of one mind, so is the Word of God. The mind gives

---

[1] Mark N. Swanson, 'Peter of Bayt Ra᾿s', in D. Thomas and B. Roggema (eds), *Christian–Muslim Relations: A Bibliographical History, volume 1* (Leiden: Brill, 2009), pp. 902–906 (p. 904).

[2] Peter of Bayt Ra᾿s, 'Book of the Proof', in Pierre Cachia (ed.), *Eutychius of Alexandria: The Book of the Demonstration*, CSCO 192 (Louvain: L. Durbecq, 1960), p. 19. See also the English translation by W. Montgomery Watt, *Eutychius of Alexandria: The Book of the Demonstration*, CSCO 193 (Louvain: L. Durbecq, 1960). Cachia and Watt accepted the identification of the author with Eutychius, Melkite Bishop of Alexandria, made by Georg Graf in his five-volume *Geschichte der Christlichen Arabischen Literatur, vol. 2* (Vatican City: Biblioteca Apostolica Vaticana, 1944–1953), pp. 35–38. However, the earliest manuscript attributes the work to Peter of Bayt Ra᾿s. See Swanson, 'Peter of Bayt Ra᾿s', p. 903.

[3] Peter of Bayt Ra᾿s, 'Book of the Proof', p. 22.

[4] ʿAmmār al-Baṣrī, 'Book of Questions and Answers', pp. 100–104.

[5] Peter of Bayt Ra᾿s, 'Book of the Proof', p. 24.

birth to the speech, yet we do not say that the mind and the speech are separated into two, but rather that they express a unity. So, likewise the Word of God is not separate from the mind of God. Peter argues,

> Concerning the union between everything that is in the mind of the one who begets (*al-wālid*) in the Word of the one who is begotten (*al-mawlūd*), who is from Him, these two are one in substance (*jawhar*) because everything that God knows about the perfection of everything is known equally by His Word.[6]

Then Peter adds the Spirit to the Word as essential components in the One God. "It is necessary for the Word to have breath because our speech also is not without breath."[7] Human breath gives the thought of the mind the opportunity to be expressed and heard by others. Likewise, the Spirit gives the Word of God the opportunity to be expressed and heard by humans. Just as human speech and human breath are different yet united aspects, so the Word and Spirit of God are different yet united aspects of God.

> Just as we understand that the Word of God exists and is not poured out and dissolved in the air … but exists by a substantial (*jawharī*) existence which has will, action and power over everything, likewise we understand the Spirit of God is inseparable from His revealed Word in His actions, yet there is a substantial (*jawharī*) power in the Spirit that is separate from the Word of God.[8]

Peter then defines the relationships between God, His Word and His Spirit. "The Spirit is sent by the Father and dwells in the Word since the Word reveals the Spirit."[9] The Spirit shares the same characteristics as the Word. "They both have existence, life, will and action … They both are eternal with no beginning or end."[10] There is a progression of the revelation from "the Father who never lacks speech" to "the Word who never lacks Spirit".[11]

He goes on to explain that the Father, Son and Holy Spirit are "the three names of three aspects (*jihāt*) in the one substance (*jawhar*) of God" mentioned by Jesus in Matthew 28:19.[12] He repeats the standard explanation of the Chalcedonian Melkite church inheritance of the relationships between them. "The Father begets and is not begotten, the Son is begotten and does not beget, and the Holy Spirit proceeds and is not begotten and does not beget … yet they are all one God. There is no separation between these three aspects (*jihāt*)."[13]

Peter develops his own understanding of John of Damascus' appeal to Q4:171 without referring to the way John uses the text. He is clearly indebted to the language of Abū Qurra in describing three aspects (*jihāt*) in one God. Rachid Haddad argues that, like Abū Qurra, Peter intends the three aspects (*jihāt*) to mean "persons". "When the author speaks of (*jihāt ma'būda*), persons who are

---

[6] Peter of Bayt Ra's, 'Book of the Proof', p. 25.
[7] Peter of Bayt Ra's, 'Book of the Proof', p. 25.
[8] Peter of Bayt Ra's, 'Book of the Proof', p. 25.
[9] Peter of Bayt Ra's, 'Book of the Proof', p. 25.
[10] Peter of Bayt Ra's, 'Book of the Proof', p. 26.
[11] Peter of Bayt Ra's, 'Book of the Proof', p. 26.
[12] Peter of Bayt Ra's, 'Book of the Proof', p. 27.
[13] Peter of Bayt Ra's, 'Book of the Proof', p. 28.

worshipped, who are the Father, the Son and the Holy Spirit, he is not signifying mere rational aspects of God. Here (*jihāt*) is surely a synonym for a person."[14]

He is similar to ʿAmmār al-Baṣrī in arguing that the Word and Spirit are essential to the nature of God, but he does not utilise the Muslim debate about the attributes of God as ʿAmmār does. We can conclude that Peter was attempting to put together a coherent account of the Christian contention that God is the one Creator in agreement with Muslims over against the teaching of Zoroastrian dualists prevalent in his area, along with a defence of the Christian belief in the oneness of the Triune God that would be acceptable to Muslims as an expression of monotheism.

Abū Zakarīyā Yaḥya ibn ʿAdī (893–974)

Abū Zakarīyā Yaḥya ibn ʿAdī wrote several treatises on the Trinity. He is distinguished among the Christian theologians reviewed so far in that he worked as a teacher of philosophy in Baghdad in the school of the Baghdad Peripatetics and had Muslim colleagues and pupils there.[15] He came from the West Syrian Miaphysite church in Takrit, which was also the home of his West Syrian theological predecessor, Abū Rāʾiṭa.

His earliest datable treatment of the Trinity comes from 940 in his 'Treatise on the Unity of God According to the Teaching of the Christians'. He begins by defining the oneness of God in an attempt to address Muslim concerns that Christians are polytheists. He agrees with the Muslim conception of the oneness of God, who is "a being who has no diversity as far as He is one".[16] He then refers to six ways to understand the concept of oneness: of genus, of species, of relation, of continuum, of indivisibility and of definition. Yaḥya argues that none of these apply to the oneness of God apart from the last.[17] How God's oneness is defined is central to the debate between Muslims and Christians. Christians wish to define the oneness of God as "one in subject but multiple in definition".[18] He uses the analogy of a human being who is one subject with multiple definitions.

---

[14] See Haddad, *La Trinité Divine*, p. 174. Haddad criticises Watt for translating *jihāt* as aspects. Watt translates, "Three names for three aspects (*jihāt*) in the substance of one God", on page 22. Haddad accuses Watt of being too literal and of ending up giving the impression that the author believes in three modes of being rather than three persons when it is clear in the context that he holds to three distinct persons (footnote, p. 174). I agree with Watt that it is important to give the English reader a sense of the value of the Arabic terminology without paraphrasing the meaning to align it with a preconceived view of the author's meaning. The author chose to use a term that normally means "face", "appearance" or "perspective".

[15] See Emilio Platti, 'Yaḥya ibn ʿAdī', in D. Thomas and A. Mallett (eds), *Christian–Muslim Relations. A Bibliographical History, vol. 2* (Leiden: Brill, 2011), pp. 390–438 (p. 390).

[16] Yaḥya ibn ʿAdī, 'Treatise on the Unity of God According to the Teaching of the Christians', in Samir K. Samir (ed.), *Le Traité de l-Unité de Yaḥya ibn ʿAdī (893–974)* (Jounieh: Patrimoine Arabe Chrétien 2, 1980), p. 196.

[17] ibn ʿAdī, 'Treatise on the Unity of God', pp. 203–207.

[18] Ibn ʿAdī, 'Treatise on the Unity of God', p. 208.

"Zayd is one subject who can be defined as "living", "rational" and "mortal".[19] This is the way that Christians think about God. He is one subject in multiple definitions. "God is one substance (*jawhar*) in three attributes (*ṣifāt*) which are goodness (*al-jūd*), power (*al-qudra*), and wisdom (*al-hikma*)".[20]

Yaḥya goes on to develop these three attributes as particularly definitive of God. In the final analysis, he believes that the power of God is behind the creation of the universe. He did not need to create anything in order to fulfil something lacking in Himself. Rather, he created the world out of his goodness and wisdom such that "His voluntary act of creation demonstrates His goodness and His wisdom".[21] Kamal Bualwan believes that Yaḥya's choice of these three attributes to define the one God is dictated by his conception of the manner of creation. "Ibn ʿAdī asserts that God, through his attributes (wisdom, power and goodness), is the cause and creator of the universe which is entirely dependent on his choice and desire."[22]

Clearly, Yaḥya is involved in debate with Muslim intellectuals who were concerned with the relationship of the transcendent God to His creation. He takes the opportunity to defend a Christian perspective on that relationship. He is able to agree with the Muʿtazilī conviction that God has no need of a creation and that His work of creation arose from his benevolence, especially towards humanity. But he introduces his own unique take on the way to define God among Christian thinkers. Rather than present the New Testament language of Father, Son and Holy Spirit, he defers to the language inherited from Greek philosophy, especially from Aristotle, that was now common currency in the school of philosophy in Baghdad. Yet his choice of three attributes is still governed by the fact that Christians hold to the Trinity. Muslims were already discussing how many of God's attributes could be defined as essential to Him. Yaḥya's selection of attributes that Muslims could recognise as being essential to God leaves the unanswered question as to why these three?

A later treatise would go some way towards answering this question. In 961, Yaḥya wrote a response to the critique of the Trinity by the Muslim philosopher al-Kindī (d. 873). He quotes al-Kindī paragraph by paragraph and gives his response. Al-Kindī understands that Christians of all sects believe more or less the same about the Trinity, that the one God is a Trinity of Father, Son and Holy Spirit. He objects to this conception of God, since there must be "composition in the Father, Son and Holy Spirit".[23] He notes that Christians speak of the one substance (*jawhar*) in three properties (*khawaṣṣ*). He then points out that this must mean that the Father, Son and Holy Spirit are composed of the same substance. Al-Kindī's definition of the oneness of God is that He is simple

---

[19] Ibn ʿAdī, 'Treatise on the Unity of God', p.209.

[20] Ibn ʿAdī, 'Treatise on the Unity of God', p.209.

[21] Ibn ʿAdī, 'Treatise on the Unity of God', p.246.

[22] Kamal Bualwan, 'Yaḥya ibn ʿAdī's Conception of "the One"', *Parole de l'Orient* 28 (2003), pp. 485–95 (p. 490).

[23] Yaḥya ibn ʿAdī, 'Treatise Showing the Errors of Abū Yūsuf Yaʿqub ibn Ishaq al-Kindi's Refutation of the Christians', in Augustin Périer (ed.), 'Un Traité de Yaḥya ibn ʿAdī: Défense du Dogme de la Trinité Contre les Objections d'al-Kindi', *Revue de L'Orient Chrétien* 22 (1920–1921), pp. 3–12 (p. 4).

without composition, and that composite bodies are part of creation and are not eternal; therefore, the Christian definition is lacking in rationality. "Each person is composed of the substance which contains them all and the properties of each in particular. Therefore, they are all composed and none of them are eternal."[24]

Yaḥya replies by defining the Trinity. "The three persons are the properties of the one substance (*jawhar*), who is good, wise and powerful. The Father is good, the son is wise, and the Holy Spirit is powerful."[25] He then disagrees with al-Kindī's complaint that Christians are left with a created deity since there is composition in God which counts against his eternal being. Yaḥya argues,

> Christians do not believe that the Father, Son and Holy Spirit are produced by composition of the substance and the properties. But they only say that the substance (*jawhar*) is qualified for each of the three attributes (*ṣifāt*) and that these attributes are eternal and not produced after never having existed.[26]

Al-Kindī also thinks that the Father, Son and Holy Spirit must be three eternal beings in the Christian conception of the Trinity. He discusses various concepts of oneness also found in Yaḥya's earlier treatise, such as oneness of genus and species, and concludes, "Christians say three is one. But this results in three eternal beings".[27] Yaḥya indicates that in his exposition of types of oneness, al-Kindī has failed to look at oneness "in relation or of numerical unity that permits subdivision".[28] Yaḥya repeats his argument from the 940 treatise that one subject can have multiple definitions. He uses once again his analogy of Zayd being one subject that contains the definition "living", "rational" and "mortal", and concludes, "This is the way that Christians speak about the Creator who is one".[29]

In another response to a Muslim critic of the Trinity, Yaḥya uses the Zayd analogy in a different way. In his response to the 'Refutation of the Three Christian Sects' by Abū ʿĪsā al-Warrāq (d. 860), Yaḥya repeatedly refers to Zayd the doctor, the accountant and the writer as a helpful analogy for the relationship between the three members of the Trinity.[30] Although this work is not dated by Yaḥya, it appears to be later than the response to al-Kindī, given the fact that the Zayd analogy is developed in this fashion.

Another treatise on the Trinity is entitled 'Treatise Concerning the Rightness of the Christian Belief that the Creator is One Substance (*jawhar*) and Three Attributes (*ṣifāt*)'. In this work, Yaḥya develops a new analogy for the Trinity that would become influential among Miaphysite Christians, particularly in the Coptic church in Egypt. He describes the three attributes as intellect (*ʿaql*), the intelligent one (*ʿāqil*) and intellection (*maʿqūl*).[31]

---

[24] Ibn ʿAdī, 'Treatise Showing the Errors', p. 4.
[25] Ibn ʿAdī, 'Treatise Showing the Errors', p. 4.
[26] Ibn ʿAdī, 'Treatise Showing the Errors', p. 5.
[27] Ibn ʿAdī, 'Treatise Showing the Errors', p. 11.
[28] Ibn ʿAdī, 'Treatise Showing the Errors', p. 12.
[29] Ibn ʿAdī, 'Treatise Showing the Errors', p. 12.
[30] See Platti, 'Yaḥya ibn ʿAdī', p. 414.
[31] Yaḥya ibn ʿAdī, 'Treatise Concerning the Rightness of the Christian Belief that the Creator is One Substance and Three Attributes', in Louis Cheikho (ed.), *Vingt Traités Théologique d'Auteurs Arabes Chrétiens (IX au XIIIe siècle)*, (Beirut: Imprimerie Catholique, 1920), pp. 70–74 (p. 71).

Yaḥya explains what he means,

> The substance (*jawhar*) of the intellect (*ʿaql*) is the essence (*dhāt*) of the intelligent one (*ʿāqil*) and the essence (*dhāt*) of the intellection (*maʿqūl*). This single essence (*dhāt*) is not multiple in itself, but is described by these three attributes (*ṣifāt*), each of which is other than the other two.[32]

This rather abstract set of definitions of the three attributes is given a more concrete form by Yaḥya a little later. He says that the Father, who is the cause of the Son and the Spirit, is the intellect (*ʿaql*) in the analogy. The Son is the one who is intelligent (*ʿāqil*) in the sense that he thinks, and the Spirit is the intellection (*maʿqūl*) in the sense that he is the thought.[33] This psychological analogy is quite different from Yaḥya's earlier analogies of goodness, wisdom and power, or Zayd as living, rational and mortal or Zayd as doctor, accountant and writer. What is astonishing about Yaḥya is his willingness to develop fresh analogies over his lifetime. This can possibly be explained as a result of problems using them in debate with Muslims in the Baghdad school of philosophy. His constant search for new analogies demonstrates his endless ingenuity as a thinker and his boundless confidence that maybe one of these analogies might convince his Muslim audience that the Trinity could stand up to intellectual rigour. There is no doubt that Yaḥya was engaged in serious discussion as an equal participant in the intellectual concerns of Muslims to determine the nature of the attributes of God. Avril Mary Makhlouf rightly indicates,

> Yaḥya's contemporaries among the Mutakallimun and the Muʿtazilites were engaged in study of the notion of the *ṣifāt Allāh*. This aspect of his environment must have been a factor in Yaḥya's decision to develop his doctrine around the use of the terms *jawhar*, *dhāt*, and *ṣifāt*.[34]

Certainly, the last analogy he developed is more in tune with Muslim sensibilities than the earlier ones. The choice of goodness, wisdom and power would have struck Muslims as arbitrary choices of attributes among many attributes of God. How could they be essential attributes when other important attributes are ignored by Yaḥya? The use of Zayd as an analogy for God is fraught with problems for Muslims in that Zayd is mortal but God is immortal. There is a disrespectful comparison being made here between three aspects of a human being and God, who is unlike anything in his creation. Maybe the later Zayd analogy was better in that the three occupations of Zayd were closer to the notion of various actions that God is engaged in, but limiting these to three raises the same problem as before, given that Zayd can be engaged in more than three occupations in his lifetime. However, the psychological analogy at least provides the idea of three essential components of the nature of the human mind as a way of understanding the essential components of the mind of God. Whether there must be only three of these is debatable. Even if the analogy is helpful for a Christian believer, the problem remains for a Muslim to accept that the Christian Trinity makes more sense in this analogy than any of the other analogies. The

---

[32] Ibn ʿAdī, 'Treatise Concerning the Rightness of the Christian Belief', p. 71.
[33] Ibn ʿAdī, 'Treatise Concerning the Rightness of the Christian Belief', p. 73.
[34] Avril M. Makhlouf, 'The Trinitarian Doctrine of Yaḥya ibn ʿAdī: An Appraisal', *Parole de l'Orient* 10 (1981–1982), pp. 37–50 (p. 45).

mind of God may work in such a way, but this has not been revealed and what the Christian seeks to say about the three essential dimensions of the mind of God does not match the notions of Father, Son and Holy Spirit.

Yaḥya does not often refer to traditional Christian language for the Trinity but prefers to develop his own distinctive voice. However, in one treatise he does refer to the language inherited from others to describe the relations between the Father, Son and Holy Spirit. In his 'Treatise Explaining How it is Right for Christians to Say that the Creator is One Substance and Three Attributes', Yaḥya says that he has read Dionysius, Basil and John Chrysostom and wishes to pass on their wisdom concerning how to speak of the Trinity.[35] He explains that Christians speak of the Trinity of Father, Son and Holy Spirit in terms of fatherhood (*ubuwwa*), sonship (*bunuwwa*) and procession (*inbiʿāth*).[36] In this treatise he does not refer to his earliest description of the Trinity as goodness, power and wisdom. Therefore, this piece of writing seems to be much later in Yaḥya's life. The issue for Muslim thinkers in this more traditional depiction of the relations within the Trinity would no doubt be that Christians have introduced unpalatable aspects into the nature of the one God, since fatherhood and sonship are proscribed by the Qurʾān as descriptors for the relations between God and Jesus. Yaḥya's reluctance to use traditional Christian language stems from this awareness of Muslim sensibilities. He goes on to emphasise to his Muslim reader that the Creator is not three substances (*jawāhir*), but the reality (*maʿnā*) of each member of the Trinity is different from the reality of the other two members.[37] So, rather than leave his Muslim reader with the traditional language inherited from his predecessors, Yaḥya makes sure that he is communicating in language more acceptable to his Muslim audience.

Abū al-Faraj ʿAbd Allāh ibn al-Ṭayyib (980–1043)

Abū al-Faraj ʿAbd Allāh ibn al-Ṭayyib was a medical doctor in Baghdad who also worked as a priest and secretary to the Patriarch of the East Syrian church. He wrote three treatises on the Trinity which are similar in many respects. The earliest is actually entitled 'The Second Treatise Concerning the Trinity' and the copyist and scholars have retained this title.

The 'Second Treatise Concerning the Trinity' opens with the author's intention to establish the truth of the "necessity of Trinity in unity in describing the Creator".[38] He says he will point out what distinguishes the true religion of Christianity from other religions. "We mention what distinguishes us from those of religions which oppose us in pursuing our religious claims. We seek to clearly

[35] Yaḥya ibn ʿAdī, 'Treatise Explaining in Which Respect it is Valid for the Christians To Say that the Creator is One Substance and Three Hypostases', in Augustin Périer, *Maqālāt li-Yaḥya ibn ʿAdī: Petits Traités Apologétiques de Yaḥya ibn ʿAdī* (Paris: J. Gabalda, 1920), pp. 44–62 (p. 53).

[36] Ibn ʿAdī, 'Treatise Explaining in Which Respect it is Valid', p. 56.

[37] Ibn ʿAdī, 'Treatise Explaining in Which Respect it is Valid', p. 58.

[38] Ibn al-Ṭayyib, 'The Second Treatise on the Trinity', Michael F. Kuhn (trans.), in Ayman S. Ibrahim (ed.), *Medieval Encounters: Arabic-Speaking Christians and Islam* (Piscataway, NJ: Gorgias Press, 2022) pp. 440–48 (p. 441).

establish the goal of those claims before proving our religion, which they do not."[39] Julian Faultless says that in Ibn al-Ṭayyib's theological work there is "no explicit mention of Islam or Muslims", but this does not mean that he did not have Muslims in his sights when he writes about religions that oppose Christians, as Faultless recognises when he admits that there was "a constant need of Christians to defend themselves from the common Muslim accusation that Christians were tritheists".[40] Michael Kuhn argues that Ibn al-Ṭayyib's case against the unnamed Muslims is that "Christians seek to understand the goal of their religious claims while Muslims, in his view, practice their religion out of mere obedience" or alternatively, "his Muslim counterparts fail to understand the goal of Christian claims before rebutting them".[41]

Ibn al-Ṭayyib says that the Apostles of Christ brought the knowledge of the Trinity and unity to the various nations that received their teaching. Their writing was accepted by both simple and intellectual people as the truth. However, later on, others brought revelation in other writing to nations that did not have the same intellectual background to test the truth of what they proclaimed. The upshot of this is that "Complete assurance of their truth is illusory, as their apostles' word and the book which directs their worship has congealed hearts by its action".[42] This stark contrast between the writing brought by the Apostles of Christ and the writing brought by the unnamed Muslims shows the intention of Ibn al-Ṭayyib to argue for the truth of the former over against the falsehood of the latter. He bluntly states, "This general statement is intended to demonstrate the rationality of the truth believed by the Christians and contained in the holy gospel".[43] Ibn al-Ṭayyib also indicates that he is writing for his fellow Christians to help them be confident in defending the Trinity in the context of Muslim rule rather than to address Muslims directly. But he will proceed to answer Muslim arguments against the Trinity so that his readers can develop their own answers to Muslim objections.

He sets out his case by declaring that the Creator is both Triune and One. He notes that there is no debate over the oneness of the Creator. The debate arises over the triunity. Christians insist that the essence of God is threefold, in terms of wisdom (*al-hikma*), power (*al-qudra*), and bounty (*al-jūd*). Here, Ibn al-Ṭayyib is dependent directly on Yaḥya ibn ʿAdī's earliest definition of the Trinity from 940. While Ibn al-Ṭayyib admits that there are other attributes alongside these three, he does not attempt to demonstrate why these particular attributes are essential to the nature of God.

He then presents another argument for the triunity of God.

---

[39] Ibn al-Ṭayyib, 'The Second Treatise on the Trinity', p. 441.

[40] Julian Faultless, 'Ibn al-Ṭayyib', in Thomas and Mallett, *Christian–Muslim Relations*, pp. 667–97 (p. 670).

[41] Michael F. Kuhn, 'Abū al-Faraj ʿAbd Allāh ibn al-Ṭayyib (d. 1043): A Scholar-Priest Explains the Trinitarian Persons', in Ibrahim, *Medieval Encounters*, pp. 415–52 (p. 441).

[42] Ibn al-Ṭayyib, 'The Second Treatise on the Trinity', p. 442.

[43] Ibn al-Ṭayyib, 'The Second Treatise on the Trinity', p. 442.

> Christians also believe that the divine essence is an essence with the attribute of knowledge, as the exalted essence could not be unknowing. The essence with the attribute of knowledge manifestly knows and therefore knows itself. As it knows itself, then it is known to itself. The result is that the divine essence has the attribute of knowledge (*ʿilm*), knowing (*ʿālim*), and of being known (*maʿlūm*).[44]

This analogy bears a close resemblance to the analogy put forward by Yaḥya ibn ʿAdī when he wrote about the three attributes as intellect (*ʿaql*), the intelligent one (*ʿāqil*) and intellection (*maʿqūl*). Why Ibn al-Ṭayyib changes the language from intellect to knowledge is not clear. But it is clear that he thinks the triad proves that there must be three essential attributes. "The claim of the unity of the Creator with Trinity is clarified, as he is one essence and three attributes. As we have elucidated, the attributes cannot be two or four."[45] This argument shows that Ibn al-Ṭayyib does not follow his fellow East Syrian theologian ʿAmmār al-Baṣrī when he argued that God has two essential attributes, life and speech. For Ibn al-Ṭayyib, ʿAmmār al-Baṣrī's presentation falls short of a true description of the threefold nature of the essence of God. That there cannot be four essential attributes is Ibn al-Ṭayyib's response to the typical Muslim argument that God has multiple attributes and that arguing for only three essential attributes makes no sense.

Ibn al-Ṭayyib continues by explaining to his reader the actual terminology familiar to Christians, which has nothing to do with the language he has borrowed from Yaḥya ibn ʿAdī. He says that Christians call the essence "substance" (*jawhar*) and the attributes "properties" (*khawāṣṣ*).[46] Here he is dependent on ʿAmmār al-Baṣrī's language that shows the enduring nature of ʿAmmār's choice of Arabic terminology for the essential attributes within the East Syrian church.

He then equates his version of the psychological analogy to New Testament terminology for the Trinity.

> The attribute of knowledge they call "fatherhood" (*ubuwwa*), and the attribute of knowing "sonship" (*bunuwwa*), and the attribute of being known "procession" (*inbiʿāth*) … If the essence is taken with the entity of knowledge, the union is called the hypostasis (*uqnūm*) "the Father"; if the essence is taken with the entity of knowing, the union is called the hypostasis "the Son"; if taken with the entity of being known, the union is called the hypostasis "the Spirit".[47]

He points out that the names Father, Son and Holy Spirit are given in the writing of the Apostles and thus the only people to question their validity are "errant sophists" and not "people of truth".[48]

He returns to the Muslim objection that the attributes of God are more than three. Ibn al-Ṭayyib replies that there are two kinds of attributes, those that are essential and those that are actions. He repeats his argument that only the attributes of knowledge, knowing and being known are essential to God. He also

---

44 Ibn al-Ṭayyib, 'The Second Treatise on the Trinity', p. 443.
45 Ibn al-Ṭayyib, 'The Second Treatise on the Trinity', p. 444.
46 Ibn al-Ṭayyib, 'The Second Treatise on the Trinity', p. 444.
47 Ibn al-Ṭayyib, 'The Second Treatise on the Trinity', p. 444.
48 Ibn al-Ṭayyib, 'The Second Treatise on the Trinity', p. 445.

repeats his argument that, with respect to the created world, God has three essential attributes: goodness, power and wisdom. With respect to creation, God acts in many different ways, but these actions are not essential to his being.[49] It is rather surprising that Ibn al-Ṭayyib repeats the two lists of three essential attributes here. The reader might quite easily assume that there are six essential attributes, according to Ibn al-Ṭayyib: knowledge, knowing, being known, goodness, power and wisdom.

He goes on to demonstrate that the two rival Muslim views on the attributes of God in his time are both mistaken. He begins with those who say that the essential attributes of God are more than three.

> The first group of people of ancient law believes as do we, saying that the essence of the Creator is one while his attributes are many … They do not limit the attributes to three, but augment their number such that our difference with them concerns the number of the attributes of essence.[50]

Ibn al-Ṭayyib is referring to the doctrine of the Ashʿarites, the majority of whom, as Michael Kuhn indicates, "agreed on seven attributes of essence: will, wisdom, power, life, knowledge, seeing and hearing".[51] The second group think that the attributes are not separate from the essence but are merely descriptors of the essence. Ibn al-Ṭayyib states, "For them, the difference in the attributes arises from the speech of the describer and is not the reality of the matter". He argues that to say that human beings attribute a variety of states and actions to God but that these states and actions tell us nothing about God in Himself is manifestly false. "The result is that there would be no difference in our description of the Creator as wise and powerful. The two meanings would be the same. This is impermissible rationally and unacceptable."[52] As Michael Kuhn points out, Ibn al-Ṭayyib, in 'The Third Treatise on the Trinity', is refuting the doctrine of the Muʿtazilites, who "viewed the attributes as existing in the mind of the speaker describing God, but not in the eternal essence, who alone was eternal".[53]

The 'Third Treatise on the Trinity' repeats much of the second treatise but adds some developments in Ibn al-Ṭayyib's approach. He distinguishes the attributes of goodness, power and wisdom from the attributes of fatherhood, sonship and procession. The first three, goodness, power and wisdom, are "attributes that are communicable beyond his essence to his creatures", while the second trio, fatherhood, sonship and procession, are "attributes peculiar to him that are not communicable beyond his essence".[54] He concedes more clearly in this treatise that the fact that there are three essential non-communicable attributes is because God has revealed this to be the case in Scripture. The communicable attributes are capable of being perceived in the way creation

[49] Ibn al-Ṭayyib, 'The Second Treatise on the Trinity', pp. 446–47.

[50] Ibn al-Ṭayyib, 'The Second Treatise on the Trinity', p. 447.

[51] Kuhn, 'Abū al-Faraj ʿAbd Allāh ibn al-Ṭayyib (d. 1043)', p. 447.

[52] Ibn al-Ṭayyib, 'The Second Treatise on the Trinity', p. 448.

[53] Kuhn, 'Abū al-Faraj ʿAbd Allāh ibn al-Ṭayyib (d. 1043)', p. 447.

[54] Ibn al-Ṭayyib, 'The Third Treatise on the Trinity', Michael F. Kuhn (ed. and trans), in Michael F. Kuhn, *God is One: A Christian Defence of Divine Unity in the Muslim Golden Age* (Carlisle: Langham, 2019), pp. 238–61 (p. 240).

operates and do not depend on scriptural teaching.[55] Yet the problem that was apparent in the earlier treatise has not been resolved here. There still appear to be six essential attributes. Despite this, Ibn al-Ṭayyib goes on to apply a third set of three essential attributes, knowledge, knowing and being known, to his argument, which would bring the total to nine. But he argues that the non-communicable attributes of fatherhood, sonship and procession are synonyms for knowledge, knowing and being known, as he did in the earlier treatise.

He deals with the relationship between the communicable and non-communicable attributes by contrasting potential to act with the action itself. The Creator is described by goodness, power and wisdom, since these are observable by human beings in the created world. He has acted in these ways towards his creatures. "After creating the world, the Creator is described as wise and bounteous in actuality because the object exists in actuality, skilfully wrought."[56] Yet these three communicable attributes are equivalent to his three non-communicable attributes of fatherhood, sonship and procession, which are equivalent to knowledge, knowing and being known. This is because goodness, power and wisdom that are perceived by human beings in the created world must be potential within the essence of God even before the world came into being. "Since power is in potentiality in eternity, the skillful outworking is also potentiality in eternity. Also, if wisdom is in potentiality in eternity, the skillful outworking is also in potentiality in eternity."[57] Nevertheless, the only way to be sure and certain of this identity between the communicable and non-communicable attributes is by revelation rather by observation of the created world. We cannot be sure that God is knowing (*ʿālim*) from mere observation of the created world. "We need the grace of assured revelation lest we fall into error."[58] Revelation is required beyond observation because "What does not extend beyond his essence is concealed from human minds".[59]

In the end, it is by revelation that we come to understand the nature of God as Triune. The apostolic writing reveals the names Father, Son and Holy Spirit, and these are equivalent to knowledge, knowing and being known. "The Father, who is the essence itself with the potentiality of knowledge, is the cause of the Son and the Spirit. By this, I mean that the essence, in that it is knower and known, is the ground of its being, but not the cause of its existence."[60] Michael Kuhn believes that Ibn al-Ṭayyib was attempting to align the revealed names, Father, Son and Holy Spirit, with the analogy of knowledge, knower and being known, because he had inherited the thinking of key Christian and Muslim intellectuals and wanted to make his own contribution to that debate.

> He felt it necessary to make this connection given the philosophical context in which he labored and the intellectual currency of the triad of knowledge. Not only did Ibn ʿAdī the Jacobite refer to this triad, but Ibn Sīnā the Muslim philosopher

[55] Ibn al-Ṭayyib, 'The Third Treatise on the Trinity', p. 242.
[56] Ibn al-Ṭayyib, 'The Third Treatise on the Trinity', p. 250.
[57] Ibn al-Ṭayyib, 'The Third Treatise on the Trinity', p. 252.
[58] Ibn al-Ṭayyib, 'The Third Treatise on the Trinity', p. 252.
[59] Ibn al-Ṭayyib, 'The Third Treatise on the Trinity', p. 254.
[60] Ibn al-Ṭayyib, 'The Third Treatise on the Trinity', p. 258.

and contemporary of Ibn al-Ṭayyib made it foundational to his understanding of God.[61]

Iliyyā of Nisibis (d. 1046)

Iliyyā was Church of the East Bishop of Nisibis from 1009 until his death in 1046. He wrote several texts explaining the Trinity for a Muslim audience, including a series of dialogues between himself and a Muslim vizier, Abū al-Qāsim. These dialogues took place on three occasions between July 1026 and June 1027 and were recorded by Iliyyā in response to a request from Abū al-Qāsim, who died only four months after the final debate.[62] It is interesting to observe that Ibn al-Ṭayyib reviewed the reported debates between Iliyyā and Abū al-Qāsim in his role as secretary to the Church of the East Patriarch and declared, "The letter is extremely beautiful, orthodox, and in harmony with the ecclesial books. It is impossible for him who loves the truth to reject a single word thereof".[63]

In the letter written by Iliyyā to Abū al-Qāsim, who asked Iliyyā to write down their oral sessions, he begins by asserting that Christians believe in one God. He uses terms familiar to Muslims. "He is one God. There is no God beside Him. He has no partner in His Lordship and no peer in His divinity. He has no equal in His eternality."[64] Here, Iliyyā refers to Qur'ānic language to affirm his agreement with Muslim belief in the unity of God. He ends his statement of belief in the oneness of God in similar fashion. "The one God, one Creator, one Lord, who alone is worshipped, no god before Him and no Creator beside Him, no Lord other than Him and none to be adored but Him."[65] Michael Kuhn points out that this is a "declaration of Christian *tawḥīd* in language to which Muslims would gladly assent".[66]

Iliyyā then goes on to explain the Trinity within this definition of unity. He reports the Muslim objection to the Trinity in the following terms. "There is no known substance (*jawhar*) that does not occupy space and is contingent and no hypostases (*aqānīm*) who are not persons (*ashkhāṣ*) and no son who is not from marital relations."[67] These three objections typify Muslim reactions to the Trinity. For Muslims, the concept "substance" implies physicality and temporality, the concept "hypostases" implies personhood and the concept "son" implies sexual intercourse. Given these Muslim preconceptions of Christian vocabulary, Iliyyā reminds his Muslim interlocutor that the Qur'ān contains language that implies physicality in God. "If God has neither a body or limbs, why do you refer to his two seeing eyes or his outstretched hands, his two thighs

---

[61] Kuhn, *God is One*, p. 71.
[62] See Kuhn, *God is One*, p. 27.
[63] Kuhn, *God is One*, pp. 25–26.
[64] Iliyyā of Nisibis, 'The Book of the Sessions' (Huntingdon 240), p. 28, in Kuhn, *God is One*, p. 99.
[65] Iliyyā of Nisibis, 'The Book of the Sessions', p. 29, in Kuhn, *God is One*, p. 100.
[66] Kuhn, *God is One*, p. 99.
[67] Iliyyā of Nisibis, 'The Book of the Sessions', p. 30, in Kuhn, *God is One*, p. 100.

which he reveals, or his face which he turns in all directions?"[68] Iliyyā has the Muslim say that these anthropomorphic expressions in the Qurʾān are not to be taken literally. The Christian response is to say that the gospel records the names for the one God as three divine properties (*khawāṣṣ*), so that those who understand the three hypostases (*aqānīm*) to mean three gods, or three composite bodies (*ajsām murakkaba*), or three separate persons (*ashkhāṣ mutafarriqa*) have misunderstood them.[69] When it comes to the names "Father" and "Son" there can be no room for sexual relations in the meaning of the terms.[70] He concludes this study of Biblical and Qurʾānic terminology by stressing that both scriptures employ anthropomorphic language and that both scriptures should be interpreted in a similar way. "If we commit idolatry (*shirk*) and anthropomorphization (*tashbīh*), you also embody God (*tajassum*) and anthropomorphize by saying God has two eyes, two hands, a face and two legs."[71]

Another version of the sessions appears to have been addressed to a Muslim who wanted to know what Iliyyā and Abū al-Qāsim discussed. Abū al-Qāsim died within a few weeks of the last encounter between them and presumably had little opportunity to write down his own contribution to the debates. Therefore, Iliyyā himself must have written the account of the sessions.

Session One is taken up with the problem of the Trinity as expressed by Abū al-Qāsim, who is aware that Christians uphold the Nicene Creed, which states that God is one substance in three hypostases, Father, Son and Holy Spirit, and that this creed represents polytheism.[72] The Vizier goes on to argue that the concept "substance" entails embodiment and temporality in God. Iliyyā replies by arguing that Muslim terminology also entails embodiment and temporality in God. If Muslims say that God is living, active, powerful and knowing, then they "are obliged to concede his corporeality".[73]

The Vizier then asks for an explanation of the three hypostases. Iliyyā begins by defining God as self-existent (*qāʾim bi-nafsihi*), depending on Muslim terminology acceptable to Abū al-Qāsim.[74] He then argues that a self-existent being must be living by definition, and also that he must be a speaking being since he created other beings to whom he spoke.[75] Speech can be either the sound produced by mortal beings that embraces animals or the communication of rational beings that embraces human beings who share such a capacity with God. Therefore, God has three hypostases: self-existence, life and rational speech.[76] Abū al-Qāsim rejects adding speech and life to the essence of God because that

[68] Iliyyā of Nisibis, 'The Book of the Sessions', p. 30, in Kuhn, *God is One*, p. 100.
[69] Iliyyā of Nisibis, 'The Book of the Sessions', p. 31, in Kuhn, *God is One*, p. 100.
[70] Iliyyā of Nisibis, 'The Book of the Sessions', p. 31, in Kuhn, *God is One*, p. 100.
[71] Iliyyā of Nisibis, 'The Book of the Sessions', p. 31, in Kuhn, *God is One*, p. 100.
[72] Iliyyā of Nisibis, 'Session 1', in Samir K. Samir (ed.), 'Entretien d'Elie de Nisibe avec le Vizir Ibn ʿAli al-Maghribi sur l'Unité et la Trinité', *Islamochristiana* 5 (1979), pp. 31–117; verses 30–39 in Kuhn, *God is One*, p. 106.
[73] Iliyyā of Nisibis, 'Session 1'; verses 72–74 in Kuhn, *God is One*, p. 107.
[74] Iliyyā of Nisibis, 'Session 1'; verses 93–94 in Kuhn, *God is One*, p. 107.
[75] Iliyyā of Nisibis, 'Session 1'; verses 95–106 in Kuhn, *God is One*, p. 107.
[76] Iliyyā of Nisibis, 'Session 1'; verses 110–21 in Kuhn, *God is One*, p. 108.

leads to belief in two eternal entities in addition to God Himself.[77] But Iliyyā is able to counter this supposed difficulty by pointing out that Sunni Muslims believe that God has seven essential attributes. They say that He is living, knowing, powerful, willing, articulating, hearing and seeing. "If Christians are polytheists through their assertion that God is speaking and living, the Sunnis must also be culpable of polytheism, only to a greater degree", retorts Iliyyā.[78]

Iliyyā continues by indicating that the speech and life of God are called "Word" and "Spirit". They are not substances in themselves but are hypostases which are "equal to God's essence (*dhāt*) in substantiality and eternality".[79] The essence is named "Father", the Word is named "Son" and the life is named "Spirit". Just as the essence of the human soul and its speech and life are one human soul and the essence of the sun and its heat and light are one sun, so the essence of God and His Word and Spirit are one God.[80]

It is interesting to observe how closely Iliyyā depends on the argument of his Church of the East forbear, ʿAmmār al-Baṣrī, that God has two essential attributes, of speech and life. This contrasts with Iliyyā's contemporary in the Church of the East, Ibn al-Ṭayyib, who argued for three essential attributes rather than two. Even within the same denomination it was possible for two theologians to disagree fundamentally on the way to understand the hypostases of the Trinity.

In two later pieces of writing, Iliyyā adopts a new expression for substance (*jawhar*), given that Muslims reject it as a term suitable for the transcendent majesty of God. In a treatise written for his brother, Iliyyā suggests that Christians should cease using the Arabic word *jawhar* to refer to the essence of God because Muslims understand *jawhar* to refer to a physical body. Instead, they might adopt a Syriac term *kiyān*, which means "self-existent" but does not immediately suggest to a Muslim that this being is part of creation.[81] In a letter written to a Muslim judge who asked Iliyyā for an explanation of the Trinity, Iliyyā adopts the new strategy of avoiding the Arabic term *jawhar* in favour of the Syriac term *kiyān*. In answer to the judge, who asked how Christians could believe in God as one substance (*jawhar*) in three hypostases (*aqānim*), Iliyyā answers that Christians believe in God as a self-existent being (*kiyān*) in three hypostases (*aqānim*).[82]

Whether the judge would have understood the Syriac loan word is doubtful, but there is no extant response from him. It is intriguing that Iliyyā thought that adopting a Syriac loan word used in his Church of the East Syriac context, in which the liturgy was still recited in Syriac rather than Arabic, would be able to communicate exactly what Christians believed to Arabic-speaking Muslims. The use of the Syriac *uqnūm/aqānim* for the Greek *hypostasis/hypostases* had been

---

[77] Iliyyā of Nisibis, 'Session 1'; verses 122–24 in Kuhn, *God is One*, p. 108.
[78] Iliyyā of Nisibis, 'Session 1'; verses 130–34 in Kuhn, *God is One*, p. 108.
[79] Iliyyā of Nisibis, 'Session 1', verses 142–46 in Kuhn, *God is One*, p. 108.
[80] Iliyyā of Nisibis, 'Session 1', verses 154–59 in Kuhn, *God is One*, p. 109.
[81] Iliyyā of Nisibis, 'Treatise on Kiyān', in Samir K. Samir (ed.), 'Un Traité Nouveau d'Elie dec Nisibe sur le Sens des Mots Kiyan et Ilah', *Parole de l'Orient* 14 (1987), pp. 109–153 (p. 112), in Kuhn, *God is One*, p. 120.
[82] Iliyyā of Nisibis, 'Letter on the Oneness of the Creator in the Trinity of His Hypostases', (Huntingdon 240), in Kuhn, *God is One*, p. 121.

established as loan words in Christian Arabic writing since the early ninth century, but to suggest after two hundred years that the Arabic term *jawhar* should now be replaced by a Syriac expression *kiyān* appears to be counterproductive. Such a procedure should have been adopted at the same time that *uqnūm/aqānim* had been taken over into Christian Arabic discourse two centuries before. It was surely too late to expect that other Christians would think it wise to follow Iliyyā's advice.

Paul of Antioch (Thirteenth Century)

Paul of Antioch was a bishop of the Melkite church in Sidon whose birth and death dates are unknown but who was active after the time of Iliyyā of Nisibis, since he refers to Iliyyā's writing. The earliest references to Paul's 'Letter to a Muslim Friend' come from a refutation of his writing by the Egyptian Muslim judge al-Qarāfī (1228–1285), entitled 'Proud Answers to Insolent Questions'. Therefore, Paul may have been writing in the early thirteenth century.[83]

In his 'Letter to a Muslim Friend', Paul sets out to write an account of what European Christian leaders think of Muḥammad and his teaching. He reports that they note in the Qur'ān that Muḥammad was sent solely to the Arabic-speaking people and that the message of the Qur'ān supports Christian teaching, so there should be concord between Muslims and Christians rather than discord. There is no doubt that Paul was situated in the middle between Western Christian military attempts to overthrow Islamic dominance in the Middle East and stout Muslim defence of the territory taken in the seventh century by the original Arab forces. While he says in the opening of his letter that he has travelled widely to consult Christian leaders in Europe, the actual contents of the letter show a familiarity with the Arabic language of the Qur'ān that would have been quite remote from those European Christian leaders. In other words, Paul is promoting his own interpretation of the Qur'ān in the guise of representing European Christian voices. Perhaps he believes he is a mediator between those European voices intent on destroying the power of Islam and the Muslims he and his people are living under, such that Middle Eastern Christians like him can demonstrate that crusades by Western Christians need not be the only method of relating to Muslims.

He deals with the Trinity within the letter by representing the typical Muslim criticism of the Christian language of Father, Son and Holy Spirit. Paul reports that the European Christian leaders replied, "If only they knew that we intend by our saying this to verify the truth of the teaching that God Almighty is living and

---

[83] See David Thomas, 'Paul of Antioch's *Letter to a Muslim Friend* and *The Letter from Cyprus*', in David Thomas (ed.) *Syrian Christians Under Islam: The First Thousand Years* (Leiden: Brill, 2001), pp. 203–204. This dating has been accepted by Sidney Griffith in his English translation of Paul's 'Letter to a Muslim Friend' in Samuel Noble and Alexander Treiger (eds), *The Orthodox Church in the Arab World 700–1700* (DeKalb: Northern Illinois University Press, 2014), pp. 216–35 (p. 216). The earliest manuscript, MSS Sinai Arabic 531, was copied in 1232.

speaking they would not reject our saying this".[84] He explains that "We say that God is living in order to deny death to him" and "We say that God is speaking in order to deny ignorance in him".[85] The names, Father, Son and Holy Spirit represent the essence, life and speech of the one God. "According to us, the essence (*dhāt*) is the Father, the speech is the Son and the life is the Holy Spirit".[86] Paul relies on the long tradition among Middle Eastern Christians since John of Damascus of reading the divine attributes of Word and Spirit predicated of Jesus in the Qurʾān as upholding the Trinity. While John's interpretation was written in Greek, the form of the argument in Paul's presentation reflects the Arabic writing of ʿAmmār al-Baṣrī, as Ebied and Thomas point out.[87] It is characteristic of ʿAmmār to say that the Father is the essence (*dhāt*) or substance (*jawhar*) of God, who has two essential attributes of speech and life expressed as the Word and Spirit of God, the Son and the Holy Spirit. It is interesting to observe how Paul as a Melkite bishop does not hesitate to rely on the theology of a Church of the East writer despite serious differences between the Melkites, who subscribed to the Creed of Chalcedon, and the Church of the East, who did not. Paul might well have said that the differences lay in understanding Christology. The agreement between the two churches over the correct way to understand the Trinity meant that he could quite straightforwardly rely on Church of the East presentations of the Trinity, as he did here.

After quoting from both the Bible and the Qurʾān to confirm that God has the attributes of life and speech, Paul concludes that the attributes of life and speech are "Essential attributes (*ṣifāt jawhariyya*) which are not the same as the other, yet God is one".[88] Notice how Paul uses *jawhar* interchangeably with *dhāt* to express the essence of God, just as ʿAmmār did.

Paul then goes on to speak about the divinity of Jesus but returns to the Trinity by denying that the divinity of Jesus implies the worship of another god alongside God, as Muslims tend to argue. "We know that what we say does not involve the worship of three gods, just as when we speak about the mind, speech and life of a human being it does not involve three human beings."[89] He also refers to the commonly used analogies of the fire and the sun to support the unity of God in Trinity. "When we speak about the flame, heat and light of a fire we do not involve three fires, and also when we speak about the disk, light and heat of the sun we do not involve three suns."[90]

Paul asks the European Christian leaders to respond to the Muslim question "If your belief about the exalted Creator is that he is one, what led you to call him by three hypostases? Those who hear this will conclude that you believe that

---

[84] Paul of Antioch, 'Letter to a Muslim Friend', in Rifaat Ebied and David Thomas (eds and trans), *Muslim–Christian Polemic During the Crusades* (Leiden: Brill, 2005), pp. 54–147 (pp. 90–91).

[85] Paul of Antioch, 'Letter to a Muslim Friend', pp. 92–93.

[86] Paul of Antioch, 'Letter to a Muslim Friend', pp. 92–93.

[87] Ebied and Thomas, *Muslim–Christian Polemic*, p. 91.

[88] Paul of Antioch, 'Letter to a Muslim Friend', pp. 96–97.

[89] Paul of Antioch, 'Letter to a Muslim Friend', pp. 122–23.

[90] Paul of Antioch, 'Letter to a Muslim Friend', pp. 122–23.

God is three composite individuals, or three gods, or three parts".[91] He has the Christian leaders say,

> They, for their part, in their belief about the Creator, hold that He has no body, limbs, or organs, is not limited to one place, therefore, what led them to say that he has two eyes with which to see, two hands which he spreads wide, a leg to expose, a face which turns in every direction, and a side, and that he comes in darkest clouds. Those who hear this will conclude that God the exalted has a body, limbs and organs, and that he moves from place to place in darkest clouds.[92]

Paul represents the European Christians as having a detailed knowledge of the Qurʾān that seems unlikely. Paul then acts as a mediator for Muslims when he goes on to interpret for the Europeans the usual way that Muslims understand the anthropomorphisms in the Qurʾān. "I said, they say that the reason for our saying that God has two eyes, two hands, a face, a leg, a side, and that He comes in darkest clouds, is that the Qurʾān speaks of this, but the intention of this is not a literal meaning."[93] Paul goes as far as to argue on behalf of Muslims that anyone who takes these descriptions of God literally is condemned as an unbeliever.

Paul then allows the Christian leaders to retort in exactly the same style of argument. "Likewise, the reason for our saying that God is three hypostases, Father, Son and Holy Spirit, is that the gospel (*al-injīl*) speaks of this."[94] Paul has the Europeans using the singular "gospel" just as the Qurʾān does, but it would have been more natural for them to use the plural "gospels". He reports the Christian leaders coming to the same conclusion as the Muslims. "What is intended by the hypostases is not composite individuals (*ashkhāṣ*), or parts, or components, or similar things, that would entail polytheism and plurality."[95] The Christians condemn as an unbeliever anyone who takes such a view of the hypostases.

The similarity between Paul's presentation and that of Iliyyā of Nisibis in 'The Book of the Sessions' is obvious, which confirms Sidney Griffith's contention that Paul "alludes to and reflects his reading of the work of the writer of the Church of the East, Elias of Nisibis".[96] It may well be the case that Paul also came in contact with the thinking of ʿAmmār al-Baṣrī via the writing of Iliyyā, since his use of ʿAmmār's arguments is closely related to the way Iliyyā uses them.

Paul then speaks on behalf of Muslims about their concern that Christians use the wrong terminology in Arabic to describe the essence of God when they talk about the substance (*jawhar*) of God. He has the Christian leaders respond by defining what they mean by substance (*jawhar*).

> Nothing exists unless it is a substance or an accident. This is because, whatever thing we examine is either self-existent (*qāʾim bi-nafsihi*), needing nothing else for

[91] Paul of Antioch, 'Letter to a Muslim Friend', pp. 128–31.
[92] Paul of Antioch, 'Letter to a Muslim Friend', pp. 130–31.
[93] Paul of Antioch, 'Letter to a Muslim Friend', pp. 130–33.
[94] Paul of Antioch, 'Letter to a Muslim Friend', pp. 132–33.
[95] Paul of Antioch, 'Letter to a Muslim Friend', pp. 132–33.
[96] Sidney Griffith, 'Paul of Antioch', in *The Orthodox Church in the Arab World*, p. 216.

> its existence, which is a substance, or is dependent on something else, needing something else for its existence, which is an accident.[97]

In light of this, Paul has the Christian leaders argue that God must be self-existent and therefore it is appropriate to call Him a substance. Yet Christians are not unaware of the difference between created substances and the uncreated substance of God.

> We say that He is a substance unlike created substances, just as we also say that He is a thing unlike created things. Otherwise, His existence would depend on something else and He would need something else for His existence, which would be among the worst things that can be said about the exalted Creator.[98]

Paul then reports the reason why Muslims reject the Christian use of the Arabic term *jawhar*. "They say, we refuse to call Him a *jawhar*, because a *jawhar* is what receives an accident and occupies space."[99] Paul has the Christians reply that there are two kinds of substances, material and immaterial. Examples of immaterial substances are "the substance of the soul, the substance of the mind, and the substance of light".[100] The conclusion is that "if there are immaterial substances which do not receive accidents or occupy space, then it is the case that the Creator of both material and immaterial substances does not in any way receive an accident or occupy space".[101]

This discussion of the appropriateness of the Arabic term *jawhar* for the essence of God is unique to Paul in comparison with previous Christian writing and demonstrates that he was not simply dependent on his predecessors. For instance, he does not follow Iliyyā of Nisibis in suggesting that the Arabic word *jawhar* be dropped by Christians in favour of the Syriac term *kiyān*. Perhaps Paul was all too aware that adopting a Syriac expression would not clarify but rather confuse the meaning of Christian convictions concerning the nature of the essence of God. This somewhat involved debate about the relation between the substance and hypostases of God concludes Paul's treatment of the Trinity in his 'Letter to a Muslim Friend'.

---

[97] Paul of Antioch, 'Letter to a Muslim Friend', pp. 136–37.
[98] Paul of Antioch, 'Letter to a Muslim Friend', pp. 136–39.
[99] Paul of Antioch, 'Letter to a Muslim Friend', pp. 138–39.
[100] Paul of Antioch, 'Letter to a Muslim Friend', pp. 138–39.
[101] Paul of Antioch, 'Letter to a Muslim Friend', pp. 138–39.

3. Evaluation of Christian Presentations of the Trinity in the Era of Muslim Rule in the Middle East in the Light of Muslim Responses[1]

Christian Presentations of the Trinity in the Early Period of Muslim Rule in the Middle East in the Light of Muslim Responses

John of Damascus' effort to engage with Muslim concepts of God is the earliest example of Christian theological reckoning with a new reality in the Middle East for Christians who had lived for centuries with a rich theological tradition that generations of Christians could take for granted. They were the dominant religious community in areas such as Syria, Palestine and Egypt. The fact that John, a lay Christian, wrote a systematic presentation of the Trinity based on the best of Eastern Christian theology in the Greek language, and then produced a counter argument against the relatively recent phenomenon of Islam, is testament to his awareness of the true situation in which the churches found themselves in the early eighth century. If he had not retired to a monastery near Jerusalem toward the end of his life, he probably would not have bequeathed his systematic theology along with his apologetic argument in favour of the Trinity, appealing to a text in the Qurʾān, to subsequent generations of Middle Eastern Christians. John sought to encourage his fellow Christians, who were now under Islamic rule, to make an effort to accommodate the new religion that openly attacked basic Christian beliefs. Some kind of dialogue with Muslims was required of Christians. They needed to come up with strategies to relate to the scriptures of the Muslims that appeared to undermine the Trinity and the Incarnation. John found one text in those scriptures that might be read to support the Trinity, Q4:171: "Christ Jesus, son of Mary, was the messenger of God, and His word which He cast on Mary, and a spirit from him".

John reads the text to indicate that Christ is the Word and Spirit of God and goes on to argue that if Muslims deny that that the Word and Spirit are in God, they can be accused of cutting off these attributes of God from Him. So, while Muslims accuse Christians of associating Christ with God in an unacceptable way, Christians, for their part, can accuse Muslims of mutilating God. John is assuming here that Q4:171 actually refers to the hypostases of the Word and Spirit within the Christian understanding of the Trinity. John's appeal to Christians to use Q4:171 was to have a profound impact on future Christian dialogue with Muslims on the Trinity, as has been demonstrated in the examples

[1] See an earlier treatment of this topic in Mark Beaumont, 'Debating the Concept of God', in Douglas Pratt and Charles Tieszen (eds), *Christian–Muslim Relations*; *A Bibliographical History, vol. 15*: *Thematic Essays (600–1600)*, (Leiden: Brill, 2020), pp. 99–112.

already cited in this book. As Reinhold Glei indicates, "The significance of *De haeresibus* can hardly be overestimated. It formed the image of Islam in the Greek world and exerted wider influence among Christian readers, at least until the mid-14th century".[2]

Greek-speaking Christians were not alone in looking to Q4:171 to refer to the Son and the Holy Spirit. Syriac-speaking Christians also used this text to persuade Muslims to accept the Trinity. The earliest example in a Syriac piece of writing comes from an early eighth-century debate between a monk of the Bēt Ḥālē monastery and an Arab dignitary who visited to discuss the differences in their beliefs. In his defence of the Trinity, the monk argues that "the Qurʾān's concept of Christ as 'the Word of God and his spirit' can be traced back to Muḥammad's knowledge of the Gospel of Luke" (Luke 1:35).[3] Barbara Roggema points out that if the disputation comes from the early eighth century, then it is the oldest Christian writing to show knowledge of the Qurʾān.[4]

Thus, by the early eighth century, Christians from both Greek- and Syriac-speaking communities were reading the Qurʾān to find points of contact for Christian beliefs, despite their full awareness that Muslims read the Qurʾān to teach the sheer oneness of God that cancelled out the Christian doctrine of the Trinity.

These early approaches to using Q4:171 to support the Trinity were addressed to fellow Christians in their languages of Greek or Syriac. They were not written in Arabic, the language of the new Muslim masters. The first Christian attempt to defend the Trinity in Arabic came from the monastic community that John of Damascus joined. The *Treatise on the Triune Nature of God* (MS Sinai 154) is by an unknown author but evidently was produced within a generation of John's work and was clearly influenced by John's appeal to Q4:171. One can imagine monks in the community that John joined taking an interest in John's apologetic method towards Muslims and one of them taking the trouble to learn Arabic well enough to study the Qurʾān, to debate with Muslims and to attempt to write an explanation of the Trinity and Incarnation that might appeal to Muslim readers.

What is of note in this treatise is the commentary on various verses from the Qurʾān that relate to the Trinity. In addition to Q4:171, which proclaims, "Believe in God and His messengers and do not say 'Trinity'", the author refers to Q5:73, "They are unbelievers who say that God is one third of a Trinity". The language of the Qurʾān sets the tone of the presentation, which seeks to supply to a Muslim reader correct information concerning Christian belief in God as Triune. Thus, the author provides a Christian corrective to these verses, such that, with respect to Q4:171, Christians do not distinguish God from His Word and His Spirit, nor do they worship another god alongside God in His Word and His Spirit, and with respect to Q5:73, Christians do not say three gods, but they do say that God and His Word and His Spirit is One God and One Creator.

---

[2] R.F. Glei, 'The Heresy of the Ishmaelites', in *Christian–Muslim Relations: A Bibliographical History, vol. 1*, pp. 297–301, p. 300.

[3] B. Roggema, 'The Disputation Between a Monk of Bēt Ḥālē and an Arab Notable', in *Christian–Muslim Relations: A Bibliographical History, vol. 1*, pp. 268–73 (p. 272).

[4] Roggema, 'The Disputation', p. 272.

Therefore, by utilising the terms "word" and "spirit" found in Q4:171, the author develops an explanation of Christian belief in the Triune God that deals directly with the challenge laid down by these verses to confess the oneness of God and avoid speaking of his threeness. The author appeals to Q16:102, "The Holy Spirit has brought down from your Lord mercy and guidance", to show that the Qurʾān presents God's Spirit in a similar way to the Bible, in that the Spirit of God mediates the Word of God to humans. In the final analysis, the author is confident that the Muslims he is writing for will be persuaded that their scriptures uphold the same teaching that Christians uphold concerning the nature of God as Triune. "You find in the Qurʾān that God and His Word and His Spirit is One God and One Lord. You have said that you believe in God and His Word and His Spirit, so do not reproach us, you people, for believing in God and His Word and His Spirit."[5] Notice how the author addresses Muslims directly about the contents of their scriptures. He does not attack their veracity but appeals to a fresh reading of these texts to support Christian belief in the Trinity. In other words, if Muslims take a step back from assuming that Christians worship three gods, then they might come to recognise that Christians are worshippers of the one Creator, just like them.

What is notable about the author is his unwillingness to enter into a polemical argument against the truth of Islam, unlike his mentor, John of Damascus. Outright rejection of the divine truth of the Qurʾān by John has now become a sensitive exploration of the Muslim scriptures in order to find mirror images of the truth of the Christian scriptures. Polemic might be understandable within the Christian community, but the author sees that only an apologetic approach to the beliefs of Muslims will have any persuasive value in Christian dialogue with Muslims. In other words, this author is the earliest example of a Christian reading the Qurʾān in order to explain what Christians believe, rather than reading the Qurʾān to show how inadequate the Muslim scriptures are in comparison with the Bible. That these two approaches to the Qurʾān are found in the master and his pupil demonstrates that throughout the period of Christian–Muslim relations there have always been different possibilities for Christians who want to relate to Muslims.

In the encounter between the Caliph al-Mahdī and the Patriarch of the Church of the East, Timothy I, we see clearly how Muslims understood the Trinity towards the end of the eighth century. Timothy is asked to respond to the question posed by the Caliph, "How can someone like you, knowledgeable and wise, say that the most high God took a wife and had a son?"[6] The Caliph obviously relies on Muslims who are known for their understanding of the Qurʾān, and who have advised him concerning what questions to put to the Christian leader. Here there is evidence for the view that the Qurʾān regards the Christian Trinity as God, Mary and Jesus. When Timothy says that this would be blasphemy for a Christian, the Caliph then asks whether Christians believe in three gods. Thus, the plain reading of the Qurʾān leads inevitably to the assumption that Christians do indeed worship God along with Mary and Jesus,

[5] Gibson, *A Treatise* , pp. 77–78.

[6] Putman, *Dialogue*, p. 7.

given their belief that God the Father had intercourse with Mary to produce His Son, Jesus. The conceptual gulf between Muslims and Christians is as wide as possible here. It is a picture of sheer incomprehension on both sides. Timothy has to negotiate this false impression of the Trinity by explaining exactly what Christians hold to be true of God. Rather than attempt to attack Muslims for setting up a ridiculous understanding of Christians, in the manner of John of Damascus, he uses Q4:171, in the manner of the 'Anonymous Apology', to assert that the Christian belief in the Trinity is referenced in the Qurʾān. Timothy has his own version of John's argument that Muslims should not divide the Trinity. By pointing out that Q4:171 teaches that God has Word and Spirit, Timothy asserts, "If someone says that God exists without Word and Spirit then he blasphemes."[7] What is interesting to observe is that the leader of the Church of the East should both know and agree with the teaching of the Chalcedonian churches, as expressed by John of Damascus and the 'Anonymous Apology'. Despite the differences over the way to understand the divinity and humanity of Jesus held by these two Christian groups, there was sufficient agreement over the doctrine of God for theologians from the two groups to read and use each other's work. While Timothy used Syriac to recount his encounter with the Caliph, he was able to read Greek, since he was engaged in translating Greek writing into Arabic for the Caliph.

Timothy went beyond the 'Anonymous Apology' by explaining in detail to the Caliph how the three members of the Trinity relate to one another. The Caliph asks another question, "How are the Son and Spirit not the same, since you say that God is simple and not composite?"[8] His advisers have clearly recommended the Caliph to interrogate Timothy on the obvious weakness of Christian belief in the Trinity that makes the one God complex rather than simple. Therefore, here is an early example of Muslims pressing Christians on the needless plurality in God involved in their conception of threeness within oneness. Timothy concedes that, from one point of view, the Father, Son and Holy Spirit are simply one. Since God is one in essence, there is no distinction between the three members of the Trinity. Yet from the point of view of the three members, each of them has his own characteristics as hypostases. The Son is begotten of the Father and the Spirit proceeds from the Father. The begetting and the proceeding are without bodily separation or by means of bodily members, because God has no body and is not composed of various parts. The shared inheritance of the Greek theological tradition is seen in Timothy's explanation. His language echoes that of John of Damascus in his exposition of the Trinity. John stated that, "The three hypostases of the holy Godhead are the same as each other (for they are consubstantial (*homoousios*) and uncreated)."[9] But John argues that, from another perspective, they are not the same. "For only the Father is unbegotten, only the Son is begotten, and only the Holy Spirit proceeds from the substance of the Father, not

[7] Putman, *Dialogue*, pp. 13–14.
[8] Putman, *Dialogue*, p. 16.
[9] John of Damascus, *On the Orthodox* Faith, p. 76.

begotten but brought forth by procession."[10] Timothy reflects John's language quite precisely here.

The Chalcedonian theologian Abū Qurra also reflects the language of John of Damascus in his defence of the Trinity. He responds to those who deny the Trinity by arguing that their "reason is confused by the Christian claims that the Father, the Son and the Holy Spirit are three hypostases (*aqānīm*) in one God (*ilah wāḥid*), and that each of the hypostases is perfect God in himself".[11] He goes on to repeat John's argument that the Word and Spirit of God cannot be separated from Him. Abū Qurra poses his own question to his Muslim reader, "Do you say that God has word or not?" If he replies "no" then God is dumb, but if he replies "yes" then the Word has to be both perfect man and perfect God as Christians believe.[12] However, Abū Qurra relates the divine status of the Word to the divinity of Jesus in the Incarnation in this form of the argument. Abū Qurra regards Muslims as irrational people in their insistence that the unity of God must be preserved at all costs. Therefore, he appeals to reason to establish the truth of the Trinity and concludes that truly rational people will conclude that God is three in one. Nevertheless, this insistence that Christians are more rational than Muslims is a much more aggressive stance than that adopted by the 'Anonymous Apology' or Patriarch Timothy. Abū Qurra was in danger of taking the debate with Muslims onto a different plane and would be met by equally stern insistence by Muslims that the unity of God was best preserved logically by focusing on defending that oneness against the encroachments of threeness.

Abū Qurra deferred to analogical argument to uphold the threeness, like the 'Anonymous Apology' and Timothy, but he loaded more weight onto such analogies by relying on them as rational supports. He appeals to the analogies of three lamps in a house that each give light but the light is one and indivisible, three speakers who recite the same poem simultaneously but the hearer hears one poem, and three pieces of gold that are just one kind of gold, not three kinds. From his perspective, a Muslim would clearly have to agree that these analogies from everyday experience allow threeness to support oneness. But in order to apply these analogies to the nature of God Himself, Abū Qurra has to acknowledge that there is a gap between this world and the transcendent God, as his Muslim reader would no doubt pronounce, "There is nothing like God". For the Muslim, a rational person attends to this fundamental distinction between the Creator and the creation. The Christian who fails to do this is inevitably irrational. Abū Qurra admits this by ending his analogical argument for the Trinity by stating that the oneness of God is "purer and higher" than the oneness in any of these analogies.[13] Such an admission might readily be pounced on by a Muslim reader who might say, "Of course, God is higher than these analogies. Why don't you Christians listen to us and avoid comparing God to elements in His creation?"

---

[10] John of Damascus, *On the Orthodox Faith*, p. 76.

[11] Abū Qurra, 'Treatise on the Trinity', p. 27.

[12] Abū Qurra, 'Treatise on the Trinity', p. 44.

[13] Abū Qurra, 'Treatise on the Trinity', pp. 36–37.

Abū Rāʾiṭa was a theologian of the West Syrian church, which disagreed with the Chalcedonians and the East Syrian church over the correct way to describe the divinity of Jesus. Yet his treatment of the Trinity is in concord with these other church communities in speaking of one essence in three hypostases. He attempts to respond to Muslims who ask Christians how the one God can be three. This most basic Muslim objection to the Trinity is now discussed in terms of different definitions of oneness by the Greek philosopher Aristotle, who Abū Rāʾiṭa clearly thinks is pivotal for debates with Muslim intellectuals. This marks a new departure for Christian–Muslim dialogue and represents the impact of translations of Greek writing into Arabic that were now preoccupying Muslim thinkers. Aristotle in particular seems to have gained the most respect in this late-eighth-century period. So, Abū Rāʾiṭa asks the Muslim questioner which category of oneness is being considered in his question. He offers three possibilities based on Aristotle's *Metaphysics*: oneness as genus, oneness as species and oneness as number. This very technical discussion takes the dialogue into a rather rarified environment that would be of interest only to a tiny handful of Muslim intellectuals and moves the debate on oneness onto a shared belief in the accuracy of Aristotle's definitions rather than the plain meaning of the scriptural texts that had been the basis for previous debate. Abū Rāʾiṭa takes the three definitions of oneness by Aristotle and one by one demonstrates that none of them can apply to the oneness of God. He cannot be one in genus, since He created all types of creatures and is not one among them. He cannot be one in number, because that would imply that he can be divided into parts. He cannot be one in species, because he would then be one among several of His kind. In other words, no Aristotelian category of oneness describes the oneness of God, and this is what should unite Christians and Muslims together. The insistence of Muslims that the oneness of God is in the category of number only shows how inadequate their thinking is. Muslims need to heed Christians in taking the definition of oneness beyond Aristotle's categories. Abū Rāʾiṭa ingeniously argues that only the Christian definition of oneness will do. God is one in His essence, but this is not in number, because He is three in His hypostases. In His essence nothing in creation can be compared with Him, and this confirms the teaching of the Qurʾān and the Bible. On this, Christians and Muslims are agreed. Yet Christians wish to go further and state that in His three hypostases God encompasses all types of number, even and odd, as categorised by Aristotle.

Abū Rāʾiṭa goes on to rely on Aristotle in his discussion of the hypostases. He credits Muslims with believing in the attributes of God such as "living", "knowing", "hearing" and "seeing". Aristotle taught in his *Categories* the difference between names that are not predicated of something else and names that are related to something else. Therefore, Abū Rāʾiṭa asks Muslims whether the names of God are predicated of something else or not. He provides two possible answers. If Muslims see "living" and "knowing" as acquired by God as predicates of action then he must describe God as Creator only after He created. But if he thinks of them as belonging to God eternally, then he must describe God as eternally creating. Abū Rāʾiṭa is reporting the debate that intellectual Muslims were involved in as a result of their new-found interest in Aristotle. Some Muslim intellectuals took the view that the names of God were merely metaphors, but others held that they could either be "attributes of the essence" (*sifāt al-dhāt*) or "attributes of action" (*sifāt al-fiʿl*). Abū Rāʾiṭa is debating with the latter group here by arguing that the attributes of "life" and "knowledge" must be eternal in God because there cannot be a time when God does not have life and knowledge. They cannot be parts of God's nature but must be perfect entities that can be distinguished, but which are also united with one another in Him. Abū Rāʾiṭa describes God as one in essence (*jawhar*) and three in the individuals (*ashkhāṣ*) or hypostases (*aqānīm*). However, the isolation of two attributes does not fit easily into this definition of the three hypostases. Where is the third hypostasis? The term *ashkhāṣ* might appear to a Muslim an admission that the three hypostases are individual beings within some idealised oneness of God's essence which merely undermines that oneness. Abū Rāʾiṭa is alive to the latter problem. He puts forward the analogy of Adam, Eve and Abel as an explanation of the relationship between the three hypostases. Just as Adam is the begetter of Abel, Abel is the begotten and Eve is the one who proceeds from Adam and is neither begetter nor begotten, but all three share the same humanity, so the Father is the begetter of the Son, the Son is begotten of the Father, and the Holy Spirit proceeds from the Father, but all three share the same essence. A Muslim might say that it is clear that there are three gods involved here, but Abū Rāʾiṭa insists that just as Adam, Eve and Abel share the same human nature, so the Father, Son and Holy Spirit share the same divine essence. If the Muslim asks why there are only three hypostases and not ten or twelve, then he should be told that God has only two essential attributes, "knowledge" and "spirit". At this point Abū Rāʾiṭa has changed the attribute of "life" to "spirit" but it is not clear why he has done this. It is interesting to observe that he never thinks of isolating three essential attributes, such as "knowledge", "life" and "spirit".

Abū Rāʾiṭa responds to a Muslim who asks why the Father who causes the Son and the Spirit in the Christian conception of the Trinity should not be praised much more than the Son and the Spirit. In reply, he indicates that the Son and the Spirit are no less than the Father from whom they originate, since they are "two perfect beings (*dhātān*) from one perfect being (*dhāt*)". This use of the Arabic *dhāt* could easily confuse his Muslim questioner. If *dhāt* is used by Abū Rāʾiṭa to describe the essence of God, then it is surely not appropriate to use the term to describe the two hypostases. Indeed, Abū Rāʾiṭa has used the Arabic term *jawhar* to denote the essence of God but here uses *dhāt* as a synonym. The Muslim could ask why Abū Rāʾiṭa does not wish also to refer to two perfect beings (*jawharain*) from one perfect being (*jawhar*). This language may sound to a Muslim all too much like a description of three perfect divine beings and merely confirms that Christians really do worship three gods.

ʿAmmār al-Baṣrī from the Church of the East sets out to respond to Muslim questions concerning the Trinity that may well have been posed by the leading Muslim intellectual in Basra, Abū al-Hudhayl al-ʿAllāf, who wrote a refutation of ʿAmmār's writing. The opening question has to do with the problem of threeness in God: since the Creator is one, how can one be three and three one? ʿAmmār replies that there is one eternal essence (*jawhar*) in three essential properties (*khawāṣṣ jawhariyāt*) that are not differentiated or separated. The Creator lives and speaks, so "life" and "speech" can be attributed to Him. "The principal essence (*jawhar al-ʿayn*) has the attributions of His life and His speech; His speech is the source of His wisdom and His life is the source of His spirit."[14] ʿAmmār appears to be naming the Creator "the principal essence" who has two attributes: "life" and "speech". By selecting "life" and "speech" he shows the influence John of Damascus continued to have on the presentation of the Trinity, even by a theologian from a different denomination. Q4:171 with its references to a Word and Spirit from God was key to ʿAmmār's explanation of the members of the Trinity. His description of the hypostases as "essential properties" (*khawāṣṣ*) of the "principal essence" shows how he was determined to avoid the kind of language used by Abū Rāʾiṭa to explain hypostases as "individuals" (*ashkhāṣ*), lest Muslims think that the hypostases are a cover for three deities. There is no doubt that ʿAmmār is much more in tune with Muslim linguistic preconceptions than Abū Rāʾiṭa or Abū Qurra in his choice of Arabic terminology. Nevertheless, his way of describing the Creator as the "principal essence" means that there are only two hypostases of the Creator in consideration. The tradition of appealing to Q4:171 for the Word and Spirit of God to be the Son and Holy Spirit means that the Father appears to be identified with the Creator Himself. Yet this apparent identification of the Creator with the Father was central to John of Damascus' exposition of the Trinity and was the basic inheritance of the Greek tradition, going back to the debates of the Cappadocian Fathers in the fifth century. So, ʿAmmār is not alone in constructing his explanation of the three hypostases in such a way. It is a feature of the whole Eastern way of thinking about the Trinity.

In answer to the Muslim who asks why Christians call the three properties "individuals" (*ashkhāṣ*), he says that he does not agree with Christians who do this, because the term (*ashkhāṣ*) applies only to beings with physical bodies and the hypostases do not belong to a being with a physical body but to the Creator Himself. He distances himself from Abū Rāʾiṭa at this point but goes on to agree with him by appealing to Aristotle's *Categories* to define "hypostases", as Abū Rāʾiṭa does. ʿAmmār says in addition to the three categories of Aristotle's essence (*jawhar*), power (*quwa*) and accident (*ʿarḍ*), there should be a fourth category called hypostasis (*qunūm*). He agrees with Aristotle that power and accident both depend on something else for their existence. But he wants to add hypostasis to essence as two categories that do not depend on anything else for their existence.

ʿAmmār answers the Muslim who challenges Christians for claiming that the Father, Son and Holy Spirit are "each perfect God". Christians must either believe in three gods or three parts of one perfect God, according to the Muslim. ʿAmmār answers that the three distinct members of the Trinity share the same perfect essence (*jawhar kāmil*), just as Abraham, Isaac and Jacob share the same human nature but are distinct persons. There are not three perfect essences or three perfect gods, but "each of them in his property (*khāṣṣa*) is perfect God".[15] ʿAmmār seeks to hold in tension a middle way between the two Muslim assumptions concerning the three members of the Trinity. They share the same

---

[14] ʿAmmār al-Baṣrī, 'Book of Questions and Answers', p. 149.
[15] ʿAmmār al-Baṣrī, 'Book of Questions and Answers', pp. 170–71.

essence but are not three separate essences. Although ʿAmmār realises that analogies are not acceptable to Muslims, he insists on using the analogy of three men who share the same human nature although they are separate persons. The same response might have come from the Muslim as to Abū Rāʾiṭa, who uses the analogy of Adam, Eve and Abel sharing the same human nature despite being separate individuals: why use analogies from the created world to describe the Creator?

In his later work, the 'Book of the Proof Concerning the Course of the Divine Economy', ʿAmmār has a Muslim ask, "How can you call the Word and the Spirit hypostases (*qunūm*) in God, but you do not call the word of the soul and its life hypostases, nor the heat of the fire and its light, nor of the sun and its heat?"[16] ʿAmmār responds by accepting that analogies between the creation and the Creator cannot be used to imply that the nature of the Creator is to be replicated in His creation. Calling the three realities (*maʿānī*) of the Creator "hypostases" does not entitle us to call created realities (*maʿānī*) by the same name "hypostases" because they are not perfect like the hypostases of the Creator. Therefore, analogies from the created world are acceptable as long as the distinction between the imperfect nature of created things is observed. But the Muslim has a case in point here. What is the value of drawing attention to aspects of the created world, such as the make-up of a human being as a soul with its life and speech, in order to argue for a similar structure in God Himself? If the structure of God is perfect, then there can be little value in pointing to the structure of a human being, which is not perfect. Imperfection cannot lead to perfection, according to Muslim thinking. ʿAmmār has changed the Arabic term for the hypostases from his earlier work to another term here. He has removed "*khawāṣṣ*" and replaced it with "*maʿānī*" as a way of explaining the meaning of "hypostases". Muslims may have thought that the concept "properties" (*khawāṣṣ*) meant that the hypostases were merely aspects of the character of God. ʿAmmār may have concluded that the concept "realities" (*maʿānī*) would convey the sense of dynamic forces that have a life of their own, so that Muslims could more clearly understand that the life of God is His Spirit at work in creation and the speech of God is His Word incarnate in Jesus. In the beginning, ʿAmmār rejected the use of the concept "individuals" (*ashkhāṣ*) because Muslims might understand three separate divine beings. Therefore, he adopted "properties" (*khawāṣṣ*) because Muslims might understand three separate divine aspects of one divine being. But he ended up with "realities" (*maʿānī*) because Muslims might understand three dynamic forces that have a divine life of their own. ʿAmmār came full circle in his attempt to communicate in Arabic what Christians had already conceived in Greek and Syriac. He represents the best example of Christian engagement with intellectual Muslims in his time. ʿAmmār's concern to find the best Arabic terminology for the hypostases is a response to Muslim interrogation of the Trinity.[17]

---

[16] ʿAmmār al-Baṣrī, 'Book of the Proof', p. 50.

[17] See Mark Beaumont, *The Theology of ʿAmmār al-Baṣrī: Commending Christianity Within Islamic Culture* (Piscataway, NJ: Gorgias Press, 2021), for a fuller comparison

While Abū al-Hudhayl al-ʿAllāf's refutation of ʿAmmār is no longer extant, there are two examples of Muslim critique of the Trinity that have survived. The first of these is 'The Refutation of the Christians' by the Zaydī Imam Al-Qāsim ibn Ibrāhīm (d. 860), which he wrote after debating with Christians in Egypt between 815 and 826.[18] He quotes from the Qurʾān those verses that criticise those who associate with God other persons worthy of worship, especially Q112:1–4, "Say, He is God the One, God the Eternal, who does not beget and who is not begotten, and there is no one like Him." Then he challenges Christians to pay heed to them. "Whoever talks about God having a son, all those who associate anyone with God, among Jews, Christians, and any other people, should listen to God's clear arguments against them concerning this."[19] When he turns to the way Christians speak of the Triune God, he has a very accurate understanding of the kind of terminology used by Abū Qurra and Abū Rāʾiṭa. "All the Christians claim that God is three separate individuals (*ashkhāṣ*), and that these three individuals have one similar nature (*ṭabīʿa*) ... Father, Son and Holy Spirit."[20] He recounts the analogies of the sun and of human nature used by Christians, and says that Christians depend on them to argue that there is "one essence (*dhāt*) and one nature (*ṭabīʿa*) which joins together the three hypostases (*aqānīm*)". Al-Qāsim does not develop a particular critique of any of this, since the burden of his refutation is directed at the notion of the divinity of Christ, but it is clear to him that the Trinity goes beyond the boundaries set by the Qurʾān by associating other beings with God. David Thomas points out that Al-Qāsim emphasises the individuality of the hypostases, "unlike the Arabic speaking Christians who emphasise the identity between them".[21] This Muslim understanding of the hypostases would explain ʿAmmār's rejection of the terminology of three individuals (*ashkhāṣ*) in favour of three properties (*khawāṣṣ*) shared by the one essence.

The second example is 'The Refutation of the Trinity' by Abū ʿĪsā al-Warrāq (d. 860), which is certainly the most thorough of any of the Muslim refutations that are extant from the early Islamic period. He is aware that different Christian communities disagree over their understanding of the uniting of the divine and human in Christ but that they basically agree over the definition of the Trinity as "one essence (*jawhar*), three hypostases (*aqānīm*)", and that the three hypostases

---

of ʿAmmār's theological method with his contemporary Christian theologians in relation to Islamic presuppositions.

[18] See W. Madelung, *Der Imām al-Qāsim ibn Ibrāhīm und die Glaubenslehre der Zaiditen* (Berlin: De Gruyter, 1965), pp. 88–90.

[19] Al-Qāsim ibn Ibrāhīm, 'Refutation of the Christians', in I. di Matteo (ed.), 'Confutazione Contro I Cristiani dello Zaydati al-Qāsim b. Ibrāhīm', *Rivista degli Studi Orientali* 9 (1921–1922), pp. 301–64 (p. 310).

[20] Al-Qāsim ibn Ibrāhīm, 'Refutation of the Christians', pp. 314–15.

[21] See David Thomas, 'The Doctrine of the Trinity in the Early Abbasid Period', in Lloyd Ridgeon (ed.), *Islamic Interpretations of Christianity* (London: Routledge, 2001), pp. 79–95 (p. 84).

are Father, Son and Spirit.[22] He reports that they have different terms for the hypostases, properties (*khawāṣṣ*), individuals (*ashkhāṣ*) or attributes (*ṣifāt*), yet "despite their differences over explanation and terminology they keep more or less the same meaning, as they themselves admit".[23] Unlike Al-Qāsim ibn Ibrāhīm, Abū ʿĪsā al-Warrāq does not quote from the Qurʾān to support his argument but depends solely on logical reasoning. So, he subjects the language of the Trinity to a sustained assault based on the presupposition that God must be one, and that the definition of oneness necessarily excludes threeness.

He develops a mirror argument to that of John of Damascus and his successors, that God's Word and Spirit are eternally of God, by showing the Christians that if the three hypostases are equivalent to the essence, then the threeness of the hypostases must attach to the one essence. "Every number attaching to the properties will attach to the essentiality (*jawhariyya*)."[24] Christians end up having to admit three essentialities rather than one and thus the Trinity is negated. The same applies to the concept of divinity. If Christians claim that Father, Son and Holy Spirit are divine, then there are three divinities that must share the one divine essence, and the result is that there must be two definitions of divinity: one for the essence and the other for the hypostases.[25] This principle also applies to the characteristics of the three hypostases. If fatherhood is essential to the Father and not the Son, then the Son lacks an essential quality and so is less than God in his essence. If fatherhood and sonship are eternal qualities then they must be shared by each, so the Son must be Father too.[26]

Abū ʿĪsā does not usually refer to individual Christian writers but prefers to speak about the teaching of the three main Christian communities of his time, although he says that "one Trinitarian theologian (*mutakallim*) has presented arguments in support of the essence (*jawhar*) and the hypostases (*aqānīm*), that the one he worships lives eternally by 'life' and speaks eternally by 'speech', and that life and speech are two properties (*khāṣṣatān*) which confer perfection on His essence".[27] This choice of life and speech as the essential properties of God reflects ʿAmmār al-Baṣrī's way of writing among the theologians studied above, and it may be that he is the unnamed *mutakallim* here. Abū ʿĪsā counters this by examining the essence (*jawhar*) in this presentation. If the essence is specified by "life", then the definition of any essence in the created world must also be specified by "life", and even stones would have to be specified as "living", which is absurd. But if the essence is specified by "life" by a cause (*ʿilla*) which is other than the essence, then an eternal cause other than the essence and the hypostases has been established, and this falsifies the argument.

---

22 Abū ʿĪsā al-Warrāq, 'Refutation of the Trinity: The First Part of the Refutation of the Three Christian Sects', in David Thomas (ed. and trans.), *Anti-Christian Polemic in Early Islam* (Cambridge: Cambridge University Press, 1992), pp. 66–181 (pp. 66–67).
23 Al-Warrāq, 'Refutation of the Trinity', pp. 68–69.
24 Al-Warrāq, 'Refutation of the Trinity', pp. 78–79.
25 Al-Warrāq, 'Refutation of the Trinity', pp. 112–13.
26 Al-Warrāq, 'Refutation of the Trinity', pp. 126–29.
27 Al-Warrāq, 'Refutation of the Trinity', pp. 130–31.

He finds the appeal to the generation of word from intellect, light from the sun and heat from fire as analogies for the generation of the Son from the Father to be useless to support the Christian case for the Trinity. No matter whether Christians intend to compare the generation of the Son by the Father directly or only approximately with these other types of generation, they cannot escape from giving the eternal Father the same status as a created being or object.[28] Abū ʿĪsā, like other Muʿtazilī Muslim thinkers, rejected analogies from the created and temporal world for the uncreated and eternal God, since there is nothing like Him (Q112:4). The problem with Christians is precisely that they think it appropriate to compare God with what He resembles, with the result that "they are openly introducing anthropomorphism (*tashbīh*), and they do not remove anthropomorphism from their teaching".[29]

These two Muslim reactions to Trinitarian theology show the challenge faced by Christians in the period of early Islamic dominance. The traditional consensus of all the denominations that God is one essence in three hypostases was put to the test by the Islamic belief that the unity of God precludes His enumeration in three properties. When Christians appealed to analogies of unity in enumeration in the observable world to support the rationality of threeness in oneness, Muslims rejected the application of the analogy to the eternal and timeless One with whom nothing and no one can be compared. The Christian apologists struggled to express the Trinity in similar terms in the Arabic language of the Muslims. Abū Qurra chose nature (*ṭabīʿa*) or essential being (*dhāt*), whereas Abū Rāʾiṭa and ʿAmmār al-Baṣrī agreed on essence (*jawhar*) to translate the Greek term *ousia*. There was even greater divergence in translation of the Greek term *hypostases*. All three apologists writing in Arabic transliterated the Syriac *qenômê* as *aqānīm*. Abū Qurra much more frequently used *wujūh*, a translation of the Greek *prosopon*, meaning person, and Abū Rāʾiṭa preferred *ashkhāṣ* to indicate the individual persons. ʿAmmār realised that this emphasis on the individual persons of the Trinity was likely to play into the hands of Muslims who wanted to see three divine beings in the hypostases and argued for the necessity of using properties (*khawāṣṣ*) of the one essence to divert attention away from threeness to oneness.

When asked why there were only three hypostases and not more, all three apologists fell back on the Biblical testimony, though Abū Rāʾiṭa and ʿAmmār al-Baṣrī attempted to defend the rationality of the three hypostases by means of the distinction between "attributes of the essence" (*sifāt al-dhāt*) and "attributes of action" (*sifāt al-fiʿl*). Thus, for Abū Rāʾiṭa, God creates through His "life" and "knowledge", which are attributes of His essence, and not through "seeing" and "hearing", which are attributes of His action. For ʿAmmār al-Baṣrī, the attributes of essence become "life" and "speech", but the argument is similar. It is obvious that only two attributes are chosen here, leaving the impression that the essence has two hypostases rather than three, but this is the inheritance of Greek Trinitarian writing passed down to them, among which an early example comes

[28] Al-Warrāq, 'Refutation of the Trinity', pp. 166–71.
[29] Al-Warrāq, 'Refutation of the Trinity', pp. 168–69.

from the third century theologian Irenaeus, who wrote about the Word and the Spirit as the two hands of God.[30]

Christian Presentations of the Trinity for Muslims in the Medieval Period in the Light of Muslim Responses

The late-ninth-century Chalcedonian Melkite bishop of Bayt Raʾs continues the tradition of John of Damascus and Abū Qurra. His exposition of the Word and the Spirit closely reflects John's writing, and his explanation of the three hypostases as aspects (*jihāt*) reflects Abū Qurra's similar use of aspects (*wujūh*), although he uses a slightly different form of the same Arabic root. Perhaps Peter is aware that *wujūh* might be understood by Muslims as "faces", which might suggest three faces of three individuals, and opts for (*jihāt*) that might better be understood by Muslims as "aspects", suggesting three ways that the one God can be seen by humans. Peter, like ʿAmmār al-Baṣrī, was trying to avoid giving the impression that Christians believed in three individuals. He was concerned not to offer any encouragement to Muslims to criticise Christian vocabulary. Though there is no evidence that Peter had read ʿAmmār al-Baṣrī, they both were straining to explain the hypostases in Arabic terminology that would best preserve the sense that Christians held onto in Greek or Syriac. They had to find a way to express the personal reality of the Son and the Spirit that was the inheritance of the Eastern Greek theology that they both confessed. ʿAmmār chose properties (*khawāṣṣ*) rather than Abū Rāʾiṭa's choice of individuals (*ashkhāṣ*), because he felt that Muslims would understand "individuals" to mean three gods. By using "properties" he believed he could convey to Muslims that the three hypostases truly belonged to one divine essence. Peter seems to have thought that Abū Qurra's choice of *wujūh* to describe the three hypostases would lead Muslims to think of three faces of three individuals and so sought another way of interpreting the same Arabic root by choosing *jihāt*, which would more easily be understood as three aspects of one person.

Peter follows John and Abū Qurra in not getting involved in a philosophical discussion based on Aristotle's *Categories*. Peter was not part of the intellectual scene in Basra or Baghdad to which Abū Rāʾiṭa and and ʿAmmār al-Baṣrī belonged. It is possible that Abū Rāʾiṭa represented the West Syrian church and ʿAmmār al-Baṣrī represented the East Syrian church in debates with Jews and Muslims in the Baghdad House of Wisdom in the early decades of the ninth century. The Chalcedonian Melkites were more represented in Syria and Palestine and seem not to have been involved in House of Wisdom debates. Certainly, Abū Qurra did not write about Aristotelian definitions that were at the heart of Christian–Muslim exchange in such discussions. Thus, it is no surprise

[30] Irenaeus, *Against Heresies (Adversus Haereses)*, IV.XX.I, "In carrying out his intended work of creation, God did not need any help from angels, as if he had not his own hands. For he has always at his side his Word and Wisdom, the Son and the Spirit. Through them and in them he created all things of his own free will. And to them he says, 'Let us make man'." Henry Bettenson (trans.), *The Early Christian Fathers* (Oxford: Oxford University Press, 1969), p. 85.

that Peter does not enter into discussion of the attributes of God that preoccupied Abū Rā'iṭa and 'Ammār al-Baṣrī. Peter was more concerned with helping his own church members to confess the Trinity in the Arabic language that was central to their everyday conversation in the late ninth century. He wanted to enable them to confess the Trinity in Arabic terms that would both uphold orthodoxy as well as communicate to Muslims exactly what Christians believed. Only a tiny minority of intellectuals were concerned with Aristotle and the vast majority of people – Christian, Jew, Muslim and Zoroastrian – were concerned with the implications of their different scriptural inheritance. It is no surprise that Peter addresses the dualism of the still large Zoroastrian population in his area just as 'Ammār al-Baṣrī did, since they both lived in Zoroastrian-majority situations in the ninth century.

Muslim reaction to Christian explanations of the Trinity by the end of the ninth century can be seen in 'Refutation of the Christians' by al-Nāshi' al-Akbar (d. 904). He says that Christians "claim that the Creator is three hypostases (*uqnūmāt*) and one substance (*jawhar*), Father, Son and Holy Spirit, with the substance being the hypostases in a general way".[31] It is interesting to observe that al-Nāshi' al-Akbar does not use the usual plural form *aqānīm* for hypostases, which may suggest that he was unfamiliar with the actual writing of the earlier Christian presentations of the Trinity by Abū Qurra, Abū Rā'iṭa and 'Ammār al-Baṣrī, who all used *aqānīm* for hypostases. He also does not seem to be aware of the distinctions made by these three writers concerning the substance (*jawhar*) and the hypostases but asserts that Christians elide the substance with the hypostases when they certainly do not. al-Nāshi' continues to expound the Christian conception of the Trinity. "They claim that of these hypostases, the Father is the cause (*'illa*) of the Son and Spirit, without preceding them in essence (*dhāt*), but rather they are equal with him. They call the Son the Creator's knowledge and the Spirit his life." The switch from *jawhar* to *dhāt* does reflect the way that the earlier Christian writers also switched between these two terms for the essence of God, and the notion that the Father is the cause (*'illa*) of the Son and the Spirit reflects the usage of 'Ammār al-Baṣrī. However, 'Ammār al-Baṣrī did not name the Son "the Creator's knowledge", but rather the Creator's speech. It was Abū Rā'iṭa who said that the Son was the knowledge of God. These are indications that the very theologians who first wrote in Arabic have not been carefully consulted by this Muslim, who appears to have gained his knowledge of Christian teaching from some kind of summary made by another Muslim. David Thomas notes that Abū 'Īsā al-Warrāq's summary of Christian teaching on the Trinity is much more faithful to actual Christian writing than that of al-Nāshi' al-Akbar.[32]

After outlining the differences between different Christian groups over the correct way to define the relationship between the divinity and humanity of Jesus, al-Nāshi' turns to refuting the Trinity. His initial concern is with the idea that one hypostasis, the Father, is the cause of the other two hypostases. If

---

[31] Al-Nāshi' al-Akbar, 'Refutation of the Christians', in David Thomas (ed. and trans.), *Christian Doctrines in Islamic Theology* (Leiden: Brill, 2008), pp. 36–77 (p. 36–37).
[32] Al-Nāshi' al-Akbar, 'Refutation of the Christians', footnote, p. 39.

Christians claim that the three hypostases are equal, then they cannot claim that one of them caused the other two. He appeals to reason to refute this Christian claim.

> This is the most patent impossibility, because in practice things are surely marked out so that one possesses what another does not, and hence reason finds that they are distinguished by themselves or that one possesses what differentiates it from another. However if reason finds that they are uniform and not distinguished by themselves ... then reason has no way of claiming that one of the two is cause and the other is effect.[33]

He goes on to apply this rational argument to the Christian Trinity. "The so-called cause of the other two, the Father, is not an effect and the two so-called effects, the Son and Spirit, are not a cause, though they are not distinguished by themselves." He comments, "There is nothing more patent than the fallacy of what they teach on this".[34]

He then examines the way that Christians claim that the three hypostases share the same substance. He refers to the distinction made by Aristotle that substances are differentiated from accidents and contrasts this with the belief of the Christians in "three uniform hypostases, uniform in the substance with no distinction between them", and argues that "If the three hypostases are one substance and are distinguished, and the other substance is only distinguished by accidents and things that are different from its parts, then there are things other than the substance within the hypostases."[35] In other words, as David Thomas indicates, "If material substances are differentiated from one another by accidents, then the divine substance must also be differentiated into distinct hypostases by entities additional to it, making the Trinity a multiplicity."[36]

Al-Nāshi᾽ concludes his refutation by pointing out that Christians appeal to the created world to explain the Trinity, but the comparisons are not possible. They claim that "The Creator is knowing and living by analogy with the fact that we have never been aware of one who acts in a wise manner who is not knowing and living. Their teaching and what they base on this inference can be attacked in many ways."[37] The most obvious problem is that "They have never been aware of one who acts who is not powerful either, so they will have to confirm another hypostasis for power."[38] Here is testimony to the ongoing debate among Muslims concerning the attributes of essence that Abū Rā᾽iṭa and ʿAmmār al-Baṣrī engaged with. Both Abū Rā᾽iṭa and ʿAmmār al-Baṣrī argued that the many names given to God could be subsumed under only two essential attributes: "knowledge" and "life" according to Abū Rā᾽iṭa and "speech" and "life" according to ʿAmmār al-Baṣrī. But al-Nāshi᾽ points out that this restriction of the attributes of God to only two essential attributes is completely arbitrary, given that "power" is just as essential to God as "knowledge' and "life". Then it

---

[33] Al-Nāshi᾽ al-Akbar, 'Refutation of the Christians', pp. 66–67.
[34] Al-Nāshi᾽ al-Akbar, 'Refutation of the Christians', pp. 66–67.
[35] Al-Nāshi᾽ al-Akbar, 'Refutation of the Christians', pp. 68–69.
[36] Al-Nāshi᾽ al-Akbar, 'Refutation of the Christians', footnote, p. 69.
[37] Al-Nāshi᾽ al-Akbar, 'Refutation of the Christians', pp. 72–73.
[38] Al-Nāshi᾽ al-Akbar, 'Refutation of the Christians', pp. 74–75.

is also clear that human beings have "never been aware of someone who is one substance and three hypostases" ...and "of someone who has knowledge and life, one of which is his son and the other his spirit" ...and "of someone who has life and knowledge of which he is the cause and they are his effects".[39] It is simply not true for Christians to argue that we witness such relationships in the created world. Finally, the hypostases have to be individuals who share the same substance, like human beings who share the same substance, but Christians claim that the three hypostases share the same substance as the Creator and this is contradictory. Al-Nāshiʾ seems to be aware of the analogy from human nature that Christians used to support the sharing of the hypostases in the substance of the Creator, though he does not cite any of them. Abū Qurra used Peter, Paul and John, Abū Rāʾiṭa referred to Adam, Eve and Abel, while ʿAmmār al-Baṣrī cited Abraham, Isaac and Jacob to demonstrate that, just as these human individuals shared a common human nature, so the three hypostases share a common divine nature. Al-Nāshiʾ will not allow analogies from the created world to influence the proper understanding of the nature of the Creator.

The West Syrian Miaphysite Yaḥya ibn ʿAdī responded to Muslim criticisms of the Trinity in several treatises spanning his career as a teacher of philosophy to Christian and Muslim intellectuals. His earliest work, from 940, analysed six concepts of oneness and declared that only one of these concepts is used by Christians in their belief in the Trinity: the idea that oneness can co-exist with multiplicity. Just as a human being can be defined in multiple ways, yet be one person, so Christians define God in multiple ways, yet hold to his unity. Just as Zayd is one person who can be defined as "living", "rational" and "mortal", so "God is one substance (*jawhar*) in three attributes (*ṣifāt*) which are goodness (*al-jūd*), power (*al-qudra*), and wisdom (*al-hikma*)".[40] God created the world from his power, but he did not need to do this. His decision to use his power to make the universe was voluntary, based on his goodness and wisdom, such that "His voluntary act of creation demonstrates His goodness and His wisdom."[41] Yaḥya's choice of goodness, power and wisdom to describe the three attributes of God is certainly novel in comparison with earlier Arabic writing theologians. There is no sense that he is reflecting Q4:171 or the well-established Christian tradition of reading the Trinity into this text. If he had read Abū Rāʾiṭa, his fellow West Syrian apologist to Muslims, he did not find much inspiration from him. Thus, Yaḥya was charting a fresh course in attempting to interpret the Trinity for a Muslim audience.

In Yaḥya's response to the critique of the Trinity by the Muslim philosopher al-Kindī (d. 873), written in 961, he quotes al-Kindī rejecting the Trinity of Father, Son and Holy Spirit because there must be "composition in the Father, Son and Holy Spirit".[42] When Christians speak of one substance (*jawhar*) in three properties (*khawaṣṣ*), they must admit that the three properties are composed of the same substance. But this is the fundamental flaw in the Christian definition

---

[39] Al-Nāshiʾ al-Akbar, 'Refutation of the Christians', pp. 74–75.
[40] Ibn ʿAdī, 'Treatise on the Unity of God', p. 209.
[41] Ibn ʿAdī, 'Treatise on the Unity of God', p. 246.
[42] Ibn ʿAdī, 'Treatise Showing the Errors', p. 4.

of God that results in a God who is no longer simple but complex. The Muslim definition of God is his simplicity, because only created bodies are composite and contingent. "Each person is composed of the substance which contains them all and the properties of each in particular. Therefore, they are all composed and none of them are eternal."[43] Al-Kindī refers to ʿAmmār al-Baṣrī's description of the three properties (*khawaṣṣ*) and appears to be influenced by Abū ʿĪsā al-Warrāq's work. Yaḥya replies to al-Kindī by repeating his definition of the Trinity from his 940 treatise and goes on to reject al-Kindī's argument that Christians have a time- and space-bound deity since they believe there is composition in God that only created beings have in reality. Yaḥya says that the three attributes (*ṣifāt*), goodness, power and wisdom, are eternal and were never composed of the substance (*jawhar*) after the world came into being.

Al-Kindī discusses various concepts of oneness also found in Yaḥya's earlier treatise, such as oneness of genus and species, and concludes, "Christians say three is one. But this results in three eternal beings".[44] Yaḥya points out that al-Kindī has failed to look at oneness "in relation or of numerical unity that permits subdivision"[45] and repeats his argument from the 940 treatise that one subject can have multiple definitions. He uses once again his analogy of Zayd being one subject that contains the definition "living", "rational" and "mortal" and concludes, "This is the way that Christians speak about the Creator who is one."[46] By clinging steadfastly to his own particular definition of oneness in multiplicity, Yaḥya seeks to uphold the rationality of the Trinity in the face of Muslim insistence that, if oneness may contain multiplicity in created things, then the Creator Himself cannot be defined in such a way.

In his response to the 'Refutation of the Three Christian Sects' by Abū ʿĪsā al-Warrāq (d. 860), Yaḥya defends the Christian concept of oneness in multiplicity once again. This treatise appears to come after the reply to al-Kindī because Yaḥya develops a new analogy for the three attributes in Zayd the doctor, the accountant and the writer. Thus, the one God operates in three different ways but is still the same being. The advantage of Yaḥya's choice of Zayd as living, rational and mortal, or doctor, accountant and writer, is that Yaḥya is not tied to the traditional Christian teaching that God the Father is the cause of the Son and the Spirit, expressed by Abū Rāʾiṭa' as the substance of God having two essential attributes of knowledge and life, or by ʿAmmār al-Baṣrī as the substance of God having two essential attributes of speech and life. Yaḥya recognises that there must be three attributes rather than two if the Christian doctrine of the Trinity is to be maintained correctly. He refuses to equate the attribute of the Father with the substance of God, as the tradition had insisted. Yet like the tradition he has rejected, Yaḥya still has to justify to Muslims why God has only three essential attributes rather than several more, but he declines to get involved in this debate, since he accepts the tradition from the New Testament that God is Father, Son and Holy Spirit. The maintenance of

---

[43] Ibn ʿAdī, 'Treatise Showing the Errors', p. 4.
[44] Ibn ʿAdī, 'Treatise Showing the Errors', p. 11.
[45] Ibn ʿAdī, 'Treatise Showing the Errors', p. 12.
[46] Ibn ʿAdī, 'Treatise Showing the Errors', p. 12.

threeness in oneness is dictated by the scriptural inheritance, but he does not need to follow the standard Greek theological interpretation from Irenaeus onwards of God the Father having his two hands, the Son and the Spirit.

Nevertheless, Yaḥya undergoes a kind of conversion to the Irenaean notion of the two hands of the Father in a later treatise, in which he describes the three attributes as intellect (*ʿaql*), the intelligent one (*ʿāqil*) and intellection (*maʿqūl*).[47] He puts forward this new analogy to explain the relationships between the Father, Son and Holy Spirit. He says that the Father who is the cause of the Son and the Spirit is the intellect (*ʿaql*), the Son is the one who is intelligent (*ʿāqil*) in the sense that he thinks, and the Spirit is the intellection (*maʿqūl*) in the sense that he is the thought.[48] Thus, towards the end of his life, Yaḥya accepted the tradition that the Father is the cause of the Son and the Spirit and develops his own unique way of expressing this belief. So instead of Zayd acting in three different ways as doctor, accountant and writer, there is the human mind that thinks and the thought that results. Rather than the equality expressed in the Zayd analogy, there is the subordination of thinking and thought to the mind that performs such actions. Perhaps Yaḥya was criticised by other Christians for his abandonment of the tradition dearly held by all Middle Eastern Christians that the Father was the cause of the Son and the Spirit and became resigned to representing that tradition, despite his many years of ignoring it, but he does not admit that this was the reason for his new psychological analogy. In a later treatise, Yaḥya gives a hint of his conversion to traditional explanations of the Trinity when he says that he has read Dionysius, Basil and John Chrysostom and wishes to pass on their wisdom concerning how to speak of the Trinity.[49] He explains that Christians speak of the Trinity of Father, Son and Holy Spirit in terms of fatherhood (*ubuwwa*), sonship (*bunuwwa*) and procession (*inbiʿāth*).[50] The language of the Trinity as goodness, power and wisdom, or Zayd as doctor, accountant and writer, is absent here. However, even in this late work, Yaḥya emphasises for his Muslim reader that the Creator is not three substances (*jawāhir*), but the reality (*maʿnā*) of each member of the Trinity is different from the reality of the other two members.[51] This choice of *maʿnā* for the three attributes reflects ʿAmmār al-Baṣrī's usage in his 'Book of the Proof' and indicates that part of Yaḥya's conversion to a more traditional explanation of the Trinity was his reading of ʿAmmār al-Baṣrī's writing, to which he alludes in his 'Dialogue with al-Maṣrī'.

A late-tenth-century Muslim discussion of the Trinity comes from the Baghdad judge Abū Bakr al-Bāqillānī (d. 1014), who included a refutation of Christian teaching in a larger work on variant religious views. He is particularly concerned with the Christian assertion that God is a substance (*jawhar*) and begins his discussion with Christians by asking "Why do you say that God is a

[47] Ibn ʿAdī, 'Treatise Concerning the Rightness of the Christian Belief', p. 71.
[48] Ibn ʿAdī, 'Treatise Concerning the Rightness of the Christian Belief', p. 73.
[49] Ibn ʿAdī, 'Treatise Explaining in Which Respect it is Valid', p. 53.
[50] Ibn ʿAdī, 'Treatise Explaining in Which Respect it is Valid', p. 56.
[51] Ibn ʿAdī, 'Treatise Explaining in Which Respect it is Valid', p. 58.

substance?"[52] He offers four different responses by Christians. Firstly, since all things are either substances or accidents, then God cannot have accidents and so is a substance. Secondly, God must be self-subsistent, not depending on anything else for His existence, so we call Him a substance. Thirdly, God acts and is not acted upon, so is a substance and not an accident. Fourthly, God is too noble to be dependent on anything else, so is a substance. The second statement more closely corresponds to Christian writing about God as a substance.[53] Both Abū Rāʾiṭa and ʿAmmār al-Baṣrī used the term substance (*jawhar*) to express the reality that God is self-subsistent and does not depend on anything else for His existence. They based this principle on Aristotle's *Categories*. Al-Bāqillānī begins his refutation of the Christians by questioning the validity and appropriateness of attributing substance (*jawhar*) to God. According to Wadi Z. Haddad, "This seems to be a reference to the use of the term by Yaḥya ibn ʿAdī, among other Christian philosophers and theologians. Yaḥya had stated that 'one of the first principles of philosophy is that all existent things consist of either substances or accidents, and since God cannot be an accident He must be a substance'".[54] However, al-Bāqillānī does not engage with Yaḥya's writing to any extent and it seems unlikely that he had read much of Yaḥya's unique contribution to Christian theology. It is much more likely that Haddad is right to say that al-Bāqillānī is dependent on "al-Kindī's 'Refutation of the Trinity' in which he argues that the three persons must of necessity be categorized as genus, species, persons, or accidents and thereby not eternal".[55] In other words, al-Bāqillānī was probably reading previous Muslim refutations of the Trinity rather than Christian presentations of the Trinity.

Al-Bāqillānī objects to the Christian use of the Arabic term *jawhar* because he understands *jawhar* to be "a basic component of material objects that can be characterised by accidents".[56] In other words, describing God by terminology locked into ways of describing the created world is futile. The danger of applying what is observed in the creation to the nature of the Creator is that not only is this futile but seriously misleading. He asks the Christians, "If the almighty eternal One is a substance, you must admit that he is like substances that are known, and of their kind, receiving accidents as they do".[57] Naturally, if the presupposition of al-Bāqillānī is accepted, then Christians are in deep trouble, for then God has to be part of the world He created. Al-Bāqillānī wants Christians

---

[52] Abū Bakr al-Bāqillānī, 'Refutation of the Christians in the Book of Introduction', in Thomas, *Christian Doctrines in Islamic Theology* (Leiden: Brill, 2008), pp. 144–203 (pp. 144–45).

[53] Al-Bāqillānī, 'Refutation of the Christians', pp. 144–47.

[54] Wadi Z. Haddad, 'A Tenth-Century Speculative Theologian's Refutation of the Basic Doctrines of Christianity: Al-Baqillani (d. A.D. 1013)', in Yvonne Yazbeck Haddad and Wadi Z. Haddad, *Christian–Muslim Encounters* (Gainsville: University of Florida Press, 1995), pp. 82–94 (pp. 87–88). He quotes from Augustine Périer, *Maqālāt li-Yaḥya ibn ʿAdī: Petits Traités Apologétiques de Yaḥya ibn ʿAdī* (Paris: J. Gabalda and Paul Geuthner, 1920), p. 53.

[55] Haddad, 'A Tenth-Century Speculative Theologian's Refutation', p. 88.

[56] Thomas, *Christian Doctrines in Islamic Theology*, footnote, p. 145.

[57] Al-Bāqillānī, 'Refutation of the Christians', pp. 148–49.

to abandon the term substance (*jawhar*) and confess with Muslims that "The eternal One exists and is not a substance or accident, and is not like things that exist in the observable sphere, just as he is not like substances".[58]

Al-Bāqillānī turns to the notion of hypostases and asks Christians, "Why do you claim that God almighty is three hypostases (*aqānīm*), but do not claim that he is four or ten or more than this?"[59] Notice that al-Bāqillānī uses the term *aqānīm* that Christians themselves used, unlike al-Nāshiʾ al-Akbar, who used the term *uqnūmāt* that Christians did not use. But he does repeat al-Nāshiʾs conceptualisation of the relationship between the three hypostases as "the existent One who has knowledge and life".[60] Once again, Abū Rāʾiṭa's explanation of the hypostases surfaces in a Muslim refutation of the Trinity, without the Muslim writer having any awareness of the origin of this way of describing the hypostases. Al-Bāqillānī then responds to this Christian explanation by asking "Why do you deny that the hypostases are four? For we say that the eternal One is existent, living, knowing and powerful".[61] He puts into the mouth of a Christian the reply that "power is life, so they are one hypostasis", and replies, "Why do you deny that knowledge is life, so that the Creator would then be two hypostases?"[62] Like al-Nāshiʾ al-Akbar, he attempts to demonstrate the arbitrary choice of attributes of God made by Christians in the restriction of such attributes to three. He then points out that Muslims list several more than three attributes of God. "We say: The Creator is existent, living, knowing and powerful, and we say: He is willing, everlasting, hearing, seeing and articulating." Al-Bāqillānī includes himself among the followers of Abū al-Ḥasan al-Ashʿarī (d. 936), who disagreed with Muʿtazilī Muslim intellectuals who said that the names given to God are only metaphors for His being that cannot be compared to characteristics in the created world. Al-Ashʿarī, who began his career as a Muʿtazilī, came to believe that God does have attributes that are essential to His being and that these are life, knowledge, power, will, speech, seeing and hearing. Wadi Z. Haddad notes that al-Bāqillānī adds an eighth attribute to this list of seven attributes: that of "everlasting".[63] Thus, al-Bāqillānī is the first Muslim scholar to discuss the Ashʿarī conception of essential attributes in God with Christians.

Al-Bāqillānī goes on to discuss the relationship between the substance and the hypostases in the Christian doctrine of the Trinity. Here he seems to repeat arguments from 'The Refutation of the Three Christian Sects' by Abū ʿĪsā al-Warrāq, as David Thomas has indicated.[64] He repeats Abū ʿĪsā al-Warrāq's argument that the Christian belief that "The substance is other than the hypostases" implies that "The substance is divine, and the three hypostases are divine … and the Divinity is thus four, substance and three hypostases other than

---

[58] Al-Bāqillānī, 'Refutation of the Christians', pp. 148–49.
[59] Al-Bāqillānī, 'Refutation of the Christians', pp. 152–53.
[60] Al-Bāqillānī, 'Refutation of the Christians', pp. 152–53.
[61] Al-Bāqillānī, 'Refutation of the Christians', pp. 152–53.
[62] Al-Bāqillānī, 'Refutation of the Christians', pp. 154–55.
[63] Haddad, 'A Tenth-Century Speculative Theologian's Refutation', p. 86.
[64] Thomas, *Christian Doctrines in Islamic Theology*, footnote, p. 159.

it".[65] He then develops his discussion by quoting a Christian asking, "But do you not yourselves say about the attributes of the Creator that they are not identical with Him or different from Him? So then why do you deny that the substance is not identical with the hypostases and not different from them?"[66] David Thomas points out that this Christian is reporting the view of the followers of Ashʿarī, "that the attributes of God are neither God nor other than him".[67] Al-Bāqillānī replies that the situation is not identical between the Christian view of the attributes and the Muslim view he espouses.

> We do not claim that God is identical with his attributes in any respect. But you claim that the substance is identical with the hypostases in substantiality, and is thus identical with them through itself, and is also different from them in hypostaticity through itself. So there is something of a difference between our teaching and yours.[68]

Here al-Bāqillānī shows that the Ashʿarī doctrine "that the attributes of God are neither God nor other than him" means that Muslims are not able to assert that they know what the attributes of God consist of, so he thinks that Christians are guilty of making assertions about the attributes of God that are untenable. He wants Christians to join him in adopting an "agnostic" position with respect to speaking about God. While he does not want to agree with the Muʿtazilī position that the attributes are only metaphors, in practice he is not willing to state that the attributes exist in any real sense, since the Ashʿarī doctrine states that God has attributes, but we do not know how he has them.

Ibn al-Ṭayyib's first treatise on the Trinity shows direct borrowing from Yaḥya ibn ʿAdī's earliest definition of the Trinity from 940, when Ibn al-Ṭayyib says that Christians believe that the one God is threefold as wisdom (*al-hikma*), power (*al-qudra*) and bounty (*al-jūd*). Later in the treatise, he alludes to another of Yaḥya's analogies for the Trinity when he says that the divine essence has the attribute of knowledge (*ʿilm*), knowing (*ʿālim*) and of being known (*maʿlūm*).[69] Ibn al-Ṭayyib has altered the components of Yaḥya's set of three attributes, intellect (*ʿaql*), the intelligent one (*ʿāqil*) and intellection (*maʿqūl*), but it is obvious that Yaḥya's late psychological analogy is being refreshed here by Ibn al-Ṭayyib, who does not feel any contradiction between Yaḥya's two quite distinct analogies. After all, the early group of wisdom (*al-hikma*), power (*al-qudra*) and bounty (*al-jūd*) all refer to attributes of God found both in the Bible and the Qurʾān, but the later group of knowledge (*ʿilm*), knowing (*ʿālim*) and of being known (*maʿlūm*), or intellect (*ʿaql*), the intelligent one (*ʿāqil*) and intellection (*maʿqūl*), are not scriptural descriptions of God.

Surprisingly, Ibn al-Ṭayyib diverts attention from these analogies by indicating that Christians call the essence "substance" (*jawhar*) and the attributes

---

[65] Al-Bāqillānī, 'Refutation of the Christians', pp. 160–61. See Al-Warrāq, 'The Refutation of the Three Christian Sects', pp. 80–83.
[66] Al-Bāqillānī, 'Refutation of the Christians', pp. 164–65.
[67] David Thomas, *Christian Doctrines in Islamic Theology*, footnote, p. 165.
[68] Al-Bāqillānī, 'Refutation of the Christians', pp. 164–67.
[69] Ibn al-Ṭayyib, 'The Second Treatise on the Trinity', p. 443.

"properties" (*khawāṣṣ*),[70] which he has taken from his fellow East Syrian theologian ʿAmmār al-Baṣrī. Yet he does not follow ʿAmmār's argument that God has two essential attributes of life and speech. Ibn al-Ṭayyib amalgamates previous Christian presentations of the Trinity from ʿAmmār al-Baṣrī and Yaḥya ibn ʿAdī into his own synthesis of the best of the past without paying much attention to any contradictions that might arise from doing this.

When he deals with the Muslim argument that there are many more than three attributes in God, Ibn al-Ṭayyib appeals to the distinction between attributes that are essential to God and those that are actions He performs. Thus, only the attributes of knowledge, knowing and being known are essential to God in His being. But the attributes of goodness, power and wisdom are essential to Him in His relationship with the created world. There are other actions that God takes with respect to His creation, but these actions are not essential to His being.[71] There appear to be two forms of the Trinity. There is the inner trinity of God's own psychology that describes His inmost reality of knowledge, knowing and being known, and in addition there is the outer trinity of God's activity towards His creation, seen in his goodness, power and wisdom. How these two forms of Trinity relate to one another is not explained by Ibn al-Ṭayyib, but a Muslim could quite easily say that there appear to be six attributes on display here rather than just three, for the attributes of knowledge, knowing and being known do not directly correspond to goodness, power and wisdom.

Ibn al-Ṭayyib's third treatise on the Trinity is an attempt to clarify his use of different analogies for the Trinity. He calls goodness, power and wisdom "attributes that are communicable beyond his essence to his creatures", but fatherhood, sonship and procession are "attributes peculiar to him that are not communicable beyond his essence".[72] Ibn al-Ṭayyib then says that the non-communicable attributes of fatherhood, sonship and procession are synonyms for knowledge, knowing and being known, as he did in the earlier treatise. What might at first sight seem to be an advocacy of nine attributes is reduced to six: three non-communicable and three communicable attributes.

The basic difference between communicable and non-communicable attributes lies in our human ability to perceive them. Whereas the communicable attributes of goodness, power and wisdom may be experienced by human beings, the non-communicable attributes cannot be directly experienced. In the final analysis, human beings can only discover the non-communicable attributes of God from scriptural revelation. He is revealed as Father, Son and Holy Spirit, which are equivalent to knowledge, knowing and being known, but without revelation we would not be aware of this. Revelation is required beyond observation because "What does not extend beyond his essence is concealed from human minds."[73] Yet it is not clear that the attributes of knowledge, knowing and being known are revealed in the Bible in the way that the Father, Son and Holy Spirit are revealed. How Ibn al-Ṭayyib can be sure that his analogy

---

[70] Ibn al-Ṭayyib, 'The Second Treatise on the Trinity', p. 444.

[71] Ibn al-Ṭayyib, 'The Second Treatise on the Trinity', pp. 446–47.

[72] Ibn al-Ṭayyib, 'The Third Treatise on the Trinity', p. 240.

[73] Ibn al-Ṭayyib, 'The Third Treatise on the Trinity', p. 254.

is a correct piece of scriptural hermeneutics is doubtful. His reliance on Yaḥya ibn ʿAdī obscures the latter's lack of interest in such matters, but it shows that Ibn al-Ṭayyib was not willing to go back to the more scripturally based argument of ʿAmmār al-Baṣrī, that the Father who is the principal attribute has the two essential attributes of His speech, who is His Son, and His life, that is His Spirit. Presumably, Ibn al-Ṭayyib did not think that ʿAmmār's way of presenting the Trinity was adequate in debate with Muslims in his own time.

Iliyyā, the Church of the East Bishop of Nisibis, who was a contemporary of Ibn al-Ṭayyib, was more dependent on previous Church of the East tradition than Ibn al-Ṭayyib. He gives a succinct statement of Muslim reservations about the Trinity. "There is no known substance (*jawhar*) that does not occupy space and is contingent and no hypostases (*aqānīm*) who are not persons (*ashkhāṣ*) and no son who is not from marital relations."[74] There are the three basic objections that Muslims typically made against the Trinity. As can be seen in the critique of Abū ʿĪsā, al-Kindī and al-Bāqillānī, a *jawhar* is for Muslims an aspect of the created world so cannot be a term that is suitable for the eternal Creator, who is beyond space and time. The three hypostases must be individual persons who are equivalent to three divine beings, and thus the unity of God is compromised and the terms Father and Son are unsuitable for the majesty of the Creator, who is beyond procreation.

Iliyyā responds to these Muslim rejections of inappropriate terminology by reminding Muslims that the Qurʾān presents God in anthropomorphic terminology. He has two eyes, two hands, two thighs and a face. Yet Muslims say that he has no body at all because he is beyond His creation. Muslims tend to say that these descriptions of God in the Qurʾān are metaphors and are not to be taken literally, reports Iliyyā, who goes on to apply a similar logic to the New Testament terminology of Father and Son, which do not imply sexual relations. As for the names Father, Son and Holy Spirit, these are given in the gospel as names for three divine properties (*khawāṣṣ*), so that those who understand the three hypostases (*aqānīm*) to mean three gods, or three composite bodies (*ajsām murakkaba*), or three separate persons (*ashkhāṣ mutafarriqa*) have misunderstood them.[75] Iliyyā is dependent on ʿAmmār al-Baṣrī's Arabic terminology for the hypostases (*aqānīm*) as properties (*khawāṣṣ*) and demonstrates how ʿAmmār's description of the Trinity has become a tradition in the teaching of the Church of the East.

This dependence of Iliyyā on ʿAmmār al-Baṣrī is further seen in his use of speech and life as the two essential attributes of God, whom he defines in Muslim terms as self-existent (*qāʾim bi-nafsihi*). He argues that a self-existent being must be defined as living and speaking. Therefore, God has three hypostases: self-existence, life and rational speech.[76] This is a replica of ʿAmmār's argument that God has Word and Spirit that are speech and life. Iliyyā reports his Muslim dialogue partner, the vizier Abū al-Qāsim, objecting to the addition of speech and life to the essence of God because that would mean believing in two eternal

---

[74] Iliyyā of Nisibis, 'The Book of the Sessions', p. 30, in Kuhn, *God is One*, p. 100.
[75] Iliyyā of Nisibis, 'The Book of the Sessions', p. 31, in Kuhn, *God is One*, p. 100.
[76] Iliyyā of Nisibis, 'Session 1', verses 110–121 in Kuhn, *God is One*, p. 108.

entities in addition to God Himself.[77] However, Iliyyā turns this objection back on Abū al-Qāsim by pointing out that Sunni Muslims believe that God has seven essential attributes: living, knowing, powerful, willing, articulating, hearing and seeing. "If Christians are polytheists through their assertion that God is speaking and living, the Sunnis must also be culpable of polytheism, only to a greater degree", retorts Iliyyā.[78] Here is a parallel with Ibn al-Ṭayyib, who made the same argument. These two Church of the East theologians show how, by the beginning of the eleventh century, Sunni Muslims had come to accept the Ashʿarī teaching that God has seven essential attributes.

Iliyyā shows his concern to meet Muslim objections to applying the term *jawhar* to God. He adopts a Syriac term *kiyān*, which means "self-existent", so that Muslims would no longer understand the Arabic term *jawhar* to mean that Christians believe that God is a part of his creation. This innovation parallels the adoption from the Syriac of *aqānim* for hypostases that Christians had made in the late eighth century. However, it was probably too late to give up on the Arabic word *jawhar* for substance that had also been used by Arabic-speaking Christians since the late eighth century.

Paul of Antioch, who was a bishop of the Melkite church in Sidon in the early thirteenth century, presented the Trinity in his 'Letter to a Muslim Friend'. He relies on ʿAmmār al-Baṣrī's argument that God is living and speaking and the names Father, Son and Holy Spirit represent the essence, life and speech of the one God. "According to us, the essence (*dhāt*) is the Father, the speech is the Son and the life is the Holy Spirit."[79] The longevity of ʿAmmār's description of the Trinity is noteworthy and demonstrates the profound impact that this ninth-century Church of the East theologian had on Arabic-speaking Christians generally and not just on members of his own denomination. Paul, a Chaledonian Melkite bishop, had no difficulty embracing the Trinitarian teaching of ʿAmmār.

Paul also repeats the argument of Iliyyā of Nisibis, who responds to the Muslim supposition that Christians believe that God is three composite individuals, or three gods, or three parts, by referring to the way the Qurʾān represents God as having two eyes, two hands, a leg and a face. Christians might conclude that Muslims believe "that God the exalted has a body, limbs and organs".[80] Paul has the Muslim respond that "the Qurʾān speaks of this, but the intention of this is not a literal meaning".[81] Then the Christian reply is a mirror image of the Muslim one. "The reason for our saying that God is three hypostases, Father, Son and Holy Spirit, is that the Gospel (*al-injīl*) speaks of this", but "What is intended by the hypostases is not composite individuals (*ashkhāṣ*), or parts, or components, or similar things, that would entail polytheism and plurality".[82] This presentation reflects the writing of Iliyyā of Nisibis quite precisely. Paul has no problem depending on an eleventh-century

---

[77] Iliyyā of Nisibis, 'Session 1', verses 122–124 in Kuhn, *God is One*, p. 108.
[78] Iliyyā of Nisibis, 'Session 1', verses 130–134 in Kuhn, *God is One*, p. 108.
[79] Paul of Antioch, 'Letter to a Muslim Friend', pp. 92–93.
[80] Paul of Antioch, 'Letter to a Muslim Friend', pp. 130–31.
[81] Paul of Antioch, 'Letter to a Muslim Friend', pp. 130–33.
[82] Paul of Antioch, 'Letter to a Muslim Friend', pp. 132–33.

Church of the East bishop for his approach to Muslim questions about the Trinity. So, while Paul says he is reporting what Western Christian leaders say about Islam, it is clear that he is relying on previous Middle Eastern Christian writers for his own writing rather than properly reporting what Western Christian leaders think for themselves.

Paul also refers to Iliyyā's treatment of the concept "substance" (*jawhar*). Muslims hold that a *jawhar* in Arabic always refers to a physical body in the created world so cannot be used to describe the eternal Creator. Like Iliyyā, Paul responds by defining God as "self-existent" and not needing to rely on anything else. It is in this sense that Christians call Him a substance *jawhar*. However, Paul develops his own explanation of "substance", which appears to be original to him. He argues that there are two kinds of substances, material and immaterial. Examples of immaterial substances in the created world are "the substance of the soul, the substance of the mind, and the substance of light".[83] In other words, if it is appropriate to find immaterial substances in our world that do not receive accidents, then it is possible to understand that God can be an immaterial substance that does not receive accidents. Thus, the concept "substance" (*jawhar*) can be attributed to the Creator.

Paul's 'Letter to a Muslim Friend' was given a new lease of life in the early fourteenth century when a revised version of his letter was sent to two leading Muslim intellectuals in Damascus from Christians in Cyprus, who added significant portions to Paul's original letter but did not alter Paul's writing to any great extent. The additions are mainly quotations from the Qurʾān and the Bible and the sections of Paul's letter on the Trinity are preserved without additional arguments. Therefore, when the two Damascus Muslim scholars wrote their replies to the letter from Cyprus, they were responding directly to Paul's presentation of the Trinity. Taqī al-Dīn Aḥmad Ibn Taymiyya received a copy of the letter from Cyprus in 1316 and Shams al-Dīn Muḥammad ibn Abī Ṭālib al-Anṣārī al-Dimashqī received a copy in 1321. Both of these men wrote replies to the letter. Ibn Taymiyya wrote a substantial book entitled, 'A Sound Reply to the One who Changed the Religion of the Messiah', and al-Dimashqī wrote 'A Response to the Letter from the People of Cyprus'.[84]

Ibn Taymiyya quotes Paul of Antioch section by section and gives his response. When he turns to Paul's statements about the Trinity, Ibn Taymiyya notes that Paul attempts to argue that God has life and speech as essential attributes, but in reality Christians believe in the Trinity of Father, Son and Holy Spirit because it is revealed in their scriptures. "The origin of their belief is what they claim to have been received from revealed religion, not that they have proved the life and speech of God, which they then assert by these expressions".[85] Their scriptures do not mention life and speech as essential attributes of God, yet

---

[83] Paul of Antioch, 'Letter to a Muslim Friend', pp. 138–39.

[84] See Rifaat Ebied and David Thomas, *The Letter from the People of Cyprus and Ibn Abi Talib al-Dimashqi's Response* (Leiden: Brill, 2005), pp. 1–35.

[85] Taqī al-Dīn Aḥmad Ibn Taymiyya, 'A Sound Reply to the One Who Changed the Religion of the Messiah', in Thomas F. Michel (trans.), *A Muslim Theologian's Response to Christianity* (New York: Caravan Books, 1984), p. 255.

they rely on rational argumentation to alter what is revealed. "This is in spite of the fact that there is nothing in the divine books which indicates such things; rather they contain what proves the contrary."[86] When Paul argues that Jesus taught his disciples to baptise people in the name of the Father, the Son and the Holy Spirit, Ibn Taymiyya retorts, "Christ and the apostles never commanded them this observation by which they claim their view is determined".[87] What Christ actually meant by this command was not what Christians think he said. "The meaning of 'Baptise people in the name of the Father, the Son and the Holy Spirit' is that they command people to believe in God and His prophet which God sent and in the angel by which God sent down the revelation which he brought".[88] Notice that Ibn Taymiyya interprets this saying of Jesus by means of the teaching of the Qurʾān. Jesus confirms the teaching of all the other messengers sent by God and therefore it is impossible for him to teach that God is Triune. Rather, he taught "them to believe in God and His angels, books, and messengers. This is the truth to which sound reason and correct religion give evidence".[89] Ibn Taymiyya here quotes Q2:285, "All believers believe in God, His angels, His books and His messengers". In other words, from a Qurʾānic perspective, the books of God must proclaim His oneness, and any books that diverge from this cannot be deemed to teach the truth. Ibn Taymiyya appears to be arguing that the report of Jesus commanding his disciples to baptise in the name of the Father, the Son and the Holy Spirit is a misrepresentation of his teaching in the scriptures of the Christians and provides evidence that they departed from his true teaching. This is simply an example of the real Jesus being covered up by those who wrote the account in the Christian gospels.

After he quotes Paul's explanation of the hypostases, Ibn Taymiyya states that the books of the Christians do not mention *aqanim*. "Rather this is a term which they have invented."[90] In any case, Christians say that only three names of God are essential to Him but, "Since the names of God are many, such as the Loving, the Powerful, and others, to limit them to three without the others is wrong".[91] He cites analogies that Christians have put forward to support their claim that God has three essential names. Firstly, he mentions Yaḥya ibn ʿAdī's analogy of Zayd the doctor, accountant and writer, and responds,

> Zayd here is one substance having three attributes of medicine, accounting and writing. There are not three substances here, but each attribute offers a definition which the other does not. No intelligent person says that the attribute is equal to that which is described in the substance.

Emilio Platti points out that Yaḥya ibn ʿAdī's attempt to argue that there are three substantial attributes akin to three activities was not well received by Ibn Taymiyya. "It is clear that Ibn Taymiyya's comment on Yaḥya's position is pointing towards a fundamental difference between Muslim thinkers and Yaḥya

[86] Ibn Taymiyya, 'A Sound Reply', p. 156.
[87] Ibn Taymiyya, 'A Sound Reply', p. 259.
[88] Ibn Taymiyya, 'A Sound Reply', p. 262.
[89] Ibn Taymiyya, 'A Sound Reply', p. 262.
[90] Ibn Taymiyya, 'A Sound Reply', p. 264.
[91] Ibn Taymiyya, 'A Sound Reply', p. 267.

in defining 'substance' and 'substantial attributes' and to a potential weakness in Yaḥya's position."[92]

Secondly, he refers to the analogy from the heat and light of the sun used by Christians. But Ibn Taymiyya rejects this comparison as false because, "The heat and light which subsist in the air, and on walls are accidents subsisting in something other than the sun, whereas the Word and the Holy Spirit, according to them, are two substances (*jawharan*)".[93] Thus, according to Ibn Taymiyya, the analogy of the heat and light of the sun does not perform what Christians wish for it. They wish to find a comparison for two substantial attributes in God within the created world, but the attributes of light and heat coming from the sun are not essential to the sun but rather to the air or walls. However, Christians believe that the Word and the Spirit are essential to God rather than being merely actions that he takes, like other actions of God. But this desire to isolate two actions as essential to God distorts their understanding of the multiple attributes of God.

Al-Dimashqī opens his letter with praise to God for sending down the Qur'ān which, among other things, erased the erroneous teaching about "substances" (*jawāhir*) and "hypostases" (*aqānīm*) that "led to open polytheism about the lordship of God".[94] It is obvious how this Damascus Muslim scholar understands the rejection of the Trinity within the Qur'ān, despite the fact that the Qur'ān does not refer to substances and hypostases. He quotes Q4:171, which tells Christians not to say three when speaking of God and Q5:73, which says that those who say that God is a third of three are unbelievers.[95] He eventually replies to the Christian presentation of the Trinity by accusing them of deviating from belief in one God. They "divided the one, single Divinity into three Divinities, hypostases in a Trinity, and named them Father, Son and Holy Spirit, accepting them as one Divinity".[96] Notice how al-Dimashqī thinks that Christians developed their concept of the hypostases before giving them the names Father, Son and Holy Spirit. Of course, the historical reality is otherwise, since Christians received the names from the lips of Jesus himself and only borrowed the concept of hypostases from Greek thought much later, but al-Dimashqī is not concerned to construct a historical account of Christian deviation from belief in the oneness of God. He later repeats this criticism of the Christians and adds, "You said that the three are one, not realising the whole world's marvelling at you and laughing at the ignorance of people who had no idea of what divinity is".[97]

When he responds to the presentation of the Trinity in the letter, al-Dimashqī notes that the Christians intend to

---

[92] Platti, 'Yaḥya ibn ʿAdī', p. 414.

[93] Ibn Taymiyya, 'A Sound Reply', p. 273.

[94] Ibn Abī Ṭālib al-Anṣārī al-Dimashqī, 'Response to the Letter from the People of Cyprus', in Rifaat Ebied and David Thomas, (eds and trans), *The Letter from the People of Cyprus and Ibn Abi Talib al-Dimashqi's Response* (Leiden: Brill, 2005), pp. 150–497 (pp. 154–55).

[95] Al-Dimashqī, 'Response to the Letter', pp. 186–87.

[96] Al-Dimashqī, 'Response to the Letter', pp. 296–97.

[97] Al-Dimashqī, 'Response to the Letter', pp. 316–17.

> list the names of the attributes of essence (*ṣifāt al-dhāt*), the three names of the attributes, thing, living and articulate, as names of the one Being named by them, one God, one Lord, and one Creator. Then you follow this explanation by saying, 'Essence, Life and Speech – to us the Essence is the Father, the Speech is the Son, and the Life is the Holy Spirit'.[98]

Then he simply rejects this construction.

> You have chosen this mockery entirely yourselves in the face of reason and revelation … This apportioning of names of yours proves that the moment you embark on speculation and search for understanding about God the exalted through intellectual means you truly are the unbelievers among the People of the Book, according to the witness of the Qurʾān.[99]

He instructs the Christians to pay heed to the clear testimony of the Qurʾān that "The blessed One is living, knowing, willing, powerful, hearing, seeing and speaking". Al-Dimashqī confidently reports that rather than just three essential attributes, God has seven of them, demonstrating that the teaching of the tenth-century al-Ashʿarī was firmly embedded in this Sunni account from the fourteenth century.

Al-Dimashqī attempts to explain the origin of the Christian conception of the Trinity by giving the honour to Paul, who was "neither a contemporary, nor a companion. Nor a disciple of Christ, and between him and the time of Christ there were almost a hundred and fifty years".[100] He invented the idea that "God is three hypostases, attributes and characteristics, Father, Son and Holy Spirit".[101] This gives him the permission to deny that Christ confessed belief in the Father, Son and Holy Spirit. "Your claim that Christ said to you, 'Say the third of three, and baptize the world in the name of the Father and the Son and the Holy Spirit' is a lying claim and false allegation. It is completely out of the question that Christ would have commanded the world to associate any other with God."[102] Notice how al-Dimashqī blends Q5:73 with Matthew 28:19.

Al-Dimashqī responds to the argument that there are substances in the created world that are immaterial and do not receive accidents. He reports discussions about the soul and the intellect in human beings and believes that every soul and intellect "is bounded within a space".[103] But there can be no comparison between God and these human realities. "God is a thing unlike others, is existent absolutely, is a non-spatial substance, is a pure essence, is self-subsistent not in any object."[104] This is why the Christian doctrine of the Trinity is profoundly false, according to al-Dimashqī. "You say, the Father exists by his essence, the Son speaks by his essence, and the Spirit lives by his essence, and each of the three is independent and eternal in one respect, and dependent and temporal in another."[105] In other words, the whole reason for believing in the Trinity stems

---

98 Al-Dimashqī, 'Response to the Letter', pp. 330–31.
99 Al-Dimashqī, 'Response to the Letter', pp. 330–33.
100 Al-Dimashqī, 'Response to the Letter', pp. 396–97.
101 Al-Dimashqī, 'Response to the Letter', pp. 398–99.
102 Al-Dimashqī, 'Response to the Letter', pp. 430–31.
103 Al-Dimashqī, 'Response to the Letter', pp. 448–49.
104 Al-Dimashqī, 'Response to the Letter', pp. 448–49.
105 Al-Dimashqī, 'Response to the Letter', pp. 450–51.

from the desire of Christians to make the essence of God bound to space and time. Al-Dimashqī ends with a statement of astonishment at the foolishness of such people. "The three are one, according to your false claim, but what a scoundrel to hold such an opinion, belief and thought about his Lord! Praise be to God for guidance!"[106]

---

[106] Al-Dimashqī, 'Response to the Letter', pp. 450–51.

PART TWO

DIALOGUE ON THE TRINITY IN THE ERA OF GLOBAL CHRISTIANITY

Debate with Muslims over the Trinity was confined to the Middle East. Western Christians who were enthusiastic to fight against the Muslim infidel in a series of crusades from the eleventh century onwards found little enthusiasm for discussion with the enemy. This was to change once the Dominican and Franciscan orders started missionary work among Muslim communities in the thirteenth century. The leader of the Dominicans, Ramon de Penyafort (d.c. 1275), asked his fellow Dominican Thomas Aquinas (d. 1274) to write a training manual for Dominican missionaries who were being schooled in Arabic and Islam in Murcia in Spain and in Tunis in North Africa. Aquinas responded with his four-volume *Summa Contra Gentiles*, written between 1259 and 1264.

In this work, Aquinas understands that Muslims reject the Bible, so he recommends that Christian missionaries approach them first of all by the rationality that is shared by all human beings. Yet reason has limitations.

> The Mohammedans and the pagans, do not agree with us in accepting the authority of any scripture, by which they may be convinced of their error. Thus, against the Jews we are able to argue by means of the Old Testament, while against heretics we are able to argue by means of the New Testament. But the Mohammedans and the pagans accept neither the one nor the other. We must, therefore, have recourse to natural reason, to which all men are forced to give their assent. However, it is true, in divine matters natural reason has its failings.[1]

The Trinity is one of those divine matters that can only be discerned by revelation.

> Since natural reason ascends to a knowledge of God through creatures and, conversely, the knowledge of faith descends from God to us by a divine revelation … We must treat of the things about God Himself which surpass reason and are proposed for belief: such is the confession of the Trinity.[2]

When Aquinas presents his understanding of the Trinity, he repeats Augustine's definition. "There is in the divine nature God unbegotten, who is the source of the whole divine proceeding, namely the Father; there is God begotten

---

[1] Thomas Aquinas, *Summa Contra Gentiles, vol 1:2*, AC Pegis (trans.), (Notre Dame IN: Notre Dame University Press, 1975), p. 62.
[2] Thomas Aquinas, *Summa Contra Gentiles, vol 4:1*, CJ O'Neil (trans.), (Notre Dame IN: Notre Dame University Press, 1975), p. 39.

by way of a word conceived in the intellect, namely the Son; there is God by way of love proceeding, namely the Holy Spirit."[3] Clearly there is little thought given to how such a conceptualisation of the Trinity be communicated to Muslims in particular. This can be explained by the fact that Aquinas had read Muslim philosophers but had not read Middle Eastern Christian debate with Muslims on the Trinity. The very resource the Dominican missionaries needed was unknown to the person who was writing a training manual for them. John Tolan indicates that Aquinas had a very limited view of what Muslims actually believed. "There is no evidence that he had ever seen a Latin translation of the Qur᾽ān or that he had read any major Latin polemical text against Islam."[4]

Ramon Llull (d. 1316) is an example of those who attempted to present the Christian message to Muslims in this period. He had initially been attracted to the Franciscans but ended as an independent missionary to Muslims in North Africa from his home in Majorca, where he set up a training school for missionaries to learn Arabic and Islamic thought. Unlike Aquinas, Llull believed that Muslims could be persuaded to accept the Trinity by reason as well as revelation, as can be seen in 'The Book of the Gentile and the Three Wise Men', written between 1274 and 1276. The Gentile is a man who has no faith, and the three wise men are a Jew, a Christian and a Muslim. Llull has the Gentile asking questions of the three wise men, who each attempt to persuade him of the truth of their religion.

> In the first book we prove that God exists. In the second book the Jew tries to prove that his belief is better than those of the Christian and the Saracen. In the third book the Christian tries to prove that his belief is worthier than those of the Jew and the Saracen. In the fourth book the Saracen tries to prove that his belief is worthier than those of the Jew and the Christian.[5]

When the Christian presents the Trinity to the Gentile, he uses the following argument to prove the Trinity.

> If in God there exists one begetting good which is infinite goodness, greatness, eternity, power, wisdom, love, perfection, and which begets a good infinite in goodness, greatness, power, wisdom, love, perfection, and if from this begetting good and this begotten good there issues forth a good infinite in goodness, greatness, power, wisdom, love, perfection, then the flower is greater in God than it would be if the above-mentioned things did not exist in God … Therefore, the Trinity, by what we have said above, is demonstrable.[6]

Llull's picture of the flowering of goodness by means of a good God begetting goodness which becomes begotten in his creation is an attempt to show that the

---

[3] Aquinas, *Summa Contra Gentiles, vol 4:1*, p. 146.

[4] John Tolan, 'Liber de Veritate Catholicae Fidei Contra Errores Infidelium qui Dicitur Summa Contra Gentiles', in David Thomas and Alex Mallett (eds), *Christian–Muslim Relations: A Bibliographical History, vol. 4* (Leiden: Brill, 2012), pp. 523–27 (p. 526).

[5] Ramon Llull, 'The Book of the Gentile and the Three Wise Men', in A. Bonner (trans.), *Selected Works of Ramon Llull (1232–1316), vol. 1* (Princeton: Princeton University Press, 1985), p. 111.

[6] Llull, 'The Book of the Gentile', p. 194.

Incarnation and infilling of the Spirit in humans are essential to the way God is to be understood.

However, he allows the Muslim to reject the Trinity when he makes his presentation of the truth about God to the Gentile by arguing that the oneness of God precludes the Christian belief in the Trinity.

> Rather, in every way He is one, without there existing in Him any Trinity or plurality. For if there did, then He would have to be compound, and His goodness, greatness, eternity, power, wisdom, love, would have to be contrary to perfection; and since this is impossible, it is therefore evident that God does not exist in Trinity.[7]

Llull makes no room in his dialogue for the Christian to respond to the Muslim denial of the Trinity. Therefore, this piece of writing is not exactly a dialogue between a Christian and a Muslim, but it does demonstrate that some missionaries were willing to engage in discussion based on a rational understanding of the world. Llull hoped that the persuasive powers of the Christian presentation about the flowering of goodness would not only impact the Gentile but the Jew and Muslim also.

Despite the fact that the Dominicans and Franciscans actively worked in Muslim communities in North Africa and the Middle East, they discovered over time that Muslims were not easily persuaded of the truth of the Christian faith. The general view began to prevail that there was little hope of Muslims responding positively to Christianity. When the Jesuit missionary order was founded by Ignatius Loyola in 1534, the expectation was that Jesuits would not actively seek to work among Muslims.

The Protestant Reformation did not initially produce a groundswell of interest in mission beyond Europe. Eighteenth-century revival movements within Protestant churches had a profound influence on mission beyond Christendom, such that a new interest in proclaiming the gospel to Muslims sprang up. The state churches in Protestant Europe were reluctant to organise mission beyond their territorial jurisdictions but voluntary societies were formed by enthusiasts. Within the Church of England, individual evangelicals organised the Church Missionary Society in 1799, but this society was not officially supported by the Church of England. The Basel Missionary Society was formed in 1815 for German-speaking Protestants from Lutheran or Reformed churches in Switzerland and Germany who could join together to preach the gospel and plant churches without being hampered by denominational structures.

The following chapter analyses the presentations of the Trinity for Muslims by five missionaries in the modern era: Karl Pfander, a German Lutheran who joined the Basel Missionary Society and then the Church Missionary Society, Kenneth Cragg, an English Anglican who began his career teaching in the American University in Beirut, David Brown, another English Anglican who joined the Church Missionary Society, Giulio Basetti-Sani, an Italian who joined the Franciscans, and David Shenk, an American Mennonite who joined the Mennonite Mission Network.

---

[7] Llull, 'The Book of the Gentile', pp. 259–60.

4. Missionaries to Muslims
Presenting the Trinity to Muslims

This chapter analyses five missionaries who wrote about the Trinity for Muslims. Karl G. Pfander, a German Lutheran, wrote a substantial treatise on the Trinity in Urdu in the mid-nineteenth century, in which he attempted to defend monotheism within the Trinity. He had a good awareness of the problems Muslims had with the Trinity and engaged with their concerns that the Qurʾān forbids multiplicity in God. He relies on the Middle Eastern terminology of three hypostases in one substance but lacks immediate knowledge of the theologians from the Middle East surveyed earlier here. Kenneth Cragg was an English Anglican who dialogued with Muslim intellectuals in Lebanon and Egypt in the mid-twentieth century. He wanted to demonstrate the dynamic life of the Trinity via the reality of the Incarnation and was not concerned to uphold traditional creedal statements that he regarded as outdated and not contextualised for a modern world. Another English Anglican, David Brown, described in the mid-twentieth century the way that the early Christians came to believe in the Trinity through their experience of Jesus as God's eternal Word and their experience of God's Spirit within them. They realised that God was from eternity related as Father, Son and Holy Spirit and that they were privileged to relate to the Triune God. He trusts that Muslims can come to experience the Trinity just as the early Christians did. The Italian Franciscan, Giulio Basetti-Sani, worked in Egypt in the mid-twentieth century, where he had a transforming experience in his attitude to Muslims. From first regarding them as followers of the Antichrist, he came to see them as seekers after the truth which would culminate in them coming to believe in the Trinity. He argued that the Qurʾān does not criticise the orthodox Trinity but only heterodox versions, so it is the task of Christians to point this out to Muslims, who may then be able to embrace the fulness of truth. Finally, the American Mennonite David Shenk published a dialogue with a Muslim scholar in Nairobi in the 1980s in which he presents the New Testament foundations of the Trinity and defends the Trinity against accusations of tritheism made by Muslims.

Karl Pfander (1803–1868)

The arrival of Karl G. Pfander in India in 1841 marks a new beginning in Christian presentation of the Trinity to Muslims. This Pietistic Lutheran had studied Islam in Switzerland and was able to draw on the academic study of Islam that had been established in European universities. He had already written *The Balance of Truth*, in Armenian in 1831, in Persian in 1835, while he was living on the border of Persia, and in Urdu in 1843, after his move to India. *The*

Balance of Truth presents arguments for the trustworthiness of the Bible and for the Incarnation and the Atonement. A subsequent book published in Urdu in 1844 deals with the Trinity. *The Key of Mysteries: A Treatise on the Doctrine of the Trinity in Unity* is the first serious attempt by a Christian missionary in the modern era to expound and defend the Trinity for a Muslim audience.[1]

Pfander appeals firstly to a Christian readership to explain why he wrote the book. In his introduction he states that he writes to convince Muslims of the truth of the deity of Jesus and the Trinity. The first half of the book is devoted to establishing the divinity of Jesus on which the Trinity depends. Pfander points out to his fellow Christians,

> Our Muslim brethren have never sufficiently and without prejudice studied the subject as it is stated in the Old and the New Testament. They have been prevented from doing so by the unfounded fancy that the holy Scriptures of the Jews and of the Christians have been annulled, or at least corrupted. A complete refutation of this illogical and ignorant assertion is given in the *Balance of Truth*, where it is proved that this idea is contrary to the clear teaching of the Qur᾽ān as well as opposed to historical facts. Now that this stumbling-block is removed, the writer of this tractate hopes that the Most Merciful God will use this little book to enable Muslims to see the true dignity and divine nature of Him whom they themselves acknowledge to be "The Word of God".[2]

The second part of the book is entitled "Statement and Proof of the Doctrine of the Most Holy Trinity in the Divine Unity Proved from Old and New Testaments". He once more addresses Christians. "We, Christians, believe, at least as firmly as Muslims do, in one Almighty God, creator of heaven and earth and of all things, visible and invisible."[3] This dual audience of fellow Christians and possible interested Muslim readers pervades the presentation of the Trinity, and suggests that Pfander felt the need to persuade Christians of the value of the exercise of addressing Muslims concerning such a contentious issue as the Trinity. In this introductory section Pfander adds to the revelation of the unity of God in the Bible with the belief that the triune nature of God is also revealed there. "Besides revealing to us His divine unity in the Holy scriptures, the most merciful God has also revealed his most holy nature in the same holy scriptures as existent in three Hypostases (*Aqanim*), the Father, the Son and the Holy Spirit."[4] Here Pfander turns to his Muslim reader by referring to "the most merciful God", a description common in the Qur᾽ān. He also uses the Arabic term for hypostases, *aqanim*, which was familiar to Urdu-speaking Muslims since it had been taken over into Urdu from Muslim Arabic texts that described the Christian teaching about three hypostases.

He then swings back to his Christian readership when he enlightens them about Muslim beliefs concerning the Spirit of God. He indicates that "the Holy

---

[1] For biographical details see Clinton Bennett, 'The Legacy of Karl Gottlieb Pfander', *International Bulletin of Missionary Research* 20 (1996), pp. 76–81.

[2] Karl G. Pfander, *Miftahu'l-asrar – The Key of Mysteries: A Treatise on the Doctrine of the Trinity in Unity*, W. St Clair Tisdall (trans.), (London: Christian Literature Society for India, 1912), pp. 3–4.

[3] Pfander, 'Key of Mysteries', p. 132.

[4] Pfander, 'Key of Mysteries', p. 133.

Spirit is not the angel Gabriel, as our Muhammadan friends fancy, nor is He any created being".[5] Pfander shows his awareness of the Qur᾽ānic references to the Spirit of God as being normally understood by Muslims to be the angel Gabriel, a created being. His style of writing suggests that he wants to engage Christians in a dialogue with Muslims, by teaching them about Muslim convictions arising from their interpretation of the Qur᾽ān, so that Christian engagement with Muslims will be sensitive to Muslim presuppositions. Given that Pfander's treatment of the Trinity is the first Protestant missionary attempt to explain the Trinity to Muslims, it is understandable that he has fellow Protestant missionaries in mind as he writes.

Pfander summarises the scriptural teaching about the Trinity.

> The Father not only created the universe through the Son, and through the Son preserves and guards it, but through Him also does He deliver His servants from sin and eternal destruction and bestow upon them everlasting salvation and true happiness hereafter. Through the Holy Spirit God enlightens and purifies them, guides them to the true knowledge of Himself, leads them to belief in the Lord Jesus Christ, and enables them to do good.[6]

He goes on to acknowledge that the teaching about the actions of God as Father, Son and Holy Spirit is named the doctrine of the Trinity, but that this name is not found in the Bible. "It is true that the word Trinity does not occur in the holy Scriptures, but the doctrine which is expressed thereby most assuredly does."[7] This is because the way God has revealed Himself in the Bible means that His unity is expressed in Trinitarian terms.

> We Christians have learnt, through the revelation of God given unto all men in the holy scriptures, that between Father, Son and Holy Spirit there is some distinction, because of which there are three Hypostases (*Aqanim*), and not merely one Hypostasis (*uqnum*), yet we have also learnt that they are not three distinct natures. There is but one divine nature, and only one God, as we have already proved from both the Old and the New Testament; hence to say that there are three Gods would be blasphemy.[8]

Again, Pfander uses the Arabic terminology developed by Christians in the early Islamic period to describe the hypostases of the Trinity. One hypostasis is an *uqnum* and three hypostases are *aqanim*. But this Urdu terminology, transliterated from Arabic, is mediated through Muslim writing about Christian beliefs. The long legacy of the Christian engagement with Islam in the Arabic-speaking world of the Abbasid Middle East filters through to Protestant missionary encounter with Muslims in South Asia. He also recognises the Qur᾽ānic rejection of threeness in God as fundamental to Muslim perceptions of the Christian teaching about threeness. The Qur᾽ānic injunction, "Do not say three" is in the foreground here.[9] To say that God is three or the third of three is indeed blasphemy and Pfander has no doubt heard this from Muslims with whom

[5] Pfander, 'Key of Mysteries', p. 134.
[6] Pfander, 'Key of Mysteries', p. 135.
[7] Pfander, 'Key of Mysteries', p. 135.
[8] Pfander, 'Key of Mysteries', p. 135.
[9] As in Q4:171 and Q5:73.

he has dialogued. He wishes to emphatically state that Christians do not divide the unity of God by teaching that his "nature" is three. They guard the unity of God's nature when they posit three hypostases in that one nature.

Having elaborated what Christians believe about the Trinity, Pfander goes on to explain and defend what Christians believe. He has a second section entitled "Considerations which Tend in Some Measure to Explain the Doctrine of the Most Holy Trinity".[10]

The first consideration is the rationality of the Trinity.

> There are some people that regard the doctrine as untrue and contrary to reason. In the present section we hope to show, by God's grace, that it is by no means contrary to reason, when rightly understood, nay rather that reason demands some such doctrine to remove the difficulties which the dogma of the oneness of God otherwise causes to the thoughtful mind, and to enable man to attain to any true knowledge, without which there can be no true religion, no vital piety.[11]

Pfander is convinced that a rational person can hold to the Trinity without denying the unity of God. But he understands the basic Muslim objection that threeness destroys oneness. He puts the typical Muslim rejection of the Trinity down to the basic contradiction between oneness and threeness. "The objection to the doctrine of the Trinity is often stated in such words as these: 'How is it possible that in the one divine nature there should exist a Trinity of Hypostases, and that in unity there should be plurality? Since these are absolutely contrary the one to the other?'"[12] In answer to this dilemma, Pfander argues that in the created world there are examples of threeness not cancelling out oneness. He accepts that analogies from creation cannot prove the Trinity, but he wants to argue that they give rational support to maintaining that God's unity is not compromised by his Triune state.

> We shall try to show that the idea of plurality does not necessarily conflict with that of unity. We must beg our readers to remember that we fully admit that no perfect analogy can be drawn between God Most High and any of His creatures and that we are not now endeavouring to prove by these illustrations the truth of the doctrine of the Trinity.[13]

Pfander lists the sorts of analogies from the created world that were also popular among the Arabic-speaking Christians who defended the Trinity in the Abbasid era. He appeals to the nature of fire and the nature of a human being.

> Fire consists of three things, heat, light and combustion. These three are different from one another, yet combined they form only one fire ... Man himself may be said to consist of body, soul and spirit, yet this plurality does not make him three men, nor does it conflict with the oneness of his personality.[14]

---

[10] Pfander, 'Key of Mysteries', p. 157.
[11] Pfander, 'Key of Mysteries', p. 157.
[12] Pfander, 'Key of Mysteries', p. 157.
[13] Pfander, 'Key of Mysteries', p. 160.
[14] Pfander, 'Key of Mysteries', p. 162.

He then adds an analogy unknown to his Middle Eastern theological ancestors. "A single ray of sunlight is now known to consist of the three primary colours, red, green and blue, yet its unity is not destroyed by this plurality."[15]

Pfander continues his defence of the reasonableness of the Trinity by appealing to Muslim belief about the attributes of God. Since Muslims hold that the many names of God represent his attributes, they are familiar with the notion of plurality in God. The plural attributes do not affect the unity of God, according to Muslim tradition. Christians too, believe in a plurality of attributes in the one God. Therefore, both Muslims and Christians believe that it is not irrational to hold that the oneness of God is not undermined by the plurality of God's attributes.

> All thoughtful Muslims agree with us in recognizing that reason teaches that it is impossible to conceive of God Most High as a mere unity, devoid of all attributes. The many most excellent names which they give to God express His possession of a plurality of excellent attributes ... If plurality of attributes be admitted, why should it be asserted to be contrary to reason to hold the scriptural doctrine that, besides plurality of attributes, there exists also in the divine unity a trinity of Hypostases?[16]

Here Pfander echoes the kind of argumentation witnessed in the apologetics of the earlier Arabic Christian theologians. But he does not develop the argument found among them that God has two essential attributes of speech (Word) and life (Spirit) that encompass several of his non-essential attributes. This is probably because he only had access to the writing of those Arabic theologians through brief summaries.

Pfander has a third section entitled "Importance of the Doctrine of the Trinity in Unity, in Connexion with the Knowledge of God and with Obtaining Salvation". He begins by pointing out that belief in one God does not automatically bring devotion to Him.

> Belief in one Almighty God cannot of itself bring eternal salvation, for even the devils believe, and tremble. Belief in God's almighty power may terrify men's hearts, but it cannot render them tender and warm with love for God. It is only when the hard heart is melted by the conviction of God's love for us that it can be stamped with the seal of the Holy Spirit and run into God's mould, so that the man may be renewed in the image of His holy Creator and Redeemer. This change in a man is what is called the new birth.[17]

Here Pfander presents an argument based on various New Testament texts. James 2:19, "You believe that there is one God. Good! Even the demons believe that – and shudder", is joined with Romans 5:5, "God has poured out his love into our hearts by the Holy Spirit, whom he has given us", and with John 3:3, "Jesus declared, 'I tell you the truth, no one can see the kingdom of God unless he is born again'".

He elaborates on the role of the Son as the manifestation of God the Father to illustrate how the Trinity functions.

---

15 Pfander, 'Key of Mysteries', p. 162.
16 Pfander, 'Key of Mysteries', p. 164.
17 Pfander, 'Key of Mysteries', pp. 193–94.

> God was in Christ reconciling the world to himself. He did not inflict suffering upon an innocent creature but bore it Himself in the person of His eternal Word … Right reason assures us that, if unselfish love and the perfection of self-sacrifice for the good of others be virtues, they must somehow exist in God, and that the Almighty must be able to manifest these gracious and most holy qualities. The doctrine of the Trinity in Unity alone shows how this is possible.[18]

Here Pfander refers to 2 Corinthians 5:19, "God was reconciling the world to himself in Christ", and combines this with John 1:14, "The Word became flesh", and also with 1 Peter 2:21, "Christ suffered for you" and 1 Peter 2:24, "Christ bore our sins in his body on the tree, so that we might die to sins and live for righteousness; by his wounds you have been healed". From these Biblical assertions he argues that a rational person will conclude that God Himself must have the attributes of unselfish love and self-sacrifice for the good of others, and that He desires to reveal these attributes to humanity. If this is the case, then the Trinity is the logical outworking of these attributes. God reveals Himself in the Word who became flesh, who sacrificed himself for the sake of others to reconcile them to God. Pfander then adds the role of God's Spirit in this reconciling work. "It is through God's Spirit that believers receive the impulse to do everything good, and power to perform good deeds".[19] The Spirit completes the revelation of the Trinity by making real to human beings the love of God the Father in the self-sacrifice of the Son.

Pfander concludes his presentation of the Trinity.

> Since, therefore, the doctrine of the Trinity of Hypostases in the Unity of the divine nature enables us to understand in some measure the incarnation of the Lord Jesus Christ, the way of salvation through him, and the gracious influence of God's Holy Spirit on the hearts and lives of those who truly believe in Christ, and since we find thus revealed to us in the holy Scripture God's holiness, justice, mercy and love, as far as any man has capacity to grasp these great truths, therefore, it is clearer than the sun at noonday that this doctrine of the Trinity in unity is true.[20]

Pfander confidently proclaims the Biblical teaching concerning the actions of the Father, Son and Spirit as having the power to convince Muslims as true. Yet, he does not go on to defend the patristic developments of the Biblical data expressed in the creedal statement that God is one in nature with three hypostases. He merely claims that the creedal definition helps us to understand "in some measure" the reality of the work of God in us. Once again, the lack of knowledge of the Arabic theologians of the Abbasid era hampers the Lutheran missionary. Their attempts to defend the oneness of God in the light of his Triune identity would have given Pfander a model with which to argue for the truth of the unity of God within his triunity, the very issue that would have dominated the response of his Muslim readers.

---

[18] Pfander, 'Key of Mysteries', pp. 196–97.
[19] Pfander, 'Key of Mysteries', p. 210.
[20] Pfander, 'Key of Mysteries', pp. 210–11.

Kenneth Cragg (1913–2012)

Kenneth Cragg was ordained as a Church of England minister before moving to Beirut in 1939 to teach philosophy at the American University. His interaction with Muslim intellectuals led him to find ways to communicate his Christian faith to Muslims on ground familiar to them. His earliest writing, *The Call of the Minaret*, was published in 1956 when he was teaching Christians preparing to work in the Muslim world at Hartford Seminary in Connecticut, USA. The book encourages Western Christians to seek to share their beliefs with Muslims by identifying with Muslim beliefs as much as possible. They should speak about their convictions "in terms that Muslims can understand".[21]

Cragg turns to the doctrine of God late on the book, under the title, "Interpreting the Christian Doctrine of God". He demonstrates his understanding of Muslim convictions at the outset of his presentation.

> The Christian faith in God as Father, Son and Holy Spirit is not a violation of faith in God's Unity. It is a way of understanding that Unity – a way, the Christian would go on to say, of safeguarding that Unity. Perhaps our largest duty with the Muslim mind lies just here. For the Muslim, faith in God as Father, Son, and Holy Spirit does violence to the Divine Unity. For the Christian, it expresses and illuminates the Unity.[22]

Here, Cragg posits the direct opposition between Muslim insistence that the Trinity negates the unity of God and the Christian insistence that the Father, Son and Holy Spirit express His unity. From the Muslim point of view, the Christian is a violator of God's oneness. How then should Christians defend the very belief that is detestable to Muslims?

Cragg continues by reminding his Christian reader of the New Testament witness to the Triune God. After surveying the apostolic belief that God was in Christ, Cragg summarises, "The doctrine of the Trinity is no more and no less than the idea of God as being in relationship with man, God Whose will sustains, Whose love redeems, and Whose Spirit orders and indwells the world of human life".[23] It is notable that Cragg sums up the apostolic teaching about the Trinity by making God the centre of the action. He recommends to Christians that they focus on the revelation of God as Sustainer, Redeemer and Indweller. He steers clear of the language of the New Testament which speaks of God the Father, and Jesus the Word of God and Son of God. Cragg believes that avoiding terminology that is offensive to Muslims is the wisest approach for Christians in their engagement with them. He is recommending that Christians try to express their experience of God as the One who sustains, redeems and indwells them.

Cragg reminds Christians that the Apostles themselves learned about God through their experience of His activity in their lives.

> It is profoundly significant that the sweetest and perhaps the earliest statement of this Christian faith places it in the context of experience where theology ends as it

---

[21] Kenneth Cragg, *The Call of the Minaret* (New York: Oxford University Press, 1956), p. 257.

[22] Cragg, *The Call of the Minaret*, pp. 278–79.

[23] Cragg, *The Call of the Minaret*, p. 285.

> should in doxology: "The grace of our Lord Jesus Christ and the love of God and the fellowship of the Holy Spirit be with us all evermore" (2 Cor. 13:14).[24]

Here Cragg does not recommend that modern Christians simply repeat the apostolic testimony in the way that Pfander was content to do. It would be better to avoid terminology that can easily be misinterpreted by the Muslim who is listening to the Christian testimony. Let the Muslim experience God without imposing Biblical terminology that is beyond his comprehension. How then can the New Testament witness become valid for a Muslim? The answer is as follows: "The principle is that we must strive to introduce the Muslim heart to the faith within the Christian doctrine by the same path that the church itself followed".[25] But this does not make clear to his Christian reader how exactly a Muslim can come to experience the Triune God.

Cragg points to two obstacles in this process for a Muslim. Firstly, a Muslim may well understand the Trinity to involve the Virgin Mary, and secondly, a Muslim may reject the Trinity on the grounds that one cannot be three.

The first obstacle refers to the Qurʾān criticising Christians for believing in a trinity of God, Jesus and Mary in Q5:116-117. "God said, 'Jesus, son of Mary, did you tell people: take me and my mother as two gods alongside God?' Jesus replied, 'May you be exalted. I would never have said what I had no right to say … I told them only what you commanded me to say: worship God, my Lord and your Lord'". Cragg knows how influential this Qurʾānic passage is in the minds of the Muslims he has encountered. When a Christian listens to Muslims, then he will hear this Qurʾānic perspective as representing what Christians believe. For Muslims there appears to be a union between God and Mary in the production of Jesus that Christians assume makes both Jesus and Mary share the divinity of God. Cragg comments, "The Christian Trinity is God the Father, God the Son, and God the Holy Spirit. It does not consist, as there has been a tendency among Muslims to suppose, of God, Jesus, and the Virgin Mary".[26] Cragg does not go on to elucidate how Christians can answer this Qurʾānic accusation apart from merely denying that it is true for Christians. The whole question of the kind of Christians that Muḥammad may have encountered in Arabia and which influenced the dialogue found in the Qurʾān is not one that Cragg wishes to deal with. Yet he was no doubt familiar with Western scholars who held that Q5:116-117 reflects the beliefs of a sect that did offer worship to Mary and that Muḥammad mistakenly believed that all Christians did too. This reticence with regard to questioning the Qurʾān and Muḥammad is characteristic of Cragg's advice to his Christian readers.

The second obstacle is the Muslim conviction that the oneness of God is denied by the Trinity. Cragg does not refer to Q4:171, where Christians are told "Do not speak of Trinity … God is only one God" or to Q5:73, "Those who say that God is the third of three are deviant. There is only one God". But he acknowledges that Muslims cannot get past the illogicality of turning one into three. "Reflection makes it clear that the idea of the Divine Unity cannot be

---

[24] Cragg, *The Call of the Minaret*, p. 285.
[25] Cragg, *The Call of the Minaret*, p. 286.
[26] Cragg, *The Call of the Minaret*, p. 286.

enforced in a mathematical sense, and that enforcement in such sense is the ground of most Muslim antipathy to the Christian Trinity."[27] Nevertheless, he does not give his Christian audience any assistance with a method to deal with this Muslim presupposition.

Cragg did not return to the issue of the Trinity in his many subsequent pieces of writing. His substantial work *Jesus and the Muslim: An Exploration*, published in 1985, briefly mentions how the Incarnation is placed within a Trinitarian view of God, and that the begetting of the Son by the Father does not negate the unity of God, but he does not elaborate how to make this case to a Muslim.[28]

David Brown (1922–1982)

David Brown was a Church of England minister who served with the Church Missionary Society in several Muslim nations and who wrote *The Divine Trinity* with Muslim readers in mind while in Jordan, after having studied Arabic and theology at the University of London. In the preface, he writes, "My deepest hope is that those Muslim friends who have taught me much about the Unity of God may through reading it catch a fresh glimpse of the divine glory in the face of the Messiah".[29]

He begins by placing Christian belief in the Trinity within the Jewish conviction that God is one. He quotes Deuteronomy 6:4-5, "Hear, O Israel: Yahweh our God is the one Yahweh. You shall love Yahweh your God with all your heart, with all your soul, with all your strength", and comments,

> This creed was repeated in the time of the Messiah by pious Jews twice a day, on waking and before retiring at night, and there can be little doubt that the Messiah himself did this, as well as his Apostles … Its acceptance by the Church has ensured that Christian beliefs about God have always been in agreement with the principles of monotheism and that Christians have always asserted the unity of the Godhead, even though they were led on to discern a certain complexity within that fundamental unity.[30]

He goes on to explain how Jesus' followers came to distinguish him from prophets that God had sent to Israel. One can discern that Brown is fully aware of the Qur᾽ānic belief that Jesus was one of a long line of prophets whose message was essentially the same, that humans should worship the one God who had created everything that exists. Without referring to the Qur᾽ān he argues that Jesus' disciples believed that Jesus himself was the Word of God and did not simply deliver a message from God as the rest of the prophets did.

> The Messiah was for them the living Saviour who had brought them the true knowledge of God, who had brought them back into the family of God through his love and self-sacrifice, and who now lived in heaven as their Lord and Master …

---

[27] Cragg, *The Call of the Minaret*, p. 287.

[28] Kenneth Cragg, *Jesus and the Muslim*: *An Exploration* (London: George, Allen &Unwin, 1985), p. 294.

[29] David Brown, *The Divine Trinity* (London: Sheldon Press, 1969), preface.

[30] Brown, *The Divine Trinity*, p. 21.

> The whole life of Jesus had been a gift to them from God, and thus they discerned an essential difference between Jesus and the prophets: the prophets had carried the divine message to mankind, the Messiah had himself been the message.[31]

Brown continues to express what was going on the minds of the disciples. As a result of Jesus' referring to God as his Father, they called him "Son of God".

> It was the conviction of the Apostles, created by their living, personal experience of God's gifts to them in the Messiah, that the Messiah had come from God to men, and they expressed this conviction by using the title "Son of God" … It had been given an altogether new dimension of meaning by the Messiah himself, when speaking about his unique relationship to God. This new dimension made it possible for the Apostles, by using the title, to express their belief that the relationship of the Messiah to God was one which had existed from eternity, and that his birth at Bethlehem was an act of humility on the part of God's Son by which he had become man as well as God.[32]

Immediately, Brown acknowledges the difficulty that Muslims have with the sonship of Jesus.

> The metaphor of "sonship", however, was not a wholly satisfactory one to use in expressing the conviction that the Messiah had come from God, for, as the history of Christian–Muslim relations shows only too clearly, it can easily be misunderstood to suggest the idea of *physical* paternity. Such an idea was far from the minds of the Apostles but it is present in the idea of sonship and to that extent makes "Son of God" a difficult term to explain. The Apostles also used other terms to express their conviction about the unique and eternal relationship of the Messiah to God and one of the most fruitful was the term "The Word of God".[33]

Here, Brown refers to the history of Muslim relations with Christians but does not mention the Qurʾānic denials of a father–son relationship between Jesus and God on which the history of those relations depends. His preference for the title "Word of God" is not worked out in any detail. Perhaps his intention in writing was to explain the New Testament witness to Muslim readers rather than get involved in the very history of Christian–Muslim relations he referred to. It is certainly the case that the apostolic writings use the title "Son of God", and that "Word of God" is associated particularly with the Johannine testimony.

Continuing his exposition of the New Testament writings, Brown points to other titles given to Jesus.

> Only very rarely did the Apostles call the Messiah "God", and never did they call him "GOD", in any absolute sense. Normally they called him "Jesus the Messiah", or "The Lord Jesus", or variants of these, and they thought of him always as the one who had saved them from evil and brought them into a living relationship with God. They worshipped him together with God but as the Saviour who had accomplished among men the purposes of God.[34]

This summary of the apostolic belief in Jesus would most likely disturb a Muslim reader, who would see the worship of Jesus as a complete denial of the

[31] Brown, *The Divine Trinity*, p. 36.
[32] Brown, *The Divine Trinity*, p. 37.
[33] Brown, *The Divine Trinity*, p. 38.
[34] Brown, *The Divine Trinity*, p. 39.

Qur'ānic prohibition in Q5:116-117, where Jesus denies asking people to worship him. "I told them only what you commanded me to say, 'worship God, my Lord and your Lord'". Brown does not attempt to dialogue with the Qur'ān in his presentation, but he seems to have felt that it would be more positive to explain the Christian Trinity from the experience of the disciples of Jesus rather than to engage in a comparison between Jesus in the Qur'ān and Jesus in the New Testament. Yet his approach does not make it easy either for a Muslim reader or for a Christian who is reading in order to gain insight into how to talk to a Muslim, because the Muslim voice is hardly heard.

Brown goes on the explain the Holy Spirit to his Muslim reader. In a chapter entitled "The Indwelling Spirit", he expounds the activity of the Spirit of God in the Old Testament and concludes, "According to the Old Testament Scriptures, therefore, the Spirit of God was given to particular individuals, to warriors and judges, to craftsmen and prophets, on particular occasions, to enable them to serve God better than they could in their own strength or wisdom".[35] The Holy Spirit was given to Jesus to perform his miraculous ministry, according to Brown. "The Lord Jesus preached and healed by the enabling of the Spirit of God: 'It is God's Spirit who gives me power to drive out demons', he said, 'which proves that the kingdom of God has already come upon you' (Matthew 12:28)".[36] Then this empowerment by God's Spirit was given to the followers of Jesus after his ascent to heaven.

> After the ascension of the Messiah, however, a radical change occurred and the Spirit of God was now given, not to special individuals, but to all the members of God's household. This was in accordance with a promise which the Messiah made to his disciples shortly before his death, when he promised that the Spirit would come to replace him as their guide and helper.[37]

Brown does not stop to engage with the Muslim perception of God's Spirit being the angel Gabriel, given that Gabriel is referred to as the Spirit of God in the Qur'ān. Q16:102, "The Holy Spirit has brought revelation with truth from your Lord" is interpreted in Muslim tradition as the angel Gabriel bringing the Qur'ān to the Prophet Muḥammad in stages. Brown does appear to avoid relating his message to Muslim assumptions at key points. He seems to want to avoid controversy. In this he shares Cragg's approach to communicating Christian beliefs to Muslims. Like Cragg, he wants Muslims to hear how the early Christians came to believe in the Trinity. Like Cragg, he does not want to get embroiled in the history of Christian–Muslim relations, which would entail debate about how Christians came to understand the oneness of God within threeness as one nature in three hypostases.

However, Brown appeals to the experience of the followers of Jesus as the reason for the Trinity.

> The Apostles and others who wrote the New Testament Scriptures made no attempt to express these beliefs in any formal statement, nor to deal at length with any difficulties which they occasioned. Their beliefs were simply the expression of their

---

[35] Brown, *The Divine Trinity*, p. 44.
[36] Brown, *The Divine Trinity*, p. 44.
[37] Brown, *The Divine Trinity*, p. 45.

> own experience of God, and they wrote in order to share this experience with others. Their experience was one in which all three divine "Persons" played a vital part: they worshipped the one living God, they had been brought into his community by Jesus the Messiah, and they served him in daily life by the constant help of the Spirit. When they baptized new converts as members of the Church, they baptized them in the *one name* of "the Father and of the Son and of the Holy Spirit" (see Matthew 28:19), and when they blessed each other they did so by invoking the same three Persons in one blessing: "the grace of the Lord Jesus Messiah, the love of God, and the fellowship of the Holy Spirit be with you all" (2 Corinthians 13:13).[38]

However, finally, Brown does bring up the Qurʾānic denial of the Trinity.

> In asserting that their experience of God was an experience of three divine Persons, Christians have exposed themselves to the risk of being accused of worshipping three separate gods. It is this conception of the Christian faith which apparently underlies the Qurʾānic protest: "they are guilty of unbelief who say, 'God is the third of three': there is no god but One God" (Qurʾān 5:73, 116; 4:171).[39]

Brown then gives a definition of the Trinity that he says Christians have believed. "Christians have conceived of the Godhead, of Divinity, as a Unity of Being, which, from eternity, has been composed of three centres of personal consciousness, each in constant and living relationship with the other two."[40] This social theory of the Trinity reflects the Greek patristic way of describing the relations between the members of the Trinity. Brown is evidently drawn to the Eastern rather than the Latin Western way of conceiving the Trinity, which contrasts with Cragg's adherence to the one God acting in three different ways, so much more in tune with Western tradition.

Brown then offers analogies for the Trinity from our experience of life, not to prove the Trinity but to support it. He gives the definitions of a human being and the human family. "Man is neither simply his body, nor his mind, nor his spirit, but a unity of these three exceedingly complex elements, which are normally integrated together so that he lives and acts as a single person."[41]

> A family is not simply the sum-total of one man, one woman, and so many children, but it comes into being as the man and woman are in a living relationship with each other, not only physically, but also, and perhaps with even greater importance, emotionally, intellectually, and spiritually as well. Although a family depends for its existence on such a complex of relationships, it is nevertheless a unity which is very robust and can survive many disasters and misfortunes, as well as joys and prosperity.[42]

Brown appeals to the family as a way of understanding the unity of the three persons of the Godhead. He understands that Muslims focus on mathematical oneness in their belief in the unity of God. Therefore, he addresses this Muslim conviction in the following argument from the unity of a family as an analogy for the unity of the three divine persons.

---

[38] Brown, *The Divine Trinity*, pp. 50–51.
[39] Brown, *The Divine Trinity*, p. 59.
[40] Brown, *The Divine Trinity*, p. 60.
[41] Brown, *The Divine Trinity*, p. 60.
[42] Brown, *The Divine Trinity*, p. 60.

> If such complex but real unities as are seen in good families may be created by finite and sinful human beings, it is not impossible to suppose that a unity of even deeper complexity and reality may exist within the Godhead. The perfection of such a unity would not then consist in the perfection of being undifferentiated, like the figure "one" in the mind of the mathematician, but in the perfection with which the several centres of consciousness are integrated with and related to each other. Among men partial integration comes only by intense effort and is often marred by human failure and sin, but in the Godhead such a unity would be perfect and eternal.[43]

Brown does go on to interpret for his Muslim reader how Christians have understood the relations between the divine persons.

> In asserting the essential identity of being shared by the three divine Persons, Christians have been careful to say that the relations between them are eternal relations and that they did not originate at any particular moment of time. There never was a time when the Son and the Spirit were not there, in the one eternal being of God.[44]

Brown does not share his fellow Anglican Cragg's reluctance to get into details about the way the church has talked about the Trinity. By stressing the eternal nature of the relations between the three persons, Brown wants his Muslim reader to know that God has always existed as Father, Son and Spirit, so that the Muslim will not think that the Son is subordinate to the Father.

> The three Persons of the Divine Trinity are believed to have been in a mutual relationship of love towards each other and to have shared in the one unity of the divine being from eternity, and the terms "Son" and "Word" do not imply the subordination which they suggest in a human context.[45]

In the final analysis, Brown does contrast the conception of God by Muslims directly with that by Christians.

> A solitary centre of personal consciousness would have had no activity beyond the contemplation of himself and this, we imagine, would have been barren and fruitless. The divine being, however, conceived in terms of the Divine Trinity, would have found the fullest and most fruitful of activity in the mutual and ever-loving relationships of the three centres of personal consciousness within the divine being.[46]

Without naming Muslims in this contrast between a solitary God and a relational God, Brown concludes his treatment of the Trinity for a Muslim readership. He hopes that, rather than confusing his Muslim reader, he has made the Christian doctrine of the Trinity not only intelligible but attractive.

Giulio Basetti-Sani (1912–2001)

Giulio Basetti-Sani was born in Italy and became a member of the Catholic Franciscan order in 1935. Having been inspired by Francis of Assisi's dialogue

---

[43] Brown, *The Divine Trinity*, p. 61.
[44] Brown, *The Divine Trinity*, p. 62.
[45] Brown, *The Divine Trinity*, p. 63.
[46] Brown, *The Divine Trinity*, p. 80.

with the Sultan of Egypt during one of the medieval crusades, he worked for over twenty years teaching in the Seminary for Franciscans of the Coptic Rite near Cairo in Egypt. He mentions that studying under Louis Massignon in Paris helped him "understand the necessity of a profound love for Muslims".[47] However, it was not until 1947 back in Cairo that Basetti-Sani took Massignon's attitude to Muslims seriously. Up till then, he had the view that "Mohammed was an instrument of Satan",[48] and that "Islam is the actualization of the kingdom of Satan and functions as an antichurch".[49] As a result he believed that "The Trinity of the Christians has no point of contact with the Koranic Allah for he is excluded absolutely and explicitly from the Trinity".[50] What turned him in Cairo in 1947 was "the sight of so many Arabs prostrate on the ground in devotion at the hour of prayer. This moving and edifying spectacle invariably caused me to reflect on my ideas and reactions. My conclusion that these people were in reality adoring Satan began to seem a great outrage to charity and truth".[51]

In 1952, Pope Pius XII declared in a radio address, "Make it clear that whatever is just and good in other religions finds its deepest meaning and its final perfection in Christ." Basetti-Sani says he "took these words as a divine command for the orientation of my study of the Koran".[52] He began to ask,

> If Islam is really the Abrahamitic mystery of the descendants of Ishmael, then it had to have an actual, though mysterious, relationship to the mystery of Christ. The words of the Pope set me on the way. In what way does the Koran conserve and conceal elements which could recapture their profound meaning in the mystery of Christ?[53]

He set out to understand, "by means of the Koran, the development of Mohammed's spiritual journey in chronological order".[54]

> Mohammed now appeared as a man in the grip of a profound religious feeling and taken with the idea of establishing the reign of God among the idolatrous Arabs … I more and more narrowed the gap between Mohammed's psychology and spirituality and those of Abraham in regard to faith and of David in regard to the defence of God's rights – by means of a holy war. In the light of Old Testament morality, or more exactly that of patriarchal morality, it is easier to understand his Deuteronomic kind of religion, his moral life, and his ideas on marriage with limitations imposed by the development of his moral consciousness. Following this line of research, it seemed to me, from then on, that a surprisingly real though slow progress toward the knowledge of God and of Jesus Christ could be discovered in the Koran. This knowledge, without doubt, is embryonic, and, as it were, limited.

---

[47] Giulio Basetti-Sani, *The Koran in the Light of Christ* (Chicago: Franciscan Herald Press, 1977), p. 6. He mentions Louis Massignon's *Les Trois Prieres d'Abraham* (Tours: Arrault imprimeur, 1935), as encouraging a more positive attitude to Muslims.
[48] Basetti-Sani, *The Koran in the Light of Christ*, p. 11.
[49] Basetti-Sani, *The Koran in the Light of* Christ, p. 12.
[50] Basetti-Sani, *The Koran in the Light of Christ*, p. 13.
[51] Basetti-Sani, *The Koran in the Light of Christ*, p. 16.
[52] Basetti-Sani, *The Koran in the Light of Christ*, p. 24.
[53] Basetti-Sani, *The Koran in the Light of Christ*, p. 24.
[54] Basetti-Sani, *The Koran in the Light of Christ*, p. 27.

> It needs development and enrichment. This is what Islam has lacked, and that during thirteen centuries of contact with Christianity.[55]

Basetti-Sani came to believe that "Mohammed never knew the doctrine of the Catholic Church, of orthodox Christianity; hence he was unable to reject it. He rejected *distortions* of Christianity".[56] These heretical views of Jesus were held by Monophysites and Nestorians, and this implies that Muḥammad's "systematic refusal to accept a heretical Christianity and his combating its two forms condemned by the Church (Monophytism and Nestorianism) should allow us to see, at the bottom of his soul, a longing and desire for a true, genuine knowledge of Jesus Christ".[57]

The role of Christians is to enable Muslims to read the Qurʾān in such a way that the fulness of truth emerges from it.

> When Mohammed makes use of a particular word or concept, by an inspiration coming hypothetically from God, it is not claimed that he perceives the entire extension of meaning, the totality, which that expression could carry, because of the very use Judeo-Christian revelation had previously made of that word or concept. Thus we Christians are able to understand it more profoundly, in its truer and fuller meaning, than the Muslims have been able to grasp it up to the present. Here we must consider all that Catholic exegetes have emphasized about the so-called *sensus plenior* in the Koran, which Christians are able to track down in its reading and can fraternally point out to Muslims. Thus the "Christian light" gives the true key to the interpretation of the Koran, permitting us to include, in some manner, the prophetic mission of Mohammed in the context of the history of Christian revelation.[58]

The Qurʾān is delivered to "pagan Arabs, Ishmael's descendants. It is the beginning of a journey in the direction of God", according to Basetti-Sani,[59] who argues that the Qurʾān teaches that Jesus is the Messiah. Yet the full knowledge of Jesus is not revealed there. Basetti-Sani speaks of "a mysterious evolution toward Christ",[60] beginning with the way Mary is introduced as his mother.

> Mary is much more detailed in portrayal than Jesus. This fact seems clear: it is Mary who presents her son; the figure of Jesus remains very vague. Hence we may say that there is only the hesitant beginning of a presentation of Jesus in the Koran, which should have been clearly brought out by Christians. It was not given to Mohammed to have knowledge of the mysteries of God, and so, to this very day, Islam is still blocked from making its journey to Christ.[61]

Basetti-Sani thinks that "It is certain that there were some elements of Monophysite and Nestorian doctrine in Arabia, and these formulas lead us to think that the Christians in question must have been of these groups. The same must be said about the rejection and condemnation of a trinitarian teaching which

---

55 Basetti-Sani, *The Koran in the Light of Christ*, p. 30.
56 Basetti-Sani, *The Koran in the Light of Christ*, p. 31.
57 Basetti-Sani, *The Koran in the Light of Christ*, p. 31.
58 Basetti-Sani, *The Koran in the Light of Christ*, pp. 102–103.
59 Basetti-Sani, *The Koran in the Light of Christ*, p. 137.
60 Basetti-Sani, *The Koran in the Light of Christ*, p. 138.
61 Basetti-Sani, *The Koran in the Light of Christ*, p. 138.

bears no relation to the orthodox Christian formula".[62] The Qur᾽ān rejects, not the orthodox doctrine of the Trinity, but a heterodox version. "We have a statement and formulation of the tritheism which seems to have been professed by some Christian heretics in Arabia, who believed in a 'trinity' composed of God (the Father), Mary, as a goddess and 'wife' of God (the Holy spirit), and Jesus (the Son of God and Mary)".[63] Basetti-Sani refers to the comments of Jerome in his commentaries on Isaiah and Micah that some heretics understood the words "This is my beloved son, with whom I am well pleased" at Jesus' baptism to be spoken by the Holy Spirit, whom they identified with Mary, since the Spirit was thought to be feminine.[64]

Basetti-Sani concludes,

> The fact, therefore, that Mohammed condemned such formulations of tritheism does not at all imply what Muslim theology and Christian apologetics erroneously thought: that Mohammed rejected the Christian dogma of the Trinity that there is one God in three persons, or the dogma of the Incarnation of the second Person of the Trinity.[65]

He has his own explanation for the warning of the Qur᾽ān not to speak of three because there is only one God. The Qur᾽ān is actually addressing Jews rather than Christians.

> When the messiahship of Jesus was introduced with the formula "He is a Word and a Spirit proceeding from God," the Jews of Medina jeered at Mohammed (and the Christians), throwing in his face the remark that there are now three Gods instead of one! The text is a reproach of this sneering twist that they gave to the formula.[66]

If this is truly the case, then both Christians and Muslims have misunderstood the teaching of the Qur᾽ān, according to Basetti-Sani. "Hence to claim – as have all Muslim theologians and all Christian apologists for thirteen centuries – that this text repudiates the Trinity is to take it and similar texts out of the context its surroundings."[67]

He summarises his approach to the Qur᾽ānic rejection of saying three when God is one.

> The Christian doctrine of the Trinity has often been ridiculed by Jews by the telling of various stories which always end with the number three. In Mecca, too, they mocked Christians by calling out: "three, three, three." So the Koran reproves this, since, in fact, the mystery of the Trinity does not mean three gods, or that two other beings are associated with God: "Say not: 'Three'! It is enough and will be better for you! For God is one God! May He be exalted!"[68]

In the final analysis, Basetti-Sani is convinced that a new era has emerged in Christian–Muslim relations based on a fresh interpretation of the Qur᾽ān that should enable a fresh conversation on the Christian doctrine of the Trinity. How

---

[62] Basetti-Sani, *The Koran in the Light of Christ*, p. 143.
[63] Basetti-Sani, *The Koran in the Light of Christ*, p. 144.
[64] Basetti-Sani, *The Koran in the Light of Christ*, p. 144.
[65] Basetti-Sani, *The Koran in the Light of Christ*, p. 144.
[66] Basetti-Sani, *The Koran in the Light of Christ*, p. 175.
[67] Basetti-Sani, *The Koran in the Light of Christ*, p. 176.
[68] Basetti-Sani, *The Koran in the Light of Christ*, p. 176–77.

that conversation might develop was not the concern of Basetti-Sani when he wrote his book. It was enough for him to attempt to get a hearing for his novel interpretation of the Qurʾānic texts that repudiated talking of God as three.

David W. Shenk (1938–2023)

David Shenk was an American Mennonite who was born in Tanzania of missionary parents and worked in Somalia and Kenya. He co-authored *Islam and Christianity: A Muslim and a Christian in Dialogue* with the Muslim scholar Badru D. Kateregga, who taught Islamic history and theology alongside David Shenk, who taught Christian history and theology at Kenyatta University College in Kenya at the time of the writing of the book. In the preface, they write, "Both of us have taught comparative religion together in a team-teaching relationship. Often the team-teaching was a dialogue, a witness from one faith to another in the presence of our students".[69] They wrote the book in two sections. Kateregga wrote part one as a Muslim and Shenk wrote part two as a Christian. Each of the twelve chapters in parts one and two include a response from the other writer.

Shenk's presentation of the Trinity comes within his first chapter in part two, entitled, "The Lord God is One". He quotes Deuteronomy 6:4, "The Lord our God is one Lord" and refers to Jesus' confirmation of this text in Mark 12:29. He says, "both the Torah of the Prophet Moses and the Gospel (*injil*) of Jesus the Messiah agree that God is one. We are commanded to love that one God".[70] Here we can observe Shenk's deference to Qurʾānic terminology concerning the prophet Moses bringing the Torah and Jesus bringing the *injil* to the children of Israel.

He then goes on the develop the ways that God has acted in his creation. Firstly, Shenk appeals to the name "Father" as referring to his care for humanity. "One way in which the Bible refers to God the Creator of mankind is 'Father'. God as Father cares for His creation, and especially for mankind."[71] He does not give any Biblical references but presumably he has in mind the teaching of Jesus expressed in Matthew 5:26, where he reminds his listeners that God as their heavenly Father provides for them as He feeds the birds. Secondly, Shenk mentions God revealing His Word through prophets as the Spirit who came upon them, as in Ezekiel 2:2, where Ezekiel speaks of the Spirit coming into him and speaking to him. Thirdly, Shenk appeals to the revelation of God in Jesus the Messiah as Saviour in Matthew 1:21, which speaks of Mary giving birth to a son who will save his people from their sins.

The revelation of God in Jesus is central to the Christian understanding of God, writes Shenk.

> Christians believe that through God's revelation in Jesus the Messiah, all the dimensions of God's revelation through nature, prophets, or history are fulfilled and enlightened. Through Jesus we recognize in a most specific and special way

---

[69] Badru D. Kateregga and David W. Shenk, *Islam and Christianity: A Muslim and a Christian in Dialogue* (Nairobi: Uzima Press, 1980), p. xvii.
[70] Kateregga and Shenk, *Islam and Christianity*, p. 83.
[71] Kateregga and Shenk, *Islam and Christianity*, p. 84.

> that God's revelation to mankind is a drama of self-giving love. That is the key to understanding God as the Father Who is the Creator, God as the Spirit Who reveals Himself through the words of prophets, God as the Saviour Who acts in history.[72]

Shenk's Trinity is Father, Spirit and Saviour, based on the history of God's self-revelation. He reveals Himself first of all in time as the caring Father of all human beings, then as the Spirit who inspires the prophets within Israel, and ultimately as Jesus the Messiah, who came at a subsequent point of history to reveal God as the one who saves human beings from their wrongdoing.

He appeals to the concept of love as binding these types of self-revelation together. "The love of God is the fountain of life and truth out of which the Christian witness concerning God proceeds".[73] The Christian experiences the love of God, but expressing that experience is never fully adequate in human language. Shenk asks, "How does one express the awareness that God loves totally, that the very essence of God is love, that even within God Himself there is an ongoing, eternal fellowship of self-giving love, that the very unity of God is bound up in His eternal self-giving love?"[74] Shenk's Trinity is closely aligned with the Western Augustinian tradition of the Father and Son joined together in love, mediated by the Spirit. He appeals to John 17:22, where Jesus speaks of giving his disciples the glory that the Father gave him so that they may be one as Jesus and his Father are one, as a support for the notion of the "eternal fellowship of self-giving love".

He mentions that the word Trinity was first used by Tertullian in the early third century in North Africa. However, the "Trinity" ought not to alarm Muslims.

> The concept of Trinity was not intended to convey that there are three gods. Never! It is an attempt to express in a simple, but profound way, that there is one true God only Who has revealed Himself by what He has done as Creator, Saviour and Spirit; this one, true, eternal God is love. He overflows with love and gives Himself in self-giving love for mankind.[75]

Shenk does not prefer the Eastern Greek tradition of three persons who are centres of consciousness to explain the Trinity. Rather, he appeals to the human person as an analogy.

> Some people use the analogy of a person who is: mind, body, spirit. These three dimensions of the person are a perfect unity … You make things with your hands. You think through problems with your mind. Your spirit is expressed through your personality. These three dimensions of your selfhood are the one person who you are.[76]

Shenk finally admits that "no analogy concerning God is ever exactly right. No one has seen God. He must remain a mystery".[77]

---

[72] Kateregga and Shenk, *Islam and Christianity*, p. 85.
[73] Kateregga and Shenk, *Islam and Christianity*, pp. 85–86.
[74] Kateregga and Shenk, *Islam and Christianity*, p. 86.
[75] Kateregga and Shenk, *Islam and Christianity*, p. 86.
[76] Kateregga and Shenk, *Islam and Christianity*, p. 86.
[77] Kateregga and Shenk, *Islam and Christianity*, p. 87.

The response by Badru Kateregga points out the difference between the Christian concept of God revealing Himself and the Muslim belief that God reveals His will. He refers to the traditional understanding of the Trinity, as Father, Son and Holy Spirit, despite the fact that Shenk avoided talk of Jesus as the Son of God entirely.

> The Christian witness of God as "Father" is also quite different from the Muslim witness. According to the true teachings of Islam, God is not to be conceived in an anthropomorphic way. He is united in design and existence. He is above all other attributes. Since He is one and the only One, a Muslim cannot invoke Him in the name of the Father, Son, or Holy spirit. All the Divine attributes are well embedded in His perfect Unity.[78]

Shenk responded in turn. "When Christians refer to God as 'Father' they should not envisage God anthropomorphically. Christians share with Muslims the prohibition against conceiving of God in the form of an image. God as 'Father' refers, rather, to a relationship."[79] But he goes on to affirm that this relationship is of God as the Father of humanity, "a description of covenant and fellowship relationship between God and man".[80] Shenk plays down the centrality of the relationship between the Father and the Son found in the New Testament in favour of a more Old Testament depiction of God as the Sustainer of humanity.

Nevertheless, he does expound the sonship of Jesus in the chapter entitled "Jesus the Messiah".[81] Then in a chapter entitled "Salvation", Shenk does make use of the traditional Trinitarian language. "We need to believe and receive God's saving redemptive action as Father, Son, and Holy Spirit in order to experience salvation".[82] He outlines this New Testament teaching as follows,

> We experience salvation when we receive God's love and forgiveness which is revealed in Jesus the Messiah, and which is present with us now through the Holy Spirit of God … The one true God Whom we experience as Father, Son, and Holy Spirit, in perfect unity, perfect love, perfect oneness, redeems us and saves us through his self-giving love.[83]

Perhaps he kept back the references to the "Son" to this later stage of his presentation of the Trinity in order to avoid the Qur᾿ānic refutation of the Father–Son relationship, which Kateregga is not slow to mention in his response to Shenk's presentation of Jesus the Messiah. In the end, Shenk could not avoid dealing with the Muslim fear that the Father–Son relationship is simply impossible. As Kateregga asserts,

> Muslims are genuinely opposed to the belief by Christians that Isa was Divine or 'Son of God' … The Qur᾿ān explicitly states: 'No son did Allah beget nor is there any god along with Him' … The Christian view of incarnation seems to

---

[78] Kateregga and Shenk, *Islam and Christianity*, p. 89.
[79] Kateregga and Shenk, *Islam and Christianity*, p. 89.
[80] Kateregga and Shenk, *Islam and Christianity*, p. 89.
[81] Kateregga and Shenk, *Islam and Christianity*, p. 130.
[82] Kateregga and Shenk, *Islam and Christianity*, p. 135.
[83] Kateregga and Shenk, *Islam and Christianity*, pp. 139–40.

> compromise God's transcendence and sovereignty while at the same time exalting a mere man to God-like status.[84]

Shenk replies,

> Christians agree with Muslims that God did not 'beget' a son ... Jesus the Messiah, as Son of God, reveals something completely different. It reveals a perfect relationship between God and the Messiah ... Recall that Christians believe that the Messiah is the incarnation of the eternal Word of God. God does not beget his Word![85]

In the end, Shenk has to explain the Trinity by using New Testament terminology. After all, he represents a Mennonite insistence on the primacy of the scriptures in developing theological thinking. But his sensitivity to Muslim beliefs is very clear in this exposition of his faith.

---

[84] Kateregga and Shenk, *Islam and Christianity*, p. 133.
[85] Kateregga and Shenk, *Islam and Christianity*, p. 134.

5. Western Theologians Dialoguing with Muslims on the Trinity

One of the features of the contemporary reality for some Christian theologians in the non-Muslim world is a sense that Christian theology has to be related to people of other faiths that are living within their own societies. For example, when Kenneth Cragg went to Beirut in 1939 there were very few Muslims present in the UK. Nowadays, Muslims are living as significant communities in British cities. When David Shenk wrote his dialogue with Badru Kateregga in Nairobi in the late 1970s, the reality of Islam for most Americans was of a foreign religion that had little to do with the normal American way of life. However, global events, such as the destruction of the twin towers in New York in 2001 by pilots who had come from Saudi Arabia to learn to fly in the US and the subsequent war against terror waged in Iraq from 2003 instigated by President Bush, has brought relations with Muslims to the forefront. The call by significant Muslim scholars for agreement between Muslims and Christians to come to a "Common Word" in 2007 opened up the possibility for American Christians to engage in conversation with Muslims.

This chapter will examine the writing of Keith Ward, a British Anglican theologian who has taken dialogue with people of other faiths seriously. Swiss Catholic theologian Hans Küng produced a large volume on Islam that was the culmination of a long career as a Catholic theologian in dialogue with other faith traditions. The Christian reaction to the Common Word initiative is seen especially in the writing of the Croatian theologian Miroslav Volf, who led the Yale response to the Common Word. Finally, the Finnish theologian Veli-Matti Kärkkäinan has written a systematic theology that dialogues with the major global religious traditions and has attempted to present the Trinity to Muslims.

Keith Ward (b. 1938)

When Keith Ward was Regius Professor of Divinity at the University of Oxford in 1994, he published *Religion and Revelation: A Theology of Revelation in the World's Religions*. He said that he intended,

> to articulate a concept of revelation which will be true to the main orthodox Christian tradition, yet which will be open to a fruitful interaction with other traditions, and with the developing corpus of scientific knowledge. This will make possible a committed, open, and developing understanding of faith in the contemporary world ... This work is intended to lay the foundation for the holistic

and eirenic study of religious belief and practice, which is an important, even essential, task for believers and non-believers alike.[1]

In conversation with people who have other convictions about the revelation of God, it is not adequate for Christians to argue that "God makes his revelation self-authenticating; for Muslims and Jews say that as well as Christians, and they cannot all be right, since their alleged revelations disagree".[2] Previous Christian theology has tended to rely on the notion that it is self-authenticating truth. Emil Brunner argued that we know that God has spoken in His Word because it is "from God himself".[3] Ward points out that "all Muslims would say that of the Koran, all Mormons of the Book of Mormon, and all Sikhs of the Guru Granth Sahib".[4] Ward picks out what Brunner has to say about Islam.

> When Brunner comes to discuss Islam, he dismisses it in a few pages, throwing doubt on the Prophet's character, writing off its content as superficial and derivative, accusing it of legalism and moralism, and seeing it, amazingly enough, as 'a religion of the Enlightenment', when one could hardly find a religious view more opposed to the beliefs of the European Enlightenment than Islam.[5]

Ward is convinced that Christian theologians cannot dismiss other religious traditions in such a facile way. He confesses,

> I think the time has come when it is positively misleading to consider religious traditions in isolation … I am inclined to say that one cannot properly understand the mode of divine revelation within Christianity unless one can set it in the context of human religious activity in general, for only in its widest context can one discern the true meaning of such revelation … The systematic theologian must make some attempt to understand the broad sweep of religious life, before being ready to make an informed judgement about the sources and methods of Christian theology.[6]

For Ward, all theology is confessional, but it should not merely confess one particular perspective without genuine dialogue with other perspectives. He writes,

> I am writing from within one (Anglican) strand of the Christian tradition. What I say is an attempt to articulate that tradition in a global context; so it is in a sense a confessional theology. But it is also a contribution to a comparative theology of revelation from a particular perspective.[7]

He turns to Islam after examining revelation in primal religions, Judaism, Hinduism and Buddhism. After studying the Qur'ānic condemnation of making partners for God, Ward asks whether Christians are guilty of saying such a thing as Q6:137 alleges, "They falsely attribute to Him sons and daughters … How can He have a son when He has no consort?"

---

[1] Keith Ward, *Religion and Revelation: A Theology of Revelation in the World's Religions* (Oxford: Clarendon Press, 1994), pp. 1–2.

[2] Ward, *Religion and Revelation*, p. 7.

[3] Emil Brunner, *Revelation and Reason* (London: SCM Press, 1947), p. 207.

[4] Ward, *Religion and Revelation*, p. 17.

[5] Ward, *Religion and Revelation*, p. 19, commenting on Brunner, *Revelation and Reason*, pp. 230–31.

[6] Ward, *Religion and Revelation*, p. 37.

[7] Ward, *Religion and Revelation*, p. 49.

> It may seem that only those who are so ignorant as to confuse human beings and God are here being condemned. But could one not accuse Christians of precisely that confusion? "In blasphemy indeed are those that say that God is Christ and Son of Mary" (Q5:19). This too, however, is not straightforward. Any Christian who said that God, *tout court*, was Jesus, would certainly be mistaken and heretical. The important Koranic truth is that there is only one creator God, and that only God should be worshipped. With this all orthodox Christians would heartily agree, of course. They do not think that Jesus was the creator of heaven and earth, any more than they think that the Son is the Father. However, if Christians should not say that God is Jesus (meaning, nothing but Jesus), they do say that Jesus is God; more precisely, the word of God, who is one with God the Creator … Muhammad seemed to regard Christians as confused rather than actually blasphemous.[8]

Ward argues that Muḥammad was predisposed to holding to the complete transcendence of God because of his rejection of polytheism.

> For reasons to do with the historical circumstances of the prophetic calling of Muhammad, the Koran emphasizes the transcendence, unity, sovereignty, and power of God. In reaction to tribal polytheism in the Arabian peninsula, all talk of sons and daughters of God, who might divide Divine power between them and be worshipped as competitors with the Divine Father, is forbidden (Q6:100).[9]

As a result, talking about the Trinity with Muslims is fraught with difficulty because the Qurʾān sees the Trinity as polytheism.

> This largely accounts for Muslim antipathy to the doctrine of God as Trinity. Thus when the Koran says, 'They do blaspheme who say: God is one of three in a Trinity; for there is no God except one God' (Q5:76), it is polytheism which is forbidden. The Christian God is not *in* a Trinity; rather, God is a Divine Triad in himself. Moreover, this Triad certainly does not consist of God, Jesus, and Mary, as one passage has suggested to some (Q5:119).[10]

Ward admits that the gulf between Christians and Muslims concerning the Trinity is very wide.

> Muslims see the doctrine of the Trinity as a later philosophically inspired corruption of strict biblical monotheism. Christians see Muslim rejection of the Trinity as based on a misunderstanding of the insight which Jesus gave into the nature of God as essentially love. This is bound up with the fact that Muslims see Jesus as a great prophet, worthy of great honour, whereas Christians see Jesus as a manifestation of the Divine word, uniting human nature to Divine nature and so reconciling humans to God. That in turn relates to a differing perception of the relation of God to the world – whether God remains the transcendent Will, ordering all things by sovereign power; or whether God shares in created being and raises it to participate in the Divine Life by the persuasive power of love.[11]

In a subsequent 1996 book, *Religion and Creation*, Ward presents a Trinitarian doctrine of creation in dialogue with major world religions: Judaism, Islam and Hinduism. He consulted practitioners of the world religions to ask for their advice about which twentieth-century thinkers he should engage with. The

---

[8] Ward, *Religion and Revelation*, pp. 176–77.
[9] Ward, *Religion and Revelation*, p. 188.
[10] Ward, *Religion and Revelation*, p. 188.
[11] Ward, *Religion and Revelation*, pp. 188–89.

answer was Abraham Heschel for Jews, Muhammad Iqbal for Muslims and Aurobindo Ghose for Hindus.[12] He wanted to relate his Trinitarian conception of God to these writers.

> One of the things I shall emphasize and try to clarify is the distinctively Trinitarian nature of the Christian image of God. I hope it will become clear that the relations between such an image and the more unitarian views of Jews and Muslims, and the more non-dualist view of Aurobindo, are more complex than may at first be supposed, and offer opportunities for constructive interaction.[13]

Chapter 3 is entitled "The Koran" and subtitled "Muhammad Iqbal: A Muslim View of God". He opens with the characteristic rejection of the Trinity in Islam.

> If the Trinitarian concept of God is distinctive to Christianity, then Islam exists, at least in part, as a decisive rejection of that concept. Islam is a clear and insistent proclamation of the unity and uniqueness of God (the unitarian thesis), and of the impossibility of identifying any finite thing with God (the transcendentalist thesis). In that respect, its basic idea of God is a return to the perspective of the Hebrew Bible, without admitting the view that God enters into a specific covenant relation with a particular group of people.[14]

It is in this context that Ward introduces his chosen Muslim dialogue partner, Muhammad Iqbal, who, he indicates, "has been described by Fazlur Rahman as 'the most serious Muslim philosophical thinker of modern times'".[15] Iqbal published *The Reconstruction of Religious Thought in Islam* in 1934, during a period of upheaval in British-ruled India, when Muslims and Hindus were both seeking independence from British rule. Iqbal was a leading voice in the Muslim community at that time, that called for a fresh interpretation of Islamic tradition. He opens his call for a reconstruction of Islamic tradition by declaring, "During the last five hundred years religious thought in Islam has been practically stationary."[16] Iqbal challenges this stationary situation by positing his own view of the teaching of the Qurʾān. He argues, "Nothing is more alien to the Koranic outlook than the idea that the universe is the temporal working out of a preconceived plan."[17] On the contrary, the universe is a "free creative movement".[18] Iqbal says that "God is the immanent self which animates and sustains the whole".[19] This implies that human beings co-operate with the immanent God, who is at work within them, so that each human being becomes aware that, "In this process of progressive change God becomes a co-worker with him".[20]

Ward notes three different models of God in Iqbal's reconstruction.

---

[12] Ward, *Religion and Creation* (Oxford: Clarendon Press, 1996), p. 4.
[13] Ward, *Religion and Creation*, p. 5.
[14] Ward, *Religion and Creation*, p. 59.
[15] Ward, *Religion and Creation*, p. 59. Ward quotes from Fazlur Rahman, *Islam* (London: Weidenfeld and Nicolson, 1966), p. 225.
[16] Muhammad Iqbal, *The Reconstruction of Religious Thought in Islam* (Oxford: Oxford University Press, 1934), p. 6.
[17] Iqbal, *The Reconstruction of Religious Thought*, p. 48.
[18] Iqbal, *The Reconstruction of Religious Thought*, p. 48.
[19] Iqbal, *The Reconstruction of Religious Thought*, p. 54.
[20] Iqbal, *The Reconstruction of Religious Thought*, p. 140.

> First, there is the model of God as the inclusive "immanent Infinite" of which the universe is but a small part ... The second model is that of the universe as an organism or organic unity, which is construed as the "behaviour" or character of the cosmic Self, which is God ... God is the Ultimate Ego and the universe is its body, through which its character is expressed ... The third model is that of God as a creative co-worker with many finite selves. This is a more communal model than that of the self-realization of the one Ultimate ego, and both are much more personal models than that of the Infinite which unfolds in space and time.[21]

Ward goes on to suggest that there are parallels with Christian interpretations of the Trinity in Iqbal's concepts.

> It might seem unhelpful to suggest that there is something like a Trinitarian view of God at work here, since there is hardly anything which would seem more unlikely for a Muslim thinker. Yet as long as one is careful to stress the utter unity and uniqueness of God, there may be a sense, especially for Muslims sympathetic to Sufism, in which God is manifold even in unity. A Christian theologian can point without undue strain to resonances with a certain interpretation of Trinitarian views.[22]

Firstly, a Christian understanding of the fatherhood of God "as ineffable source of all being, who is yet intimately present to all things, would resonate well" with Iqbal's view of God as "the Infinite, the self-unfolding source of all things".[23] Secondly, a Christian belief in "the Sonship of God, as the Logos or eternal Wisdom of God, through which the universe is created, upon which it is patterned, and in which it is to be united and completed, would resonate well" with Iqbal's belief in "God as the Self of the world, the rational pattern of its being and the spiritual reality in which the physical universe exists, which can be characterized in some sense as a personal reality, in which all things are to be united".[24] Thirdly, a Christian understanding of God as Spirit, "as the creative energy which works within and between human spirits, guiding them into truth, creativity, and co-operative community, would resonate well" with Iqbal's belief in "God as a reality which co-operates with finite wills, guiding them towards harmonious creativity and a community of life in which creativity can be more fully exercised".[25]

Ward points out that,

> The sorts of opposition which have sometimes been said to exist between Muslim and Christian doctrines are not as straightforward as may at first seem. There can be a complex, developing, and productive interweaving of Christian and Muslim strands of thought on the question of God, in which each can illuminate and enrich the other.[26]

Yet Iqbal has not precipitated an ongoing discussion among Muslims about the relationship of God to the creation and humanity. Ward admits, "Iqbal's

---

21 Ward, *Religion and Creation*, p. 66.
22 Ward, *Religion and Creation*, pp. 66–67.
23 Ward, *Religion and Creation*, p. 67.
24 Ward, *Religion and Creation*, p. 67.
25 Ward, *Religion and Creation*, p. 67.
26 Ward, *Religion and Creation*, p. 68.

attempt at a reconstruction of religious thought in Islam has so far had few, if any, successors in the Muslim world".[27]

After several chapters on Christian discussion of the nature of God and creation, Ward sums up his own reconstruction of the doctrine of the Trinity.

> One may speak of a Triad of the depth of being, the power of being, and the manifestation of being. The depth of being is that beyond all words, the ground of all beings, the infinite potency of all things which is also a wholly and unimaginably unrestricted actuality, beyond conceptual grasp. The power of being is the creative activity which expresses the divine being, actualizing from the abyss of potency endless particular forms, without end in its creative energy. The manifestation of being is the archetypal pattern and the completed image, the matrix and completion of creative activity, fully apprehended and appreciated within the divine life. These are not three distinct subjects of awareness, but three forms of the being of God, in each of which its whole being is expressed in a different manner.[28]

Ward does not see these three aspects of divine being as three centres of divine consciousness. Here he inhabits the Western tradition of seeing God as revealing Himself in three distinct ways, rather than the Eastern tradition of viewing God as three persons in communion. He speaks of three modes of being of the one divine subject.

> There are three modes of being of the one omnipotent and omniscient will and awareness who is God. The primal being, the manifested being, and the creative being are all ways in which the one God experiences and acts. All of these coinhere, forming one subject in three centres of awareness and will, indivisibly co-acting and experiencing, each in its own way, and with its own form of awareness of the other centres. Each hypostasis of the same consciousness and will interpenetrates the others, being aware of them in its own appropriate mode and willing with them in its own distinctive modality.[29]

In this elaboration, Ward wants to make room for individuation among the three modes of divine being. While avoiding talk of "persons", Ward does speak of each of the three hypostases as having awareness and will, which takes him into the Eastern conceptualisation of Father, Son and Spirit interpenetrating each other. He seeks the best of both worlds by granting self-consciousness to the three modes of divine being while refusing to admit that the three modes are discrete individual persons. The following summary shows that Ward finds it difficult to see the Son and the Spirit as personal, since he speaks of them in impersonal terms.

> One may think of the depth of being (the Father) generating an intelligible self-expression and pattern of being (the Son), with its own form of consciousness and all possibilities. Together, they generate, through the power of being (the Spirit), with its own actualizing and evaluating consciousness, a set of supreme values, which forms the changelessly completed awareness of the Father.[30]

Ward goes on to outline how the Trinity operates in the created universe.

---

[27] Ward, *Religion and Creation*, p. 75.
[28] Ward, *Religion and Creation*, p. 336.
[29] Ward, *Religion and Creation*, p. 336.
[30] Ward, *Religion and Creation*, p. 339.

> The primordial being of God gives rise to the origin of worlds in a distinctively threefold pattern. The ecstatic abyss of potentiality engenders the archetypal intellect which forms the pattern for a particular universe, and the power of creativity which embodies that form materially. The world is created through the Divine Wisdom, the Christ, in the power of the Spirit.[31]

He upholds the Western over against the Eastern creed that "The Spirit proceeds from the Father in creative energy, and proceeds from the Father and the Son together as the Spirit shapes particular created things into the image of the archetypal Son."[32] Ward indicates the history of the actions of the three modes of divine being.

> The Father calls a particular people into fellowship. God sends the Spirit to inspire the prophets and make known the divine will. The divine being is embodied, first in Torah and then in the person of Jesus, as the incarnation of the cosmic image upon which things are patterned. The Christ is incarnated on earth as the particular historical image of divine love, responsive to created human beings, whom he guides and teaches. The Spirit, in relation to the historical process, becomes the one who makes the love of Christ present within creatures.[33]

He has a final vision of the work of the Son and the Spirit as bringing creation into the completeness of the Father.

> Finally, as creation returns to its source, the Spirit sanctifies, reconciles, and unites all things within the perfected and actualized form which is the cosmic Christ. In the Spirit and through Christ, all things return to the Father, and all the values of temporal existence are conserved in the completed experience, in which all sentient creatures can share in an appropriate way. At the end of this historical time, all created life which is responsive to God's call is taken into fellowship with the life of God, who will be all in all … purged of all evil and corruption.[34]

After his retirement from Oxford, Ward taught at the Catholic Heythrop College in London. While there in 2015 he published *Christ and the Cosmos* as a response to Christian theologians who have embraced a social theory of the Trinity. In his preface he says,

> The central argument of this book is that the idea of God as other-creating dynamic love is an illuminating one and is fully consistent with many strands of Biblical thought. But the idea of God as a sort of society is a bad idea. It is repugnant to Jews, Muslims, and many monotheists (including me), and it has great disadvantages that its proponents have not fully recognised. Among them can often be found a sort of unintended arrogance that presumes to say exactly what God is in the divine being itself, as opposed to saying how God truly appears to finite human minds. So as well as attacking the "social" view of the Trinity, I also attack the claim, sometimes made, that the phrase "Father, Son, and Holy Spirit" must be unrevisably and unsurpassably true of the divine being in itself. I think any such claim is inconsistent with the belief, also common in Christian traditions, that God

---

[31] Ward, *Religion and Creation*, p. 340.
[32] Ward, *Religion and Creation*, p. 340.
[33] Ward, *Religion and Creation*, p. 340.
[34] Ward, *Religion and Creation*, p. 341.

> is essentially beyond full human understanding – even though God can reveal the divine nature in ways suitable for human understanding.[35]

Ward shows how influenced he is by his interaction with Jews and Muslims about belief in God. In his introductory chapter he quotes Q5:76, "They blaspheme who say 'God is one of three in a Trinity'" and points out that many Jews and Muslims think of the Christian Trinity as three gods.[36] In his third chapter, entitled "The Doctrine of Divine Simplicity", Ward appeals to the teaching of Jesus that appears to undercut the Trinity.

> Anyone who thinks about God as Trinity must keep firmly in mind the statement that Mark's Gospel attributes to Jesus: "The first of all of the commandments is, 'Hear, O Israel; the Lord our God is one Lord' (Mark 12:29). Christians need to be clear that the most important commandment in the Bible, therefore, is that there is one and only one God. There are not three Gods, and nothing must be said which suggests that there are. How, then, does talk of a Trinity arise?[37]

In dialogue with Muslims, Christians discover that, for Muslims, though there are multiple attributes of God, there can be no plurality within Him. "The most rigorous Muslims accept that there are ninety-nine beautiful names of God, even though they often interpret the Arabic word *tawhid*, oneness, as forbidding any plurality within God."[38] Christians ought to agree with Muslims that there is one God who is active in different ways.

> There are different attributes of the one God … It does not compromise the unity of God to say that God thinks, feels, and wills. In fact it supports the idea that there is just one God to say that it is the same God who thinks, feels, and wills. There are not, after all, different beings who do these things. This is one main reason I am uneasy about saying that God is a "society" of three beings who think, feel, and will. That seems to undermine the belief that there is just one God. Perhaps there is an internal complexity in the one and only God … If we can establish this, we can go on to ask if the Trinity is a sort of internal complexity in God. I am going to argue that it is. [39]

Ward quotes Jürgen Moltmann and Wolfhart Pannenberg as advocates of a social Trinity.

> Moltmann points out that the Father and Son are spoken of as if they could have different desires, which implies that they have different centres of consciousness. And the difference is so great that one may even be said to forsake the other. Given that Jesus is granted divine status in the Gospels, it looks as though there are at least two divine individuals who converse with one another. John's Gospel points out that Jesus sends the Spirit, or that the Father sends the Spirit at the request of Jesus, which implies that the Spirit is different from Jesus and from the Father. The Spirit will guide the disciples into all truth. Guiding is typically something persons do.

---

[35] Ward, *Christ and the Cosmos* (Cambridge: Cambridge University Press, 2015), preface, pp. x–xi.
[36] Ward, *Christ and the Cosmos*, p. 3.
[37] Ward, *Christ and the Cosmos*, p. 11.
[38] Ward, *Christ and the Cosmos*, p. 11.
[39] Ward, *Christ and the Cosmos*, pp. 12–13.

> Moltmann concludes that there are three divine individuals who are reciprocally conscious of one another and who communicate with one another.[40]

> Pannenberg argues that if Jesus truly reveals God, and distinguishes himself from the Father, then that distinction is constitutive of the Trinity. Jesus and the Father are distinct persons – "not merely as different modes of being of the one divine subject but as living realisations of separate centres of action".[41] Taking the Holy spirit into account as well, Pannenberg also maintains that in God there are three separate centres of action and consciousness, three "persons" almost in the modern sense of conscious subjects.[42]

Ward admits that the New Testament can be read as advocating a social Trinity, but he spots problems within the scriptural portrait of Father, Son and Holy Spirit.

> The Biblical case for a social Trinity may seem to be decisive. But it has its problems. The three centres of consciousness do not seem to be equal persons. It is the Father who commands, who sends, and who ultimately controls. The Son's role is to ask, to hear, and to obey the Father's will, not to initiate any independently chosen courses of action. And the Spirit seems to be almost entirely passive, carrying out what he is sent to do but not apparently taking any part in a divine conversation about what is to happen … If these are three individuals, there seems to be a clear hierarchical line of authority between them, which makes any thought that they are three fully individual persons who are equal with one another dubious.[43]

Ward prefers the Western tradition of explaining the Trinity adopted by Karl Barth and Karl Rahner.

> Both Karl Barth and Karl Rahner, leading theologians of Reformed and Roman Catholic Christianity respectively, have suggested that it might be better to speak of one divine Subject, one centre of consciousness, knowledge, and will in God, which has three modes of being (Barth) or three modes of subsistence (Rahner), so that the one divine Lord has three different ways of possessing and manifesting Subjectivity.[44]

In his final statements concerning the Trinity, Ward wishes to separate the ways God is active in creation from any attempt to apply these actions to his divine being.

> Father, Son and Holy spirit are terms drawn wholly from, and dependent for their meaning upon, items in a specifically human world. God takes human form, God suffers and dies because of the actions of human agents, and God liberates from the endemic evil that marks human nature. Yet God did not have to create humans, humans did not have to become prey to hatred and greed, and God did not have to deliver humans by death on a cross. These things happened, and they mark ways in which God creates, humans fall into evil, and God redeems them. But these are all contingent occurrences. They did not have to happen. God might well have created

---

[40] Ward, *Christ and the Cosmos*, p. 34.

[41] Wolfhart Pannenberg, *Systematic Theology, vol. 1* (Grand Rapids: Eerdmans, 1992), p. 319.

[42] Ward, *Christ and the Cosmos*, p. 35.

[43] Ward, *Christ and the Cosmos*, p. 36.

[44] Ward, *Christ and the Cosmos*, pp. 89–90.

> other kinds of intelligent life, there could have been intelligent life that did not fall into evil, and God might have chosen another way of reuniting the human species to the divine.[45]

Since God could have related to other worlds than our own, it is not appropriate for us to determine His nature merely by superimposing our experience of His actions onto His own being. "It follows that the terms we use to describe the Trinity, insofar as they depend upon contingent matters of fact, cannot denote necessary and essential properties of God."[46] This means that what appears to be a society of divine individuals to us is not in fact what the divine being is in Himself.

> The economic Trinity, the Trinity of Father, Son, and Holy Spirit that we humans experience, is rooted in a threefoldness of subjectivity, creativity, and unitive love which is not strictly identical with the Trinity as it is expressed in the human world. That in turn is rooted in a deeper "immanent" threefoldness of primal origin, expressed thought, and beatific love. It is not a society of three distinct individuals.[47]

Finally, Ward argues that the Trinity is a valid response to the revelation of God, which can be found in many different human religious responses, including Islam.

> On this planet there may be diverse forms of revelation as the infinite God is disclosed to and responded to by different peoples with different histories and cultures … The Trinity is authentically known to human beings as Father, Son, and Holy Spirit. The Father brings into being free value-creating persons. They fall into alienation and spiritual death. Jesus expresses the sacrificial, agapic, love of the Father which liberates them into true freedom. The Spirit is the divine power that empowers them upwardly to prepare them for communion with the divine in a life that transcends bodily death. In this contingent history, the threefold God is known in a specific way – not perhaps the only way, but a way uniquely fitted to enable human beings to find fulfilment in God. [48]

Hans Küng (1928–2021)

Hans Küng, a Swiss Catholic theologian who was professor of theology at Tübingen, Germany, for most of his career, developed a concern for being a Christian theologian in dialogue with world religions. With respect to Islam, he dialogued with Seyyed Hossein Nasr in 1984 at Harvard University, and published *Christianity and World Religions* in 1985, in which he has a section on Christianity and Islam. His mature writing on Islam came in his large book, *Islam: Past, Present and Future*.

His presentation of the Trinity for Muslims points out to Christians that they need to ensure that the unity of God is not put in question by the way Christians advocate the Trinity. Islam has faith in one God in common with Christianity. "Whatever will have to be said about the Christian doctrine of the Trinity, this

---

[45] Ward, *Christ and the Cosmos*, pp. 249–50.
[46] Ward, *Christ and the Cosmos*, p. 251.
[47] Ward, *Christ and the Cosmos*, p. 256.
[48] Ward, *Christ and the Cosmos*, p. 261.

too certainly does not want to question belief in the one and only God but to expound it and develop it concretely."[49]

However, there is a basic difficulty with the Islamic approach to Christians that comes from Muḥammad's lack of true awareness of Christian beliefs. In his exposition of Muḥammad's career, Küng argues that Muḥammad's initial approval of Christians changed when the Byzantine army defeated the Muslims in 629, near the end of Muḥammad's life.

> Muhammad's attitude to Christians presumably deteriorated when he fought for an expansion route to Syria and was defeated by the Byzantines or their Arab allies in 629 at Muʾta. Moreover, the Qurʾan does not show the slightest comprehension of Christian dogma (the Trinity and the divinity of Jesus).[50]

This sweeping dismissal by Küng of the Qurʾānic portrait of Christian beliefs concerning the Trinity and the divinity of Jesus does not bode well for Christian presentations of their beliefs. Indeed, his traversing of the history of Muslim attitudes to Christians simply adds to the dilemma for Christians. For example, he highlights the building of the Dome of the Rock in Jerusalem in the late seventh century as propaganda against the Christian teaching of the Trinity. "With triumphalist and propagandist intent, the Dome of the Rock was therefore provided with an inscription running round it in two bands, on which the unity and oneness of God is proclaimed – over against the Christian doctrine of God as Trinity."[51]

In the Abbasid era, Muslims were particularly engaged in rejecting the Christian Trinity, Küng argues. There was intellectual interaction between Jews, Christians and Muslims, but Christians were especially attacked by Muslims for believing in polytheism.

> Muslims were bound up with Jews and Christians through faith in the one God of Abraham but nevertheless were distinct from them, especially from Christians, who could easily be accused of "polytheism" because of the Trinity. Any "association" (*shirk*) which threatened belief in the one and only God had to be fought.[52]

Küng turns to a detailed discussion of the Trinity in *Islam: Past, Present and Future*. He gives an overview of the developments of the doctrine of the Trinity after Tertullian's coinage of the term Trinity.

> A trinitarian speculation which was intellectually highly demanding and which emphasized the unity of the three entities came increasingly to be built on this (God is threefold in the "persons" but one in "nature"). The result was something like a higher trinitarian mathematics which, despite all the efforts to attain conceptual clarity, hardly led to permanent solutions. Practical preaching continued to be about the Father, the Son and the Spirit but largely passed over this doctrine of the Trinity – God in three persons but in one nature.[53]

Küng is clearly unhappy with the speculative nature of creedal definitions that marked the period of the ecumenical creeds. He wants modern Christians to draw

---

[49] Hans Küng, *Islam: Past, Present and Future* (Oxford: Oneworld, 2007), p. 90.
[50] Küng, *Islam*, p. 115.
[51] Küng, *Islam*, pp. 206–207.
[52] Küng, *Islam*, p. 278.
[53] Küng, *Islam*, p. 505.

back from such speculation today. Let us leave behind the Greek philosophical scaffolding used to build the creeds and return to the simplicity of the New Testament message, he pleads.

> Thirty years ago, I called for critical reflection on the traditional doctrine of the Trinity on the basis of the evidence of exegesis and the history of dogma. I asked whether Greek speculation, which was far removed from its biblical basis and attempted boldly to spy into the dizzying heights of God's mystery, wasn't comparable with the story in Greek mythology of the flight of Icarus, the son of Daedalus. As he came too near to the sun, his wings made of feathers and wax fell off.[54]

Küng is referring to his 1987 book *The Incarnation of God.* It is no surprise that his presentation of the Trinity for Muslims fits into this general rejection of Greek thought as a foundation for doctrine in our time. Küng prefers to return to the New Testament presentation of Father, Son and Spirit.

> The *Father* is the one and only God of Abraham, beside whom there are no other Gods and who to us is both "Father" and "Mother". Belief in one God must not be put in question indirectly either: there is no third way between monotheism and polytheism. The *Son* is none other than the historical person Jesus of Nazareth, who personally reveals the word and will of this one God: in him the one true God is really manifest, present and effective. The *Spirit* is the holy emanation, might and power of God and Jesus Christ who is exalted to him, which is effective in the believer and in the community of faith and which makes all human beings the sons and daughters of God. Thus the Spirit is not a third party between God and human beings but is none other than God himself, God's powerful spiritual presence and reality.[55]

This means, for Küng, that we can only speak of the Trinity as the way God has revealed Himself in history. There is no route to speaking about the eternal nature of the Trinity as Christian theologians have attempted to do for centuries.

> In theological terms, according to the New Testament (in contrast to later Christian Dogmatics) the issue is not an "immanent" unity of three persons in God "in himself" in his eternity, far less the identity of an eternal divine "nature". Rather, it is the salvation-historical ("economic") unity of God "for us" in history: the way in which God himself has acted, spoken, made himself known and revealed himself through Jesus in the gift of his Holy Spirit to us, to our very unholy spirit and for our salvation.[56]

If Christians could keep to the New Testament revelation of Father, Son and Holy Spirit, then dialogue with Muslims would be so much less complicated. It should be enough for Christians to explain the New Testament teaching about Jesus as the particular revelation of God along with the sending of His Spirit to us.

> Every Christian theologian should be really oppressed by the question: how can I explain, to a Muslim or a Jew, why Christians believe in this Jesus as the Messiah, the Christ, God's revelation? As a "European Christian", should I really expect them to accept the Hellenistic councils of the fourth and fifth centuries or even the

---

[54] Küng, *Islam*, p. 506.
[55] Küng, *Islam*, pp. 514–15.
[56] Küng, *Islam*, p. 515.

> Roman Catholic development of the views of Augustine and the Latin Middle Ages?[57]

However, even this appeal to the New Testament witness will not necessarily make dialogue with Muslims more straightforward. Küng's approach sounds rather Protestant, like that of Pfander and Shenk. But even a Protestant use of the apostolic testimony does not mean the Muslims will find the Trinity more attractive. The basic issue of the particular nature of Jesus' divinity and the need for the Spirit of God to be expressed as a mode of God's activity or a person with divine consciousness still remains.

Miroslav Volf (b. 1956)

Miroslav Volf grew up in Yugoslavia as the son of a Pentecostal minister. He went on to become professor of theology at Yale University, where he wrote *Allah: A Christian Response* in 2011. Volf became well known for organising the Yale response to the Common Word initiative of 138 leading Muslim scholars who invited Christian leaders to endorse their call for a dialogue on what Muslims and Christians hold in common in 2007. Volf was the primary drafter of the "Yale Response to the Common Word" published in the *New York Times* in November 2007 under the title "Loving God and Neighbor Together: A Christian Response to 'A Common Word Between Us and You'". Volf also organised various conferences between Christians, Muslims and Jews to discuss the Common Word proposal.

He indicates several reasons for writing the book. Firstly, he dedicates the book to his father, "a Pentecostal minister who admired Muslims and taught me as a boy that they worship the same God we do". But the civil war of the early nineties in Yugoslavia showed Volf that his parental inheritance was not shared by others in his homeland. So, secondly, he wrote the book for his fellow Christians to plead with them not to turn to hatred and violence. "I was born and grew up in a country that no longer exists. It was called Yugoslavia, and it was destroyed by tensions turned into wars among some of its ethnic groups. Two of these wars were between Muslims and Christians (though Christians fought fiercely among themselves as well)."[58] Thirdly, he wrote the book for Christians and Muslims to plead with them to come to agreement whenever possible. Both Christians and Muslims worship the creator of the universe who does not want them to fight against each other but to live in tolerance and good will towards each other. If Christians claim that they worship a different deity, then co-operation between Christians and Muslims will be much further away. "The claim that Muslims and Christians worship radically different deities is good for fighting, but not for living together peacefully."[59] Fourthly, he wrote for Muslims to think afresh about how they view Christians, especially how they understand Jesus. "I write for Christians, but at the same time this book is an open invitation

---

[57] Küng, *Islam*, p. 516.
[58] Miroslav Volf, *Allah: A Christian Response* (New York: HarperOne, 2011), p. 2.
[59] Volf, *Allah*, p. 8.

to Muslims to think along with me and, if so moved, re-examine their own stances toward the God of Jesus Christ in the light of what I have written."[60]

Volf had already written a book that explored the impact of the civil war in the Yugoslavia of his youth which threw up such sectarian hatred. *Exclusion & Embrace: A Theological Exploration of Identity, Otherness, and Reconciliation*, published in 1996, contains a graphic illustration of how Christians can treat Muslims with contempt. He records the testimony of a Muslim woman whose Christian neighbours turned on her during the conflict.

> I am a Muslim, and I am thirty-five years old … I am a teacher of literature … I was born in Ilijaš and I almost died there. My student, Zoran, the only son of my neighbor, urinated into my mouth. As the bearded hooligans standing around laughed, he told me: "You are good for nothing else, you stinking Muslim woman" … I do not know whether I first heard the cry or felt the blow. My former colleague, a teacher of physics, was yelling like mad and kept hitting me … I taught them to love and all the while they were making preparations to destroy everything that is not of the orthodox faith. Jihad-war. This is the only way.[61]

Volf comments,

> How many children around the globe are growing up with "jihad," "war," "crusade," "revenge," "hatred," not only inscribed in their names but woven into the very fabric of their lives! For reconciliation to take place, the inscriptions of hatred must be carefully erased and the threads of violence gently removed.[62]

In a discussion of violence, Volf commends Hans Küng's argument that "There can be no peace among nations without peace among the religions."[63] Volf argues, "without the principled assertion that it is never appropriate to use religion to give moral sanction to the use of violence, religious images and religious leaders will continue to be exploited by politicians and generals engaged in violence".[64]

Volf therefore was highly motivated by the impact of Christian hostility to Muslims in his childhood homeland to make his personal contribution in *Allah: A Christian Response* to challenge Christians to treat Muslims as fellow human beings with their own integrity. But he also wants to challenge Muslims to engage with Christians in such a way that Muslims accept the integrity of Christian beliefs. There is a double and reciprocal challenge for Christians and Muslims in their relations.

Right at the outset of *Allah: A Christian Response* Volf challenges Muslims to accept that Christians are monotheists. Their interpretation of the Qurʾān needs to be overhauled if they wish to find common ground with Christians. The denial of the Trinity in the Qurʾān is not relevant to what Christians actually believe and Muslims need to recognise this.

---

[60] Volf, *Allah*, p. 12.
[61] Miroslav Volf, *Exclusion & Embrace: A Theological Exploration of Identity, Otherness, and Reconciliation* (Nashville: Abingdon Press, 1996), p. 111.
[62] Volf, *Exclusion & Embrace*, p. 111.
[63] Volf, *Exclusion & Embrace*, p. 284. Volf quotes from Hans Küng, *Global Responsibility: In Search of a New World Ethic* (New York: Continuum, 1993) p. 76.
[64] Volf, *Exclusion & Embrace*, p. 286.

> What the Qur᾽an denies about God as the Holy Trinity has been denied by every great teacher of the church in the past and ought to be denied by every orthodox Christian today. I reject the idea that Muslim monotheism is incompatible with the Christian doctrine of the Trinity.[65]

But he also has a secular, humanist audience in mind. There are many voices in the Western world that see religious thought as detrimental to peace. Both Christians and Muslims are on trial for promoting sectarianism that inevitably leads to violence. But he calls on both Christians and Muslims to demonstrate that violence is not inevitable for those who believe in God.

> To give allegiance to the one God who enjoins humans to be loving and just to all, as Muslims and Christians do, means to embrace pluralism as a political project – the right of all religious people to articulate their views in public and the impartiality of the state with respect to all religions. I reject the idea that monotheism, properly understood, fosters violence and totalitarian rule.[66]

As Volf gets into his stride, he deals with what is both common and not common between Christians and Muslims concerning the God they worship. Muslims are ready to insist according to the Qur᾽ān that Jews, Christians and Muslims worship the same Creator. But the Qur᾽ān criticises Christians for reneging on God by associating Jesus with him as a god to be worshipped. He calls on Muslims to re-examine these conflicting views within the Qur᾽ān.

> Muslims make two affirmations that don't sit easily next to each other: (1) that Islam's God and Christianity's God are one and the same, and (2) that central Christian beliefs seriously compromise the most important characteristic of God, God's oneness. The challenge for Muslims in relation to Christian views about God is to deal with this tension.[67]

Getting Muslims to acknowledge that Christian worship of Jesus does not compromise the oneness of God is a priority for Christians in dialogue with Muslims. He illustrates this from his own experience of dialogue in the aftermath of the Yale response to the Common Word initiative. Volf relates his conversation with Sheikh Habib Ali al-Jifri in the fall of 2008 in Abu Dhabi. Volf asked, "Do you think that Muslims and Christians worship the same God?" Sheikh al-Jifri answered without hesitation: "'Yes, they do. In the Qur᾽an it is written: "Our God and your God is One."' 'But Christians believe that God is the Holy Trinity, and Muslims disagree. How do you then still affirm that the two worship the same God?' I pressed him. He smiled enigmatically and said, 'What the archbishop of Canterbury wrote about the Trinity in his response to the "Common Word' was very helpful.'" Volf reports that Rowan Williams had written a letter entitled "A Common Word for the Common Good". He wrote, "God exists in a threefold pattern of interdependent action … But Christians affirm that there is only one divine nature and reality".[68] Volf said to the Sheikh that the archbishop had said nothing new in his comments on God as the Holy

---

[65] Volf, *Allah*, p. 14.
[66] Volf, *Allah*, p. 15.
[67] Volf, *Allah*, pp. 79–80.
[68] Rowan Williams, 'A Common Word for the Common Good', letter written 14/07/2008, accessible from acommonword.com.

Trinity. "For us, the divine 'three' are one single and undivided divine essence, not three divine essences next to each other comprising some kind of a divine troika". Volf reports that they stayed up late discussing the Trinity.[69]

Volf offers to help Muslims reinterpret the Qur'ān by repeating the point that the Trinity denied by the Qur'ān of God, Jesus and Mary is not the Trinity of orthodox Christians. "In statements that address the doctrine of the Trinity, the Qur'an may well be targeting the beliefs of some Christians contrary to what the Christian creeds advocate, for what the Qur'an rejects in this regard, Christians ought to reject as well."[70] Nevertheless, Volf has heard Muslims say that worship of the Son really does mean that Christians offer worship to the Creator along with a human being. The Trinity is actually a statement of plurality in the one God, and that is always impossible for a Muslim to accept. Volf introduces a possible Muslim reaction.

> If you claim that the "Son" was incarnate, but the "Father" was not, then have you not in fact divided the Trinity? … You are simultaneously saying two contradictory things, namely, that the divine essence is undivided and that the divine "Persons" are distinguished … You actually believe in three gods. Either give up on God's unity or reject the Trinity. You can't have it both ways.[71]

In order to answer this Muslim criticism, Volf appeals to Augustine's approach to the Trinity.

> There are two related ways of understanding the intimate connection between the divine Three who are indivisibly one. First, when God acts "toward the outside" – creating, redeeming, and bringing the world to completion – God's acts are undivided, inseparable. Every act of one "Person" is always caused by all three. If this were not the case, then, as Augustine put it, "the Father [would do] some things, the Son others and the Holy Spirit yet others". The second way to think how the divine "Persons" are tied together is their *mutual indwelling* or, in technical terminology, *perichoresis*. Again, as Augustine put it, "they are always in each other and never alone." The Father and the Spirit are always "in" the Son; to be the "Son" is to be indwelled by the Father and the Spirit.[72]

Volf concludes from his Augustinian quotations that what we predicate of human beings is not identical to what we predicate of God.

> Two consequences follow: 1. With regard to the *identity* of divine Persons, you cannot simply say, "To be one is not to be the other," as you can say of creatures, including human beings. 2. With regard to the *activity* of divine persons, you cannot say that the act of one is the act of that Person alone, as you must say of human beings.[73]

Volf explains the teaching of John's gospel concerning the Word of God becoming incarnate.

---

[69] Volf, *Allah*, pp. 127–29.
[70] Volf, *Allah*, p. 136.
[71] Volf, *Allah*, p. 136.
[72] Volf, *Allah*, p. 137. He quotes from Augustine, *The Trinity*, E. Hill (trans.), (Brooklyn: New City Press, 1991), 1.8, p. 70.
[73] Volf, *Allah*, p. 137.

> Though only one Person is incarnate, all three Persons are present and act in that one Person who became incarnate. This is the consequence of saying that the "Persons" of the Trinity "mutually indwell" one another. Thus, the incarnation doesn't require any division of God's essence.[74]

Volf imagines a Muslim rejecting this language about a Triune identity of God.

> A Muslim critic might respond: "Those are just the kinds of difficulties you get into when you affirm the Trinity; then you have to use words like 'begetting,' 'Son,' and 'Person,' but can't use them properly like everybody else does." But now it may be my turn to suggest that this would be a false victory, for our difficulties in speaking of God would not go away if God were not the Holy Trinity. *All* words we use of God – such as "sustainer" and "master" or "gracious" and "merciful" (Q1:1-4) are inadequate. Why? Augustine explains: "Because the total transcendence of the godhead quite surpasses the capacity of ordinary speech."[75]

Volf admits that talk about God is ultimately talk about a mystery. Yet Christians believe that God has revealed this mystery.

> The talk of "Persons" captures something important about God, but is inadequate to express the full reality, because God transcends the notion of "person" as we have seen. The same is true of "essence," "Goodness," "love" – all to varying degrees correct and true when referring to God, but also deeply inadequate. The very reality of God is such that God always remains inconceivable, a mystery that can never be properly named or puzzled out. And yet we speak of God – guided by God's self-revelation. We have true knowledge of God, but we are capable of understanding much better what the divine Mystery is *not* than what that Mystery is.[76]

Volf hopes that the arguments he has presented will be plausible to Muslims and Christians alike. But his real purpose is to get Muslims to see that the Christian Trinity does not violate the unity of God.

> With regard to Muslims, however, my purpose here is not to persuade them that God indeed is the Holy Trinity. I have not offered a single argument in favor of this cardinal Christian belief. My purpose is more modest: to demonstrate that the rejections of the "Trinity" in the Qur'an do not refer to normative Christian understanding of God's threeness, and that the Christian doctrine of the Trinity does not call into question God's oneness as expressed in Muslims' most basic belief that there is "no god but God." What the Qur'an may be targeting is misconceptions about God's nature held by misguided Christians.[77]

Yet he now goes on to present an argument for the Trinity as a preferable way of understanding God. This is based on the concept that God is love. Volf argues that the claim that "God is love" requires the Trinity.

> How is God to be love before there were any creatures to love? Only if, in God's own very being, God loves and is love. "The doctrine of the Trinity," writes Archbishop Williams in the text that Sheikh al-Jifri so highly praised, "is a way of

---

[74] Volf, *Allah*, pp. 138–39.
[75] Volf, *Allah*, p. 139. He quotes from Augustine, *The Trinity*, 7.7. p. 224–25.
[76] Volf, *Allah*, pp. 139–40.
[77] Volf, *Allah*, p. 143.

> explaining why we say that God *is* love, not only that he shows love." For love, you need more than the sovereign and solitary one.[78]

Volf looks back to Ibn Taymiyya (1263–1328) and al-Ghazālī (d. 1111) as representative Muslim scholars who have expounded the idea of the love of God.

> Ibn Taymiyya argued that since God is perfect, God's love for creatures cannot be a consequence of a deficiency on God's part. That excludes two reasons for loving creatures. First, God doesn't love creatures because God needs them; that would be incompatible with God's self-sufficiency. Second, God doesn't love creatures simply for their benefit; that would mean that God loves them for no reason and that God's love is whimsical. He therefore concludes that God loves creatures because God first of all loves God's own self … God's self-love is the reason God created the world, and God's self-love is the source of all other loves.[79]

Volf points out that Thomas Aquinas also said that "God loves himself". "However he argued along with Augustine that God loves himself in a trinitarian way, as love among the three divine 'Persons' who are the one God of undivided essence".[80]

Volf then refers to al-Ghazālī's view that "God does indeed love people but in reality He loves nothing other than Himself, in the sense that He is the totality [of being], and there is nothing in being apart from Him."[81] Volf argues that on this interpretation,

> 1. all love is God's self-love. God loves people in that God gives them the ability to love God, and that love for God is nothing else but God's own self-love. God loves God's own self through people. 2. Creatures are illusory. In God's self-love, the absolute unity of all reality is affirmed as identical with the unity of God; all individuality, all multiplicity is then ultimately an illusion.[82]

Given these Muslim interpretations of the self-love of God, Volf argues strongly that the Trinity is required for a better understanding of the love of God.

> For the most part, Christians strenuously resist speaking about the unreality and illusoriness of creatures. As monotheists, they are able to do so coherently partly because of the doctrine of the Trinity, because they believe that the one God is internally differentiated, and that from the "beginning" God loves "the other".[83]

Since God loves Himself within the Trinity, He shows that He loves the other and not simply Himself.

> Moreover, the kind of love that is at the foundation of all reality, then, is not love that ultimately redounds to itself. Instead, it is a love that gives to the other as well as receives from the other. From this standpoint, God's creating to benefit creatures is exactly what God's love does – it gives to the other for the other's sake, and not merely for one's own sake.[84]

---

78 Volf, *Allah*, p. 148.

79 Volf, *Allah*, pp. 166–67. Volf relies on Joseph N. Bell, *Love Theory in Later Hanbalite Islam* (Albany: State University of New York Press, 1979).

80 Volf, *Allah*, p. 167. He quotes from Aquinas, *Summa Contra Gentiles*, 1:80:6.

81 Al-Ghazālī, *The Revival of Religious Sciences*, vol. 6, book 36.

82 Volf, *Allah*, p. 169.

83 Volf, *Allah*, p. 169.

84 Volf, *Allah*, p. 169.

Veli-Matti Kärkkäinen (b. 1958)

Veli-Matti Kärkkäinen is a Finnish Pentecostal theologian who worked as a missionary in Thailand before becoming professor of systematic theology at Fuller Seminary in California, USA. Between 2013 and 2017 he published a five-volume systematic theology which engages in dialogue with the major religions: Judaism, Islam, Hinduism and Buddhism. He indicates that Christian theology must engage with global concerns rather than merely with a Western mindset. He quotes Wolfhart Pannenberg's *Systematic Theology* as an example of Western-oriented theology that does not seek to engage in dialogue with world religions. Pannenberg accepts the limitations of his theology when he writes,

> An express comparison with other religions might enter into the self-explication of the content of Christian revelation to a greater degree than it does in the following presentation. A systematic comparison between the competing conception of the world religions is certainly a task that will more fully occupy systematic theology in the future. Perhaps in this field a particularly important contribution might be made to Christian theology by the Third World churches.[85]

Kärkkäinen comments,

> His excuse for not engaging religions sounds lame at best … Sadly enough, this German theologian does not differ from tradition or even contemporary practice of systematicians and other theologians. But at least Pannenberg has convincingly argued that an appropriate systematic task cannot be conducted apart from the engagement of other religions and their claims to truth and meaning.[86]

Kärkkäinen engages in dialogue with Muslim conceptions of the Trinity in the second and fourth volumes of his systematic theology. In the second volume, *Trinity and Revelation*, he outlines his methodology in the introduction.

> Theology makes space for an honest, genuine, authentic sharing of one's convictions. In pursuing the question of truth as revealed by the Triune God, constructive theology also seeks to persuade and convince with the power of dialogical, humble, and respectful argumentation.[87]

When he turns to dialogue with Islam concerning God, he summarises the Muslim view of God and His relationship to the creation. "Muslim theology of God includes the built-in dynamic between the absolute transcendence of God, because of his incomparability and uniqueness, on the one hand, and on the other hand, his presence and rulership in the world, which is a call for total obedience."[88] A second issue is the Qur'ānic teaching that the unity of God precludes any notion of threeness. "The Qur'an absolutely and unequivocally affirms the oneness of God … The Qur'anic teaching categorically rejects any notion of threeness of God."[89] Thirdly, the Qur'ān also rejects any suggestion

---

[85] Wolfhart Pannenberg, *Systematic Theology, vol. 1* (Grand Rapids: Eerdmans, 1991), preface, p. xii.
[86] Veli-Matti Kärkkäinen, *A Constructive Christian Theology for the Pluralistic World, vol. 1*: *Christ and Reconciliation* (Grand Rapids: Eerdmans, 2013), pp. 22–23.
[87] Veli-Matti Kärkkäinen, *A Constructive Christian Theology for the Pluralistic World, vol. 2*: *Trinity and Revelation* (Grand Rapids: Eerdmans, 2014), p. 5.
[88] Kärkkäinen, *Trinity and Revelation*, p. 366.
[89] Kärkkäinen, *Trinity and Revelation*, p. 372.

that God had a son through intercourse with a woman. "A foundational reason for the strict rebuttal of the Christian doctrine of the Trinity includes the absolute exaltedness of Allah and the sheer absurdity of the idea of God having a child by a woman."[90] Despite this antagonism to the Christian language of God as Father to His Son, Kärkkäinen notices that the Qur'ān does give titles to Jesus that reflect Christian convictions about him even while refuting any biological connection between Jesus and God. "What is remarkable about this rebuttal of the Trinity is that ironically it gives Jesus high status, as he is called the 'word' and 'spirit,' whatever the precise theological meanings in Islam were!"[91]

A fourth consideration is the allegation of *shirk*, that Christians associate Jesus with God in an unacceptable way. "Another major reason for the categorical rejection of the Trinity in Islamic theology is that it represents *shirk*. On this issue, we need to clarify what Christology is *not*, what *shirk* is, and what is not *shirk*."[92] In answer to the first question, what Christology is not, he points out that "When the Qur'an gives 'Praise to God who took not up a son' (17:111; 19:35; 19:92; 25:2), it must be noted that Christians also affirm this statement, as it is not about incarnation but rather about adoptionism."[93] So the answer to the second question, what *shirk* is, is adoptionism, the belief that God adopted Jesus as His Son, reflected in the words, "took up a son". Finally, the answer to the third question, what is not *shirk*, is the Incarnation. "God's gracious relation or association with humanity, the eternal Word becoming human, is not *shirk*."[94]

When he turns to advocating a Christian concept of the Trinity for Muslims, he recommends Pannenberg's solution when he states, "The doctrine of the Trinity is in fact concrete monotheism in contrast to the notions of an abstract transcendence of the one God and abstract notions of a divine unity that leaves no place for plurality."[95] Kärkkäinen also commends Pannenberg's statement about the three persons in one divine essence. "The trinitarian persons ... are simply manifestations and forms – eternal forms – of the one divine essence."[96] Kärkkäinen welcomes Pannenberg's orthodoxy in seeking to present the creedal tradition to a modern audience. He states,

> The Athanasian creed confirms this. "We worship one God in Trinity, and Trinity in Unity; Neither confounding the persons nor dividing the substance. For there is one person of the Father, another of the Son, and another of the Holy Spirit. But the Godhead of the Father, of the Son, and of the Holy Spirit is all one, the glory equal, the majesty coeternal".[97]

---

[90] Kärkkäinen, *Trinity and Revelation*, p. 372.
[91] Kärkkäinen, *Trinity and Revelation*, p. 373.
[92] Kärkkäinen, *Trinity and Revelation*, p. 373.
[93] Kärkkäinen, *Trinity and Revelation*, p. 373.
[94] Kärkkäinen, *Trinity and* Revelation, p. 374.
[95] Kärkkäinen, *Trinity and Revelation*, p. 374. He quotes Pannenberg, *Systematic Theology*, *vol. 1*, pp. 335–36.
[96] Kärkkäinen, *Trinity and Revelation*, p. 374. He quotes Pannenberg, *Systematic Theology*, *vol. 1*, p. 383.
[97] Kärkkäinen, *Trinity and Revelation*, p. 374. He quotes from Rick Brannan (ed.), *Historic Creeds and Confessions*, available at www.ccel.org., p. 5.

He then turns to the problem of the Incarnation in explaining the Trinity to Muslims. Do Muslims not see the Incarnation as implying "plurality in the Christian understanding of God: one God 'up there in heaven' and the other one 'down here on earth'?"[98] To answer this he appeals to Keith Ward, who argues that "In worshipping Jesus one does not worship another than God; one simply worships God."[99] In order to make this claim, it is important, according to Kärkkäinen, that we categorically deny what the Qurʾān "claims to be a Christian statement: 'Behold, God is the Christ, son of Mary' (Q5:72). Christian faith, rather, says that Christ is God".[100]

In summary, Kärkkäinen argues that dialogue with Muslims has a positive role in Christian theology. "In engaging another radically monotheist faith, Christian faith can also help clarify its own core beliefs and teach its members about the correct way of negotiating unity-in-diversity/diversity-in-unity."[101]

After raising the question, "Do Muslims and Christians believe in the same God?", he concludes, "to say that both etymologically and theologically both Muslims and Christians refer to the same God when they speak of the Divine is not yet to settle the issue of *what kind* of God that is".[102] He points to four issues that need to be addressed in order to answer the question, what kind of God? Firstly, Muslims claim that the Qurʾān is for all humanity, but Christians claim the same for the Bible. "Therefore, both faiths also are deeply missionary by nature."[103] Secondly, Jews claim to believe in one God along with Muslims.

> To confess one God does not require an identical understanding of the nature of that God if there are significant, wide-ranging agreements, as there are between Christians and Muslims, including the oneness of God, God as Creator, God's love, and so forth. Just consider how widely the views of various Christian traditions differ from one another. Add to the equation the third monotheistic faith, Judaism, and the differences are real – even when these three Abrahamic faiths, having their roots deeply embedded in the Jewish Bible, claim the same one God.[104]

Thirdly, "the task is to clarify the many misunderstandings about what the Christian trinitarian confession means".[105] Fourthly, "we must clarify what and how much can be said about the identity of the two monotheistic traditions' God".[106] Kärkkäinen points out that "The Common Word document quoted from the Qurʾan to affirm the identity".[107] He also indicates that the Catholic document from the Second Vatican Council in 1965, *Nostra Aetate*, "fails to give a blank affirmation of the identity of Allah and the Christian God … despite John Paul

---

[98] Kärkkäinen, *Trinity and Revelation*, p. 375.
[99] Kärkkäinen, *Trinity and Revelation*, p. 375. He quotes from Keith Ward, *Religion and Revelation*, p. 179.
[100] Kärkkäinen, *Trinity and* Revelation, pp. 375–76.
[101] Kärkkäinen, *Trinity and Revelation*, p. 376.
[102] Kärkkäinen, *Trinity and* Revelation, p. 377.
[103] Kärkkäinen, *Trinity and Revelation*, p. 381.
[104] Kärkkäinen, *Trinity and Revelation*, p. 381.
[105] Kärkkäinen, *Trinity and Revelation*, p. 382.
[106] Kärkkäinen, *Trinity and Revelation*, p. 383.
[107] Kärkkäinen, *Trinity and Revelation*, p. 383.

II believing in such an identity ... The statement is not silent about Islam's opposition to trinitarian confession in terms of Jesus' divinity".[108]

In conclusion to his treatment of the Trinity in dialogue with Muslims, Kärkkäinen says, "an authentic interfaith engagement is always a give-and-take event in which the Triune God is present. Not only can Christians contribute to and challenge the Muslim faith, but also are they challenged and enriched by the other".[109] Certainly his own attempt to take Islam seriously as a dialogue partner has enriched his own presentation of the Trinity in a way that would not have been the case if he had avoided Islam's claims altogether.

In the fourth volume of his systematic theology, Kärkkäinen discusses Muslim views of the Spirit of God in relation to the place of the Spirit in the Christian doctrine of the Trinity. He notes the references to the Spirit of God in the Qurʾān have multiple meanings. "The twenty Qurʾanic references to *ruh* can be divided into four categories. First, angels and spirits; second, Allah sharing his spirit with humans; third, the spirit linked to the command of God; fourth, the spirit of holiness."[110]

With regard to the second category, Allah sharing his spirit with humans, Kärkkäinen quotes Q4:171, His Word which He cast to Mary, and a Spirit from him. He then dialogues with Christians who want to relate the Word and Spirit to the divinity of Jesus.

> The Christian theologian has to be careful in interpreting the title Allah's "word," which has nothing to do with the theology of the divine logos; indeed, as even the immediate context indicates, the Prophet means the word that was spoken by Allah to Mary's ear that caused the birth of Jesus in her pure womb. All that said, what then is the meaning of the Qurʾanic saying that Jesus is a spirit from Allah? How much of that can be linked either to the Hebrew Bible's idea of *ruach Yahweh* as a creative principle or even semipersonified agent or to the NT idea of the creative Spirit? With regard to the latter question, the same sura gives a clear answer, as it continues immediately: "do not say, 'Three.' Refrain, it is better for you. God is but one God." Any linking of Jesus' lofty titles with divinity – and by implication with the Spirit – is categorically ruled out.[111]

Kärkkäinen has now responded to the suggestion he raised in *Trinity and Revelation* that "Word of God" and "Spirit of God" could serve as a starting point for interreligious dialogue[112] by noting the difficulties attached to these notions from an Islamic perspective. Perhaps his further reflection on the Qurʾānic use of these terms convinced him that his earlier proposal was not adequately thought through. At least, he ends on a sober note here by admitting the sheer difficulty of appealing to Qurʾānic terminology to interpret Christian terminology.

---

[108] Kärkkäinen, *Trinity and Revelation*, p. 383.

[109] Kärkkäinen, *Trinity and Revelation*, p. 385.

[110] Kärkkäinen, *A Constructive Christian Theology for the Pluralistic World, vol. 4: Spirit and Salvation* (Grand Rapids: Eerdmans, 2016), p. 134.

[111] Kärkkäinen, *Spirit and Salvation*, pp. 134–35.

[112] Kärkkäinen, *Trinity and Revelation*, p. 382.

6. Christian Theologians within the Islamic World Presenting the Trinity to Muslims

This chapter analyses three theologians living in Muslim majority nations who wrote about the Trinity for Muslims. The Egyptian Coptic priest Ibrahim Luqa defended the Trinity in the early twentieth century by depending on traditional Middle Eastern arguments of ʿAmmār al-Baṣrī and Yaḥya Ibn ʿAdī. He entered into debate with Muslim commentators on the Qurʾān over the correct interpretation of verses relating to the denial of threeness in God and the role of the Holy Spirit in order to propose that the Qurʾān does not deny the orthodox doctrine of the Trinity or the personhood of the Holy Spirit. The Anglican Malaysian theologian Albert Walters asked Malaysian Christians how they shared their faith in the Trinity towards the end of the twentieth century. He discovered that they relied on analogies, such as water being one in three forms, and recommended that they also share a belief in God as relational. The Jordanian Evangelical theologian Imad Shehadeh believes in the early twenty-first century that Muslims who hold steadfastly to the concept of God defined as Absolute Oneness may be able to believe in the concept of God as Oneness in Trinity. Christians need to show that the nature of God as eternally Father, Son and Holy Spirit in a relationship of love so that Muslims may come to realise that their experience of God as an utterly transcendent being who gives commands should be supplemented by an assurance that the Triune God wishes to pour out His love to them.

Ibrahim Luqa (early twentieth century)

Ibrahim Luqa was an Egyptian Coptic priest who published *Christianity in Islam* in 1938. Luqa writes for his fellow Christians but engages with Muslim scholars in order to dialogue with Muslims concerning the authenticity of the Bible, the Trinity, Jesus and salvation. In many respects Luqa writes in the tradition of the earlier Middle Eastern Christian apologists within their Islamic milieu.

In his section on the Trinity, Luqa begins by pointing out that Christians believe in the Trinity as essential to the nature of the Creator. "Almighty God is the one who exists in life and speech. His life and speech are not created but are eternal within him."[1] Luqa is repeating the formulation of ʿAmmār al-Baṣrī from the early ninth century. The Trinity of Father, Son and Holy Spirit is in reality a way of referring to the essential attributes of God. Luqa explains, "Christians refer to the attributes of the Father, the Son and the Holy Spirit. His existence is

[1] Ibrahim Luqa, *Christianity in Islam* (Rikon: no date), p. 76. This is a reprint of the original 1938 edition.

equivalent to the attribute of fatherhood, his speech is equivalent to the attribute of sonship, and his life is equivalent to the attribute of emanation."[2] Just like the earlier apologists, Luqa uses the analogy of fire to explain the function of the three essential attributes in God. He argues that these three attributes are essential within God just as the impact of heat and the emanation of light are essentially from the burning of fire. "Burning, heat, and light are one fire … Fire has one substance (*jawhar*) and three properties (*khawass*)."[3] His choice of the Arabic term *khawass* follows ʿAmmār's example of trying to avoid any notion of implying that the Father, Son and Spirit are discrete individuals.

He also follows the earlier Arab Christian writing in saying that the Word and Spirit are essential properties of God. However, this Middle Eastern conceptualisation of the Trinity raises the issue of the Godhead. He says that God has three essential attributes, but then defines God as one of the three. "We say that one of the divine hypostases (*aqanim*) is God (*Allah*), and we believe that the two other hypostases are necessary to him."[4] He equates God with the first hypostasis, the Father, in the usual Eastern way as the origin of the Son and the Spirit. It is not surprising that he does not notice the problem of equating the Father with God and having the Son and the Spirit as the essential attributes of the Father, given that all his Eastern forebears ignored this problem too. He can quite easily conclude by stating, "We believe that God is one substance in three essential properties."[5]

Addressing Muslim concerns that the three hypostases are in reality three divine beings, Luqa replies, "We do not say that there are three gods because adding up the properties and the attributes is not possible just as we pointed out in the previous example that it is not possible to talk about three fires."[6] Christians believe about God along with Muslims what the Qurʾān says, "there is nothing like Him". Christians agree with Muslims that this Qurʾānic text means that God cannot have "any created substance within him".[7] He quotes Muḥammad ibn al-Ṭayyib al-Bāqillānī (d. 1014) as a Muslim scholar who correctly understands the Christian doctrine of the Trinity when he states,

> If we look into the teaching of the Christians that Almighty God is one substance in three hypostases we do not find between us and them any conflict except in wording. They say that he is a substance (*jawhar*), but not like created substances, and they mean by this that he exists in his own essence (*dhat*). The meaning is clear but the wording is wrong.[8]

Luqa goes on to argue that the Qurʾān supports the doctrine of the Trinity. The Qurʾān lists several attributes of God: the living, the existent, the all-powerful, the all-knowing, the hearing and seeing. "Muslims understand God the

---

[2] Luqa, *Christianity in Islam*, p. 77.
[3] Luqa, *Christianity in Islam*, p. 77.
[4] Luqa, *Christianity in Islam*, p. 78.
[5] Luqa, *Christianity in Islam*, p. 78.
[6] Luqa, *Christianity in Islam*, p. 78.
[7] Luqa, *Christianity in Islam*, p. 78.
[8] Luqa, *Christianity in Islam*, p. 79. He quotes from Al-Bāqillānī, 'Refutation of the Christians'.

way we Christians do. They say that the substance is that which precedes the creation … We say that his substance, with respect to its existence, exists in his own essence possessing three properties which are described in the Holy Trinity."[9]

Luqa then turns to the kind of "trinity" that is opposed in the Qur᾿ān. He argues, "Islamic scholars have agreed with the thinking of true Christians about the Trinity, that it is something different from a false doctrine of tritheism (*tathlith*) which the Qur᾿ān opposes."[10] The Qur᾿ān calls Christians "people of the book" and Muslims have seen Christians along with Jews as monotheists, who are not guilty of polytheism.

Firstly, the Trinity that Islam rejects is not the Trinity of true Christians. He quotes Q 4:171, 5:60, 72-73, and 9:31, and says, "It is clear from these verses that the Qur᾿ān opposes any teaching that bears the meaning of associating anything with God or adds to his divinity … Islam opposes tritheism rather than the Christian Trinity".[11] This is because "These verses indicate that the Holy Virgin Mary is one of the three … yet even to this day Christians do not believe that the Virgin is a member of the Holy Trinity".[12] Christians are just as opposed to the deity of Mary as Muslims. "The Qur᾿ān opposes the belief that Jesus and Mary are two gods apart from God, but Christianity does not believe this about the Messiah. Rather Christians believe that the Messiah and the Father are one God without addition or division."[13]

When the Qur᾿ān attacks those who speak of God being the third of three, it is not orthodox Christians who are being criticised, but heretical groups. Firstly, "The Qur᾿ān opposes those who say that God is the third of three. This refers to the Marcionites who believed in three gods. The just god sent the Torah, the good god is revealed in the gospel, and the evil god is the devil."[14] Then there were other heretical groups who believed in two gods that are being attacked here. "Islam opposes the Manichaeans and the Daysanites who said that there are two gods, the first of which is good, with the substance of light, and the second is evil, with substance of darkness."[15] All these groups existed before the coming of Islam and were already rejected by orthodox Christians, argues Luqa. When the Qur᾿ān rejects the sonship of Jesus it always speaks of physical sonship. Luqa quotes ten occasions where the Qur᾿ān rejects physical sonship, but he avers, "Christianity is completely free from this belief".[16]

Secondly, Islamic scholars testify to the truth of the Christian Trinity. His previous quote from Abū Bakr al-Bāqillānī shows that "The meaning of this is that Islam is not opposed to the true teaching of the doctrine of the Holy Trinity

---

[9] Luqa, *Christianity in Islam*, p. 81.
[10] Luqa, *Christianity in Islam*, p. 82.
[11] Luqa, *Christianity in Islam*, pp. 84–85.
[12] Luqa, *Christianity in Islam*, p. 85.
[13] Luqa, *Christianity in Islam*, p. 86.
[14] Luqa, *Christianity in Islam*, p. 86.
[15] Luqa, *Christianity in Islam*, pp. 86–87.
[16] Luqa, *Christianity in Islam*, p. 88.

and Islamic scholars testify that the teaching of Christianity about the Trinity does not nullify monotheism."[17]

Thirdly, Christian monotheism is removed from associating anything with God. He quotes verses from the Qur'ān that affirm that Christians are monotheists such as Q2:62, "the Jews, Christians and Sabians who believe in God".[18] He concludes, "There is no doubt that Islam regards Christianity as a true faith in God almighty, a faith which is far from the accusation of associating something with God or adding something to him, and that it sees Christians and speaks about them as a monotheistic people."[19]

Fourthly, Islam verifies the truth of the Christian doctrine of the Trinity. Luqa refers to Q3:45, "The angels said, 'Oh Mary, God gives you good news of a word from him, named the Messiah, ʿIsa, son of Mary, honoured in this world and the next, and who is among the nearest to God,'" and 2:87, "We gave ʿIsa, son of Mary, signs and strengthened him with the holy spirit." He argues that these two texts confirm Christian teaching about the Word of God and the Holy Spirit. "They teach the Christian doctrine of the Trinity perfectly."[20]

Luqa argues that Q3:45 speaks clearly about the second member of the Trinity, the Word of God, but he admits that "Muslim commentators on the Qur'ān state that 'the word' is not from God but is from the power of the word of God".[21] This interpretation seeks to distance God Himself from the action of giving His word to Mary. Luqa points out that the text makes the giving from God Himself. "However, the text states that the word originates from God and shows that the father of the Messiah is not human."[22] This interpretation must be true, since Q2:87 speaks of God giving His Spirit to ʿIsa. If Muslim commentators accept that God gives His Spirit to ʿIsa, then they should be consistent in accepting that God gives His Word to ʿIsa as well in the same way. "The commentators claim is not true because the other text in Q2:87 states that the holy spirit is from God. Since the holy spirit is from God then the word must be from God as well. This proves that the source of the word is the essence of God".[23]

Luqa then goes on to demonstrate that the word is uncreated, "because it originates from God by means of begetting and origination from the intelligence not by means of creation or beginning in time".[24] This is confirmed by the Gospel of John 1:1-2, where the Word is God. Luqa offers a Trinitarian exposition of this affirmation. "The Word of God originates from God in conformity with his intelligence in his essence, and since the intelligence (*al-ʿaql*) and the one who thinks (*al-ʿaqil*) and the meaning of thought (*al-mʿaqul*) are one in God

---

[17] Luqa, *Christianity in Islam*, p. 93.
[18] Luqa, *Christianity in Islam*, p. 94.
[19] Luqa, *Christianity in Islam*, p. 97.
[20] Luqa, *Christianity in Islam*, p. 101.
[21] Luqa, *Christianity in Islam*, p. 101.
[22] Luqa, *Christianity in Islam*, p. 102.
[23] Luqa, *Christianity in Islam*, p. 103.
[24] Luqa, *Christianity in Islam*, p. 106.

Almighty, then the Word is God Almighty."[25] Here Luqa repeats Yaḥya Ibn ʿAdī's definition of the Trinity.

Luqa then turns to establishing that the Holy Spirit is from God Himself. He finds four meanings for "holy spirit" in the Qurʾān. Firstly, the Holy Spirit is Gabriel or one of the angels, as in Q97:4, "The angels and the spirit descend by the permission of their Lord". He notices that all the Muslim Qurʾān commentators he has read interpret the Holy Spirit in Q97:4 as Gabriel. The second meaning is found in Q15:29, where God is addressing his angels, "When I have fashioned a human and breathed into him of my spirit then prostrate yourselves before him." He notes that four commentators, "Razi, Jalalain, Kashaf and Baydawi interpret this to mean that God brings the human being to life. None of them understand Gabriel to be involved in this activity."[26] The third meaning is found in Q16:2, "He sends his angels by the spirit of his command to those servants he wishes." Luqa observes that there are many interpretations of this text. "The commentators say that the spirit here is inspiration, or the Qurʾān, or the book, or prophecy, or faith, or victory over enemies, or light, but mostly they say, inspiration."[27] The fourth meaning is found in Q2:87, "We gave ʿIsa, the son of Mary, clear signs, and strengthened him with the holy spirit." Luqa again notices a variety of interpretations. "The commentators state that the spirit here is Gabriel, or the spirit of ʿIsa who is free from Satan, or his being honoured by God, or the gospel, or the name given to ʿIsa when he gave life to the dead."[28] He concludes that the desire of Muslim commentators to avoid connecting the Spirit with God Himself does not do justice to what the Qurʾān actually says. "The commentators have erred when they have made the spirit originate from the hidden spiritual power and not from the essence of God … It is certain that the Spirit is from God, or he is the Spirit of God, and like his Word, he is God."[29]

Luqa quotes several texts from the New Testament to show that the Spirit is God and concludes, "The Qurʾān speaks of the secret of the Holy Trinity just as orthodox Christianity speaks of the Trinity. The Qurʾān describes God, and his Word, and his Spirit and these are the divine hypostases, one essence and substance."[30] Thus, a positive doctrine of the Triune God emerges from a proper reading of the Qurʾān. Luqa alleges that Muslim commentators have sought ways to avoid the plain meaning of the text because they have failed to understand what orthodox Christians have taught about the one essence of God in three hypostases.

Albert Walters (Late Twentieth Century)

Albert Walters is an Anglican theologian who was teaching theology at Seminari Theoloji in Malaysia when he published *We Believe in One God? Reflections on*

---

[25] Luqa, *Christianity in Islam*, p. 107.
[26] Luqa, *Christianity in Islam*, p. 110.
[27] Luqa, *Christianity in Islam*, p. 110.
[28] Luqa, *Christianity in Islam*, p. 112.
[29] Luqa, *Christianity in Islam*, p. 112.
[30] Luqa, *Christianity in Islam*, p. 115.

the Trinity in the Malaysian Context in 2002. This was based on his PhD, gained from the University of Birmingham, UK, for which he issued questionnaires to members of Methodist, Lutheran and Anglican churches in Kuala Lumpur. His seminary trained leaders for these three denominations. At that time 60% of Malays were Muslims and 9% were Christians. Walters conducted field research in 1997–1998 to discover "how ordinary lay Christians understood the Trinity using local languages and thought-forms, and how they continued to affirm their faith and live a life of witness embodying the truth and qualities of the Trinity".[31]

The context for the various Christian denominations in Malaysia was the constitution that states that there can be "no propagation of any religious doctrine or belief among persons professing the religion of Islam".[32] Added to this restriction came a further prohibition in 1981, when "The use and distribution of *Alkitab*, the Malay language Bible was banned, as was all non-Muslim religious teaching in schools, even Christian government-aided ones".[33]

> As a result of representation made by the Council of Churches of Malaysia, in a subsequent executive order dated 22 March, 1982, the ban was amended. This meant that except for Christians' personal and liturgical use, no one else is allowed to possess the Malay language Bible … The restriction placed on the use of the Malay Bible was accompanied by other legal restrictions on the use of certain Malay/Arabic words and religious terms because these are deemed to belong to the private reserve of the Islamic faith. The Ministry of Home Affairs had earlier prohibited a total of sixteen words, but this was later reduced to four. They are *Allah*, *Baitullah*, *Solat* and *Ka'abah*.[34]

Walters decided to survey members of three Christian denominations to discover how they were relating to Muslims in the light of the restrictions imposed on them by the Malay government. He knew that "There has been very little dialogue with Muslims and the churches seem to be working only among non-Muslims in Malaysia".[35] But he was concerned that Christians were not able to develop healthy relationships with Muslims because of the limitations in which they lived. His motivation to conduct the research was the need to encourage empathy for Muslims among Christians. "What is needed is mutual respect of one another's beliefs and points of view. There must be frankness, sincerity and above all empathy in understanding other people's religious values and to work together in the building up of each other's faith in a multi-religious society."[36] Therefore, he decided to examine how Christians spoke about their faith in the Trinity to Muslims. How did they find ways of contextualising their belief in the Trinity? "The main focus would be to study the need for contextualisation of the doctrine of the Trinity in the light of Christian relations with people of other faiths."[37]

---

[31] Albert S. Walters, *We Believe in One God? Reflections on the Trinity in the Malaysian Context* (ISPCK: Delhi, 2002), p. 118.
[32] Walters, *We Believe in One God?* p. 28.
[33] Walters, *We Believe in One God?* p. 76.
[34] Walters, *We Believe in One God?* pp. 76–77.
[35] Walters, *We Believe in One God?* p. 80.
[36] Walters, *We Believe in One God?* p. 85.
[37] Walters, *We Believe in One God?* p. 86.

He surveys the official teaching concerning the Trinity in the Anglican, Methodist and Lutheran churches in Malaysia. He concludes,

> We cannot fail to notice from the official position of the churches is that the church has been transported without being transplanted into the Malaysian soil. Its beliefs and practices do not convey attempts at "contextualising" the Christian faith in the local milieu. Perhaps the churches represented in this study have become comfortable and complacent with inherited statements of belief and the various Western church teachings. But this could prove detrimental to Christians when considering the religiously pluralistic context in Malaysia and especially in Christian–Muslim relations. For example, in the Lutheran *Book of Concord*, Mohammedanism is thought to be an anti-Trinitarian heresy, and the Creeds distinguish and separate Christians from others and even if they believe in the one true God they are damned forever.[38]

Walters was seeking for a more nuanced approach to professing the faith in a Muslim context, since he was concerned that the leaders of the churches were not making an effort to pursue such a contextualised approach. The results of his survey of church members showed, "Though the Trinity is of cardinal importance to Christians living in Malaysia, it is not something that could be easily explained".[39] Their belief in the Trinity was basically expressed through their experience. "Their experience was one in which all three 'Persons' played a vital part: they worshipped the one living God, they have been brought into the community by Jesus the Messiah, and they have served God in daily life by the constant help of the Spirit."[40] The majority of church members surveyed thought that "The doctrine of the Trinity is a divinely revealed truth, and that this truth is a mystery which we must believe but cannot hope to understand".[41] When they did try to articulate the Trinity to Muslims, they tended to use analogies of threeness in oneness, such as three forms of water, to support the idea that God can be three in one.

> People have made up their own picture/analogy/illustration of what Trinity means to them in an Islamic context. Thus the analogy of water found in three different forms to depict the Trinitarian idea. The evidence from the responses does not explicitly support the need to re-express the Trinity but Trinitarian thought has definitely been affected by the Malaysian context. Many of the research subjects indicated that the Trinitarian idea could be articulated using more meaningful, familiar and simpler words.[42]

Walters develops his own suggestions in the light of his research. He refers to the use of water as an analogy for the Trinity.

> Water which exists in three forms could be employed in order to demonstrate the unity and communion of the Trinity to a Muslim. And so, for Malaysian Christians

---

[38] Walters, *We Believe in One God?* p. 116.
[39] Walters, *We Believe in One God?* p. 173.
[40] Walters, *We Believe in One God?* p. 173.
[41] Walters, *We Believe in One God?* p. 173.
[42] Walters, *We Believe in One God?* p. 174.

water has meanings beyond itself. A common thing like water can signify something on a much deeper level.[43]

Walters finds support for this suggestion from David Cunningham. "This analogy of water as an alternative attempt to express the point of trinitarian doctrine finds credence in David Cunningham's example of 'source', 'wellspring', and "living water'."[44]

Walters goes on to suggest the use of hospitality and friendship as a model. "The possible starting point for a reconstruction of a Trinitarian theology for the Malaysian context is to view the image of Jesus as Friend."[45] But the drawback of friendship is that only a few Christians in the survey admitted that they had Muslim friends. "While some Christians and Muslims attempt to become more acquainted with each other's faith, efforts to build personal bridges of friendship within the two communities are few. In the absence of such friendliness, genuine and respectful dialogue is something which can hardly take place."[46] Walters sees friendship as the key to the Trinity.

As Christians, they extend friendship because Jesus has set the example by calling them his friends. The 'Trinity from below' model links Christians with their friend and companion, Jesus. And Jesus, by fully identifying himself with his fellow human beings in and through his humanity, ascends to his divinity, his Godliness.[47]

If Jesus identified with other human beings so as to call them his friends, then his relationship with his Father must be based on friendship, argues Walters. "For God to be understood as being friendly and hospitable, implies that there must exist such a relationship within the Godhead."[48] He appeals to the social Trinity as the most appropriate way of thinking about God. "God's self-disclosure in Jesus shows that the proper mode of being is in *loving communion*, exemplified in the love between the Father and the Son, and correlatively the love and friendliness between the three Persons of the Trinity."[49]

He refers to Colin Gunton's argument that the persons of the Trinity do not simply enter into relations with one another but are constituted by one another in the relations.

Father, Son and Spirit are eternally what they are by virtue of what they are from and to one another. Being and relation can be distinguished in thought, but in no way separated ontologically; they are rather part of one ontological dynamic. The crucial biblical and biblically derived concept is *koinonia* or communion. God

---

[43] Walters, *We Believe in One God?* p. 264.
[44] Walters, *We Believe in One God?* p. 264. He quotes from David Cunningham, 'Developing Alternative Trinitarian Formulas', *Anglican Theological Review*, 80 (1998), pp. 8–29.
[45] Walters, *We Believe in One God?* p. 269.
[46] Walters, *We Believe in One God?* p. 271.
[47] Walters, *We Believe in One God?* p. 272.
[48] Walters, *We Believe in One God?* p. 272.
[49] Walters, *We Believe in One God?* p. 272.

> appeared to be conceived neither as *koinonia* nor as an individual, but as a communion, a unity of persons in relation.[50]

He appeals also to Jürgen Moltmann's idea that "Trinity from below is a process of living relationships of love between friends and companions of various religious backgrounds and the three Persons of the Trinity and open to the inclusion of the world".[51]

In summary, Walters believes that,

> Such a dynamic Trinitarian concept in a religiously pluralistic Malaysia, will further strengthen the faith of the community when Christians engage with Muslims without anxiety, defensiveness or proselytism. A renewed understanding of the Trinity will move Malaysian Christians away from a tendency towards self-preoccupation to one of active social involvement in the direction of a Christian community that is more human-centred and hence more God-centred as Jesus himself was.[52]

In other words, Walters does not see much future in Christians explaining the Trinity in verbal terms using the terminology of Father, Son and Holy Spirit given in the New Testament. He believes that the Trinity can be lived out in friendship and that such hospitality towards Muslims by Christians will demonstrate the truth of the Trinity through the fruit of actions rather than by arguments or verbal testimony. How this coheres with the traditional understanding of the churches in Malaysia, Walters does not explore.

Imad Shehadeh (Twenty-First Century)

Imad Shehadeh was president of Jordan Evangelical Theological Seminary, Amman, Jordan, which he founded in 1991, when he published *God With Us and Without Us; Volumes One and Two: The Beauty and Power of Oneness in Trinity Versus Absolute Oneness* in 2020. This is a large study of the doctrine of God in which Shehadeh deliberately juxtaposes Christian Trinitarian thinking about God with Muslim unitarian thinking about God. This is certainly a brave move for a Middle Eastern, Arabic-speaking Christian working in a Muslim majority nation. But the fact that the book has been published is testimony to Jordan's much more open policy of Muslim recognition of Christian belief than many other Muslim states. After all, the Common Word initiative was sponsored by the Jordanian royal family.

Shehadeh introduces his writing as a study which "contrasts two different concepts of God, Oneness in Trinity and Absolute Oneness".[53] However, he goes on to make the disclaimer that he is not simply comparing Christianity and Islam

---

[50] Walters, *We Believe in One God?* p. 273. He quotes from Colin Gunton, *The One, the Three and the Many* (Cambridge: Cambridge University Press, 1993), pp. 214–15.

[51] Walters, *We Believe in One God?* p. 281. He quotes from Jürgen Moltmann, *The Trinity and the Kingdom of God* (London: SCM, 1981), pp. 174–76.

[52] Walters, *We Believe in One God?* p. 282.

[53] Imad N. Shehadeh, *God With Us and Without Us; Volumes One and Two: The Beauty and Power of Oneness in Trinity Versus Absolute Oneness* (Langham: Carlisle, 2020), p.1.

in his choice of the term "Absolute Oneness". He states, "The concept 'Absolute Oneness' is not confined specifically to Islam, but is the general belief of a large portion of humanity."[54] Nevertheless, he does not give any details about the large portion of humanity that holds to a belief in an Absolutely One God apart from Muslims, and his references to holders of "Absolute Oneness" throughout the book come from Muslims rather than others. For example, he says,

> The concept of Oneness in Trinity shares with absolute Oneness the belief in one necessary and sovereign creator God, without the existence of any other god or any secondary god. Again, this is the general belief of most of humanity, and is also the conclusion of philosophy.[55]

Here the philosophers must be the ancient Greeks such as Plato and Aristotle, rather than contemporary Western thinkers who embrace secularism, or the Chinese Marxists who rule the largest nation on earth, or the thinkers of the Hindu-dominated second largest nation, India, which certainly teems with a profusion of gods. Shehadeh is trying to make his dialogue concerning the Trinity a global affair without actually intending to engage with Indians, Chinese or Western humanists. In reality, he is embedded in a culture that holds passionately to a belief in God such that, in public at least, there is little room for secularism or polytheism.

Shehadeh gives his definition of Oneness in Trinity upon which he will engage in dialogue with proponents of Absolute Oneness.

> Oneness in Trinity differs from Absolute Oneness in that it goes further by believing that God revealed himself as existing in three equal but distinct persons in an unending relationship. This is the nature of God eternally, that is, from eternity past to eternity future, outside of creation, with or without its presence. In this faith, God is one in a first sense and plural in a second sense. For he is one in the sense of essence or nature, without being composed of parts. But he is also three in the sense of persons. These persons are the Father, the Son and the Holy Spirit, whereby each of them is equally God, without separation or confusion, and each is distinct from the others.[56]

Here, Shehadeh announces that he holds to a social view of the Trinity and that the social relationships between Father, Son and Holy Spirit are eternal and not merely the way that God has related to his creation. He seems to be confident that this way of believing in God will make sense to those who hold to Absolute Oneness. He does not share the reticence of earlier Arab Christian theologians who preferred to speak about properties of God rather than persons because the latter might be misunderstood by Muslims as introducing polytheism.

In chapter five, Shehadeh asks the question, is the Absolutely One God the same as the God of Oneness in Trinity? He feels the need to pose this question because there are those who argue that the two concepts are speaking of different deities. He does not quote examples, but the Common Word initiative provoked considerable debate among Christians in the West about whether Christians believed in the same God as Muslims. Miroslav Volf's positive attitude was

[54] Shehadeh, *God With Us*, p. 39.
[55] Shehadeh, *God With Us*, p. 40.
[56] Shehadeh, *God With Us*, p. 40.

opposed by others, such as Andy Bannister, a British Christian debater with Muslims, who published *Do Muslims and Christians Worship the Same God?* to argue that they do not.[57]

Shehadeh opens the chapter in an "attempt at answering the perennial question of whether the God proclaimed by the Qur᾽ān is the same as the God of Oneness in Trinity proclaimed by the Bible".[58] He quotes Q29:46, "We believe in that which has been revealed to us and revealed to you. And our God and your God is one; and we are Muslims in submission to him" and points out that Jews and Christians referred to God as Allah before the arrival of Islam in the Middle East.

> There was never an avoidance of the use of the expression "Allah" to refer to God in any of the extant Christian Arabic Bibles from their earliest appearance in history … It is safe to conclude that the expression "Allah" was used before the eighth century AD by Jews and Christians with a biblical understanding.[59]

Shehadeh then indicates that the question of whether Muslims worship the same God as Christians has to be posed in a different way. The issue is not so much the similarities as the differences. "The question whether it is possible that the God that the Qur'an proclaims is the same as the God that Oneness in Trinity proclaims may not be the right question to ask … A better question to ask is about difference."[60]

He quotes the Qur᾽ānic rejection of threeness in God and quotes the Egyptian Muslim thinker Muhammad ʿAbduh (d. 1905), "who asserted that God cannot be composed of parts because reason requires that necessity to the whole includes necessity to the parts – that is, each of the parts becomes divine as God is divine – and to him, that was unacceptable".[61] Thus, even modern Muslims with a good understanding of Christianity find the plurality embedded in the Trinity to represent the worship of three gods.

He then turns to Christians who have tried to make the Trinity align with the teaching of the Qur᾽ān. He quotes Giulio Basetti-Sani, "who argues that the Qur᾽ān does not condemn the doctrine of the Trinity but only a false tritheism of God, Jesus and Mary", but Shehadeh states, "the entire weight of Islamic tradition is against his interpretation".[62] Shehadeh is knowledgeable concerning the history of Islamic reactions to the Trinity and certainly feels that Basetti-Sani's reinterpretation of the Qur᾽ān does not go down well with Muslims.

The heart of the difference between Absolute Oneness and Oneness in Trinity for Shehadeh is, "How can the attributes of God be active eternally apart from

---

[57] See Andy Bannister, *Do Muslims and Christians Worship the Same God?* (London: IVP, 2021).

[58] Shehadeh, *God With Us*, p. 91.

[59] Shehadeh, *God With Us*, p. 95.

[60] Shehadeh, *God With us and without us*, p. 99.

[61] Shehadeh, *God With us*, p. 100. He quotes from Muhammad ʿAbduh, *Risalat al-Tawhid*, *The Theology of Unity*, Ishaq Musaʿad and Kenneth Cragg (trans), (London: George Allen and Unwin, 1966), p. 51.

[62] Shehadeh, *God With us*, p. 101. He quotes from Giulio Basetti-Sani, 'For a Dialogue Between Christians and Muslims', *Muslim World* 57 (1967), pp. 186–96 (p. 189).

the existence of creation without God existing in relationship?"[63] He gives his answer in terms of the definition of "relationship".

> The question can be explained using the example of love. If love is one of God's eternal attributes, it requires the presence of the lover and the one loved (or beloved), in addition to love itself. Simply put, how can love be active eternally without a relationship? However, if the object of God's love is outside of himself, this leads to two options. The first option is that God is in relationship with another eternal being like himself. But this is rejected because it opens the door to polytheism; for there is only one God with no partners. The second option is that God is in an eternal relationship with creation. But this is also rejected because it makes creation eternal like God, and it makes the necessary being (God) dependent on what is contingent (creation).[64]

He outlines the debate between the Muʿtazilites and the Ashʿarites in the Abbasid era, pointing out that the latter became Islamic orthodoxy by the eleventh century. He quotes the Palestinian Muslim Ismaʿīl al-Fārūqī, as a modern representative of the Ashʿarite view of "the eternality of God's attributes of action that stem, not from anything in his nature, but rather from his will to do anything he chooses".[65] Al-Fārūqī was in dialogue with Kenneth Cragg during a World Council of Churches dialogue session when he argued against Cragg's defence of God becoming incarnate in Jesus.

> The will of God is … The nature of God in so far as I can know anything about him … But God does not reveal himself to anyone. Christians talk about the revelation of God himself – by God of God – but that is the great difference … You may not have complete transcendence and self-revelation at the same time.[66]

Shehadeh sees this utter rejection of the self-revelation of God as the real difference between the Muslim and Christian concepts of God. The inability of Muslims to admit that God invests Himself in his actions towards His creation is the dividing line for Christians, who passionately believe that God was in Christ reconciling the world to Himself out of love for humanity. Shehadeh recognises that the Muslim world has never got beyond the Ashʿarites position that only the will of God is revealed and not his nature, and that it is necessary for Christians to dialogue with such a view.

> Absolute Oneness adopted the thinking of the Ashʿarites that his attributes of action spring from God's free will eternally. This resulted in the impossibility for human beings to depend on God's attributes. In contrast, Oneness in Trinity declares that the attributes of action spring, not from an unpredictable will of God, but from his revealed nature, which combines all his attributes as he is in himself. This in turn leads to the possibility of depending upon and trusting the attributes of God.[67]

Clearly, Shehadeh thinks that the Trinity is true because it upholds the revelation of God's nature as relational, and that His relationship with humanity

---

[63] Shehadeh, *God With Us*, p. 108.
[64] Shehadeh, *God With Us*, p. 108.
[65] Shehadeh, *God With Us*, p. 112.
[66] Shehadeh, *God With Us*, p. 112. He quotes from Ismaʿīl al-Fārūqī, 'On the Nature of Islamic Daʿwah', *International Review of Missions* 65 (1976), p. 405.
[67] Shehadeh, *God With Us*, p. 135.

expressed in the Incarnation is a value that Christians can present to Muslims, who he sees as trapped in a diminished concept of God. He also thinks it is essential for Christians to communicate to Muslims that the attributes of God that are demonstrated in his interaction with His creation are equivalent to His essential attributes. "Oneness in Trinity declares that the attributes of action stem from the attributes of essence. So God's temporal activity inside creation with humanity (God with us) springs from God's eternal activity outside creation in himself (God without us)."[68] He quotes with approval the view of the Catholic theologian Karl Rahner that, "The 'economic' Trinity is the 'immanent' Trinity and the 'immanent' Trinity is the 'economic' Trinity".[69] Shehadeh ends his discussion of the attributes of God with the following appeal to his Muslim readers.

> The appeal of this book to adherents of Absolute Oneness is that they begin the journey of trust in the perfection, equality and harmony of all God's attributes. This will make their faith grow so that they enter a personal relationship with God, and then become receptive to any revelation from God about his nature, no matter how difficult it is for them to change their thinking.[70]

Notice that Shehadeh hopes that the already real faith of Muslims in God will be enriched by a new perception of God's attributes such that they can begin to see God as in a personal relationship with them, a relationship of love rather than simply commanding will.

Chapter eight is entitled "Consistency of the Trinity With Logic", in which Shehadeh attempts to demonstrate that the Trinity is logically possible. He states, "The purpose of this study is not to arrive at the doctrine of the Trinity through logic, it is not to prove the doctrine of the Trinity through logic, but it is rather to demonstrate the consistency of the doctrine of the Trinity with logic."[71]

He has four affirmations. Firstly, "Logically, it is impossible for God to exist without all his attributes being eternally active".[72] The notion that some of God's attributes only exist in relation to the creation does not mean that these attributes are not already existent in Him. Secondly, "The eternal activity of his attributes presupposes a relationship between persons".[73] Shehadeh is willing to argue for personal distinctions within God, but he states that we must not predicate individuality to these divine persons as we do for human persons.

> In the case of human beings, interaction is between distinct but separate persons. However, in the case of God, interaction is between distinct persons who are not separate from one another. This is what distinguishes God, who is multi-personal, from human beings, who are unipersonal.[74]

---

[68] Shehadeh, *God With Us*, p. 143.

[69] Shehadeh, *God With Us*, p. 143. He quotes from Karl Rahner, *The Trinity* (New York: Seabury Press, 1974), p. 22.

[70] Shehadeh, *God With Us*, p. 148.

[71] Shehadeh, *God With Us*, p. 149.

[72] Shehadeh, *God With Us*, p. 150.

[73] Shehadeh, *God With Us*, p. 160.

[74] Shehadeh, *God With Us*, p. 161.

Thirdly, "The relationship is protected by Threeness of persons".[75] Shehadeh points out that in a human relationship between two people, the love they have for each other needs to go beyond, to loving others. "It is necessary for the activity exchanged between two persons to encompass shared activity with a third person. For example, the love exchanged between two extends beyond the two to become a shared love between three, thereby becoming completed love."[76] Though how such love is restricted to three persons is not explained here. Fourthly, "The Threeness of Persons is guaranteed perfection through oneness".[77] He believes that "The oneness means the absence of any deficiency in the eternal relationship … and guarantees order without subordinationism".[78]

It is in the tradition of Arab theology that Shehadeh presents his rational defence of the Trinity. But as with the tradition, it is difficult to see how the threeness can be defended as not arbitrary. How can Muslims be convinced that this appeal to reason is not just a cover for the decision already taken that there are three persons in the Godhead because Jesus and Paul thought so? If there are three persons by revelation, then no appeal to reason is necessary. Yet, of course, Muslim tradition has appealed to reason to refute the unreasonableness of the Trinity. The unity of God is much more logical than the threeness of God. Perhaps it is less surprising that a modern Middle Eastern Christian should appeal to the logic of the three persons, given that Muslims regularly appeal to logic to reject the Trinity.

Shehadeh turns to examining the attributes of God in chapters ten and eleven. Chapter ten is entitled "The Activity of the Attributes of God Without Us". He quotes the Council of Florence statement on the Trinity, "The Father is wholly in the Son and wholly in the Holy Spirit. The Son is wholly in the Father and wholly in the Holy Spirit. The Holy Spirit is wholly in the Father and wholly in the Son", as the creedal belief in the mutual indwelling of the three persons.[79] He goes on to quote Leonardo Boff, the Brazilian Catholic theologian, who writes, "Each Person contains the other two, each one penetrates the others and is penetrated by them, one live in the other and vice versa."[80] However, Shehadeh disagrees with Boff when he states,

> This understanding [*perichoresis*] excludes the monarchy of One (the substance of the Father or the unity of the divine nature) in favour of the eternal communion of a simultaneous Three who are always one in, by, with, through and for others, interpenetrating one another in love, one containing the others.[81]

Shehadeh argues that there is eternal order between the persons in submission and humility without subordinationism, "So the concept of mutual indwelling

---

[75] Shehadeh, *God With Us*, p. 163.
[76] Shehadeh, *God With Us*, p. 163.
[77] Shehadeh, *God With Us*, p. 171.
[78] Shehadeh, *God With Us*, p. 171.
[79] Shehadeh, *God With Us*, p. 251. The Council of Florence took place between 1431 and 1449.
[80] Shehadeh, *God With Us*, p. 251. He quotes from Leonardo Boff, *Trinity and Society* (Maryknoll, NY: Orbis, 1988), p. 5.
[81] Shehadeh, *God With Us*, p. 251. He quotes from Boff, *Trinity and Society*, p. 145.

does not cancel out the concept of real submission within the Trinity".[82] He explains that,

> The eternal relationship between the Father and the Son is characterized by a horizontal equally reciprocal relationship in love, knowledge, indwelling, glorifying and the association of the Holy Spirit with all the attributes active between them. The eternal relationship between the Father and the Son is also characterized by a vertical order of submission. For, in spite of the attribute of humility in each of the persons of the Trinity, the son submits to the Father in a unidirectional manner … The Father gives and the Son receives; the Father is the standard and the Son imitates; the Father shows and the Son sees; and so on.[83]

Shehadeh wants to hold on to the New Testament affirmation of the voluntary submission of the Son to the Father, which continues into the future after the Incarnation, when the Son submits to the Father in the ultimate kingdom of God.

Shehadeh finally turns to "The Activity of the Attributes of God With Us" in chapter eleven. He applies the mutual indwelling of the three persons of the Trinity to human believers. "It is astonishing that the mutual indwelling of the persons of the Trinity extends to believers. So the Father, Son and Holy Spirit dwell within believers, and believers are in the Father and the Son."[84] There is no more moving or amazing reality for us as believers, according to Shehadeh.

> The mutual indwelling of the Father and the Son without us and which is extended to believers so that it is with us expresses the deepest relationship between God and humanity and the deepest relationship between believers that begins now and continues for all eternity.[85]

It is interesting that Shehadeh talks about the attributes of God without us and with us. Whether the persons of the Trinity are the same as attributes such as love, kindness, grace and mercy is problematic. The older Arab theological discussion of the essential attributes of word and life as being represented by the Word of God incarnate and the Spirit of God outpoured is transposed by Shehadeh into a discussion of the essential attributes of fatherhood and sonship within the Godhead, and the circularity of their love expressed through the Spirit of God beyond their twofold relationship. However, the older Arab theology referred to shared assumptions between Christians and Muslims about what constituted attributes of God. There was a deliberate avoidance of fatherhood and sonship in the defence of the Trinity in order to make the Trinity comprehensible to Muslims. Shehadeh has no such anxiety about Muslim comprehension. He boldly asserts the New Testament terminology as a given reality about God without being concerned with the Muslim rejection of that very terminology.

---

[82] Shehadeh, *God With Us*, p. 251.
[83] Shehadeh, *God With Us*, p. 257.
[84] Shehadeh, *God With Us*, p. 296.
[85] Shehadeh, *God With Us*, p. 297.

7. Evaluation of Christian Presentations of the Trinity in the Modern Era in the Light of Muslim Responses

The Missionary Presentations in the Light of Muslim Responses

The impact of Western missionary engagement with Muslims can be seen in the reactions to the apologetic writing produced by missionaries. For example, Pfander's detailed work relating Christian teaching to Muslim beliefs eventually induced Indian Muslims to publish their own assessment of Christianity. Pfander was challenged to a public debate by the Sunni Muslim scholar Rahmatullah al-Kairanawi, which took place in Agra in 1854. Clearly, Rahmatullah organised the topics for debate on the basis of Pfander's *The Balance of Truth*, since the plan was to deal with the status of the Bible, the Trinity, the prophethood of Muḥammad and the status of the Qur'ān. However, the actual debate did not get beyond the first topic.[1] Nevertheless, Rahmatullah went on to write his own refutation of Pfander's writing in his *Izhar-ul-Haq*, published in Urdu in 1864 and in Arabic in 1867. In this work, he dealt with the Trinity by meticulously pointing out that the four gospels do not actually teach the doctrine, which therefore was not advocated by Jesus himself but by Paul in his letters. He had the advantage of consulting *The Life of Christ* by the radical German scholar David Strauss, published in English in 1846, through which he was able to present Jesus as advocating belief in the oneness of God in a way that was not merely the prejudice of Muslim criticism of the gospels but the most up-to-date scholarly approach by a Protestant theologian from Pfander's own Germany.[2] Part of the difficulty for Christians such as Pfander was the advance in Europe of more critical opinions concerning the gospels, summed up in Strauss's point of view that the early church overlaid the original orthodox Jewish teaching of Jesus of the oneness of God with their own assessment of his divine status within a Trinity of Father, Son and Holy Spirit, and that these early church enthusiasts put the confession of the Father, Son and Holy Spirit onto the lips of the unitarian Jesus in Matthew 28:19. Missionaries such as Pfander were ill-equipped to cope with this Muslim use of European Christian scholarship, since they mainly emerged from conservative Christian institutions that did not encourage their students to read radical critiques of the Bible.

---

[1] See Christine Schirrmacher, 'The Agra Debates of 1854', *The Bulletin of the Henry Martyn Institute of Islamic Studies* 13 (1994), pp. 74–84.

[2] See Avril Powell, *Muslims & Missionaries in Pre-Mutiny India* (Richmond: Curzon Press, 1993), pp. 248–55.

In his assessment of *Izhar-ul-Haq*, Clinton Bennett accepts that this Muslim critique of the gospels may have some ongoing validity. "Al-Kairanawi may be right to argue that the Trinity cannot be explicitly found in the Gospels."[3] However, Bennett argues, Christian belief in the Trinity is not incompatible with the message of the gospels.

> The early Christians were Jews, for whom any compromise with monotheism was unthinkable: yet God's Spirit and God's wisdom, and notions of God's Word, were already available to them. Trinity as a rigid dogma may well be incompatible with the biblical record, Trinity as the expression of what Christians experienced to be spiritually true may be biblically sound. It seemed to the first Christians that Jesus had enjoyed such an intimate relationship with God that the divine–human distinction became blurred. It also seemed that the Spirit that came upon them at Pentecost linked them powerfully to both God and Jesus, so that, although Jesus no longer walked with them on earth in physical form, he was with them in spirit. This experience resulted in the Trinity. Al-Kairanawi was not interested in understanding the experiential process that resulted in the formulation of Trinitarian theology, only in refuting it as non-biblical.[4]

Another Indian Muslim to refute the Trinity from a reading of the gospels was Sayyid Ahmad Khan (1817–1898). He published a commentary on the Gospel of Matthew in Urdu in 1865 which follows the same line of argument as Rahmatullah al-Kairanawi. For example, as Lloyd Ridgeon points out,

> Khan appealed to Matthew 4:10 to deny that Jesus saw himself as God. In Matthew 4:10 Jesus rejects the temptations offered by Satan and proclaims: 'You shall worship the Lord your God and only Him shall you serve.' Khan states that if Jesus were God, Satan's efforts to tempt him would be pointless. The temptation only makes sense if Jesus is a man or prophet.[5]

Khan believed that the doctrine of the Trinity evolved from a much later period in the history of the church, reflecting the fact that the word "trinity" was only used by Christians from the early third century. The disciples of Jesus could not possibly have misinterpreted their master so readily. The distortion of the original teaching of Jesus led to the need for "the pure revelation" that Muhammad brought.[6]

Ridgeon demonstrates that this nineteenth-century heritage of Muslim appeal to the gospels to refute the Trinity has continued in more recent times. Sayyid Abul Aʿla Mawdudi (1906–1979) referred to the Trinity in his commentary on the Qurʾān, commenced in 1942 and finished in 1973. Mawdudi had founded the Islamic Party (*Jamaʿat-I Islami*) to encourage the creation of a purely Islamic state within India and represents a twentieth-century approach to Christianity among Indian Muslims. He too appeals to Jesus' confrontation with Satan in Matthew 4:10. Mawdudi, like Ahmad Khan, declares, "The essence of *tawhid* is

---

[3] Clinton Bennett, *Understanding Christian–Muslim Relations* (New York: Continuum, 2008), p. 137.
[4] Bennett, *Understanding Christian–Muslim Relations*, p. 137.
[5] Lloyd VJ Ridgeon, *Crescents on the Cross* (Oxford: Oxford University Press, 2001), p. 9.
[6] Ridgeon, *Crescents on the Cross*, p. 9.

found in Jesus' advice in Matthew 4:10, 'You shall worship the Lord your God and Him only shall you serve'".[7]

Ridgeon gives another example of Mawdudi's manner of rejecting the Trinity.

> One reason explaining the appearance of that "insoluble riddle" which is the Trinity [Maududi, 1.117], is the confusion over the miraculous conception of Jesus. Mawdudi states that both the Qur'ān and the Authorized Version of the Bible confirm that Jesus was created of a spirit "from" God. This is in contrast to the "orthodox" Christian understanding which speaks of the spirit "of" God and thus deifies Jesus [2.116-117]. Mawdudi adds that the conception of John the Baptist was also miraculous. Jesus' birth was no more miraculous than John's and there are no grounds for referring to John as God's son [5.157]. He drives this point further by stating that if Jesus is considered such a holy figure because he had no human father, then how should Adam be regarded since he had neither a father nor a mother [1.260].[8]

Here Mawdudi refers to the gospel and the Qur'ānic parallels between the miraculous births of John the Baptist and Jesus to refute the divinity of the latter because the former was not divine, and adds that the Qur'ān makes the case that Jesus' miraculous conception without a human father is no greater than Adam's conception without either father or mother, and Christians do not consider Adam to be divine as a result. Mawdudi expounds the Qur'ānic conviction that Christians have made a grave error in attributing worship to Jesus partly because they think that his miraculous conception entitled him to the rank of divinity.

Pfander's appeal to the New Testament to establish the Trinity created a reaction among Indian Muslims that continued to have an impact for generations to come. For these Muslims, if the Jesus of the gospels could be shown to teach the unity of God, then the Trinitarian aspects of the gospels could be attributed to Christians who misunderstood their founder. And if there were scholarly Christians who basically read the gospels the way Muslims did, then the Muslim case was immensely strengthened. Christian missionaries would continue to present the Trinity as Jesus' own conviction, but the ability to relate the Trinity to Christian scholarly concerns would wait until someone was able to relate mission to scholarship. That person would be Kenneth Cragg.

Cragg was trained in a conservative Church of England environment but came to think, through mission to Muslims, from a broader perspective. Christians and Muslims alike should take note of scholarly issues to reinterpret their traditions for the modern world. There is little to be gained by simply living in the past, argues Cragg. Not for him just to sit within a Christian creedal confession formed centuries before. Rather, Christians must re-examine their ancient foundations and contextualise them for contemporary life. Muslims too, should not hide behind venerable points of view established in a bygone era. Faith is a lived experience, and any previously formed convictions should have a dynamism that empowers Muslims and Christians for life today.

---

[7] Ridgeon, *Crescents on the Cross*, p. 17. Ridgeon quotes from Mawdudi, *Towards Understanding the Qur'an, vol. 1*, Zafar Ishaq Ansari (trans.), (Leicester: The Islamic Foundation, 1988–1989), p. 255.

[8] Ridgeon, *Crescents on the Cross*, pp. 17–18.

An example of his challenge to Christians comes in his reluctance to get into discussion about the eternal nature of God in Trinity. He is happy to note how early Christians came to worship God in Trinity, but he is not willing to get engaged in a discussion of how the essence of God is in three hypostases in the language of the creeds. When Cragg points out for his Christian readers that Muslims are preoccupied with the mathematics of God, he does not give them much help in relating to Muslim anxiety about that mathematical oneness they so earnestly believe in.

An example of his challenge to Muslims comes in his dialogue with the Palestinian Muslim Isma'īl al-Fārūqī, in 1976, at a World Council of Churches sponsored dialogue. Cragg challenged al-Fārūqī to accept that God must be seen to relate to human beings more than simply by issuing commands. Cragg asked, "Is there the possibility of a relationship more tragic, more compassionate? It is possible you can be found forbidding things to God in the interest of what you trust is His dignity?"[9] Al-Fārūqī replied by denying that he was forbidding God at all. Cragg went on, "You are forbidding God the sovereign freedom of manifesting His transcendence in whatever way He chooses – which may be to condescend to man's condition in terms of incarnation."[10] Al-Fārūqī responded by referring to the Qur'ānic text, "There is nothing like unto God", and stated "It is we who must beware of what is appropriate when talking about God and about transcendence."[11] For Cragg, the Trinity is the logical outcome of the Incarnation, and once the Incarnation is accepted then the mathematical oneness of God is invested with a form of plurality. However, Cragg does not develop this argument about plurality to any extent. He probably believed that, just as the early Christians came to believe in the Trinity of Father, Son and Holy Spirit, so Muslims can come to believe in a threefold God.

An effort to demonstrate how the early Christians came to believe in a Triune God is offered by David Brown who, like Cragg, came from the Evangelical wing of the Church of England. His careful presentation of the New Testament witness is designed to relate to Muslim perceptions. Unlike, Cragg, Brown is willing to go beyond the apostolic period in showing how the creeds summed up that testimony. He is much more ready to explain the one nature in three hypostases of the Godhead. While he agrees with Cragg's appeal to the experience of the Apostles, he shows that the church had to develop teaching about the Trinity to defend the original testimony. Unlike Cragg, he devotes special attention to analogies for plurality in God from the way the world works. The Trinity is likened to a family that exists in mutual love. A complete family is more than the love that a married man has for his wife, since children are included in that love. So, the love of the Father for the Son includes His love for the Spirit. And just as a family includes the responsive love of a wife and children to the father, so the Godhead includes the responsive love of the Son and the Spirit for the Father.

---

[9] Kenneth Cragg responding to Isma'īl al-Fārūqī, 'On the Nature of Islamic Da'wah', *International Review of Mission* 65 (1976), pp. 391–409 (p. 408).
[10] Cragg to al-Faruqi, p. 408.
[11] Al-Fārūqī to Cragg, p. 408.

Brown's embrace of the social model of the Trinity goes way beyond anything that Cragg felt he wanted to say about God. Cragg was in the Western tradition of thinking about God revealing Himself in different ways, but Brown was content to speak of the Father, Son and Holy Spirit as distinct centres of consciousness, even in a book designed for Muslim readers. Clearly, Brown felt no real difficulty in confessing his faith in the three divine persons to Muslims. He seems to have thought that Muslims could come to recognise the truth of the three persons once they were presented with an argument for this. He even goes so far as to challenge his Muslim readers to see that a solitary God is less inviting than a social God.

It might be thought that Brown's long-standing relationship to Muslims in the Middle East that undergirds his presentation of the Trinity would encourage him to play down the use of analogies from the created world that Muslims find unacceptable, but Brown was sure that the right analogy had inner power to convince. Was Brown influenced by Middle Eastern Arab Christians who tended to hold to a social view of the Trinity? Cragg too lived in the Middle East but evidently did not embrace such teaching. In any case there were English Anglicans who had proposed the social model of the Trinity, so Brown did not need to rely solely on Arab theology for his view.[12] What this comparison between two missionary theologians from the Evangelical wing of the Church of England shows is that there can be considerable diversity emerging from any one particular stream of Christianity, and that the approach to Muslims can be quite different from one person to another from the same church background.

Giulio Basetti-Sani represents a very different missionary approach to Muslims from the three Protestant missionaries studied so far. In his earlier career he certainly would have been aligned much more clearly with them, but his transformed attitude to Islam and the teaching of the Qurʾān marks him out as someone who sought to align the Qurʾān with Christian teaching. Since, in his opinion, the Qurʾān disagrees with the trinity of God, Jesus and Mary, then all that remains for the Christian missionary is to point out to Muslims that Christians agree with the Qurʾān. Once Muslims have heard this carefully explained, they may come to see that the Christian Trinity fits with the revelation given in the Qurʾān.

He says that Louis Massignon influenced him to read the Qurʾān this way and to seek to converse with Muslims along the line of sharing the faith of Abraham. It is interesting that he does not mention Ibrahim Luqa's 1938 presentation of Christianity in Islam, even though he was in Egypt when the book was available. Luqa's argument that the Qurʾān does not attack the orthodox doctrine of the Trinity is precisely what Massignon and Basetti-Sani were proposing.

Muslims have tended to react against the Christian doctrine of the Trinity in terms of their deep desire to uphold the unity of God and castigate Christians for allowing plurality to enter into God's nature. Seldom have they thought much about the way the Qurʾān sees the Trinity that Christians believe in as including Mary. One recent example of a Muslim who accepts that the Trinity criticised by

---

[12] See Walter R. Matthews, *God in Christian Experience* (London: Nisbet, 1930) and Leonard Hodgson, *The Doctrine of the Trinity* (London: Nisbet, 1943).

the Qur᾽ān is not what Christians actually believe is the South African Muslim scholar Farid Esack, who argues,

> The Qur᾽an naturally dealt only with the behaviour and beliefs of those of the People of the Book with whom the early Muslim community were in actual social contact. To employ the qur'anic category of People of the Book in a generalized manner of simplistic identification of all Jews and Christians in contemporary society is to avoid the historical realities of Medinan society, as well as the theological diversity among both earlier and contemporary Christians and Jews … I do not wish to suggest that there are no Christians who believe in the concept of a triune deity. Justice, however, requires that no one be held captive to categories which applied to a community or individuals fourteen centuries ago, merely because they share a common descriptive term, a term that may even have been imposed on them by Muslims and rejected by them.[13]

Esack has heard Christians categorically deny that they believe in the kind of Trinity mentioned in the Qur᾽ān. "The qur'anic accusation of *shirk* against the Christians because of their alleged worshipping of three deities (4:171-3; 5:72-73) is a case in point; most Christians insist that the doctrine of the Trinity is not the same as Tritheism, the worship of three gods."[14]

There might be some value in Christians pointing out their agreement with the Qur᾽ān when the Trinity is being criticised there. However, the basic issue of plurality in God is still at the back of the actual critique of threeness found in the Qur᾽ān. As we have seen in the earlier Muslim opposition of the Christian doctrine of the Trinity, the issue is the dilution of the oneness of God to which the Qur᾽ān testifies. Basetti-Sani does not really deal with this utter concentration on oneness within the Qur᾽ān and therefore must be found guilty of misrepresenting the deepest convictions of the Muslim scriptures in his dialogue with Muslims. He was a Catholic missionary in Egypt but did not attempt to dialogue along with Middle Eastern Christians in their engagement with Muslims. The Jordanian Evangelical Imad Shehadeh has distanced himself from Basetti-Sani's interpretation of the Qur᾽ān, since Muslim commentators on the Qur᾽ān have not followed that way of reading the texts denouncing the Trinity that Basetti-Sani has proposed. Shehadeh argues that, "the entire weight of Islamic tradition is against his interpretation".[15] This is something of an exaggeration, as we have seen in Esack's comments, but Shehadeh is reflecting the history of Muslim criticism of the Trinity that bears down on Middle Eastern Christians. After all, Esack is a South African Muslim who has been quite liberal in his interpretation of the Qur᾽ān, unlike Arab Muslims, who have tended to repeat conservative interpretations given centuries before.

The final representative missionary to have presented the Trinity to Muslims is David Shenk, the American Mennonite. What is distinctive about his method is to have juxtaposed his own presentation with a Muslim response in the same piece of writing. While the actual dialogue between Shenk and Kateregga is limited, there is enough in the response of the latter to suggest how Muslims

---

[13] Farid Esack, *Qur᾽an Liberation & Pluralism: An Islamic Perspective of Interreligious Solidarity Against Oppression*, (Oxford: Oneworld, 1997), pp. 152–53.

[14] Esack, *Qur᾽an Liberation & Pluralism*, p. 177.

[15] Shehadeh, *God With Us*, p. 101.

respond to the Trinity in the late twentieth century. Shenk prefers the traditional Western view of the Trinity as the self-revelation of God and relies on Augustine's approach of the Spirit being the love bond between the Father and the Son. His analogy for the Trinity is based on the psychology of the human person, as Augustine preferred. In other words, Shenk does not present a social theory of the Trinitarian persons who are distinct centres of consciousness. The personality of the Spirit is subsumed under the two personalities of Father and Son, as their common Spirit. Mennonites are well known for their adherence to the New Testament as the foundation of their theology, but the willingness of Shenk to play down the personal nature of the Spirit, as presented by Paul in his letters, reflects the fact that the Mennonite tradition depends on the teaching of Jesus in the Synoptic Gospels as central to the Christian faith. Mennonite pacifism and the rejection of oath taking are examples of this rigorous concern to reflect that teaching.

Kateregga responds to Shenk's presentation of the fatherhood of God as taught by Jesus through the Qurʾānic rejection of anthropomorphic language for the Creator. His response to the sonship of Jesus is through the Qurʾānic rejection of the possibility of God needing a son. There is no discussion of the Holy Spirit by Kateregga, since Shenk does not present the Spirit in personal terms and therefore, Kateregga probably did not see any serious distinction between the Qurʾānic language about the Holy Spirit and that which Shenk was proposing. Kateregga represents his fellow Muslims well in indicating that the terminology of the Trinity is fundamentally wrong.

What this publication demonstrates is that a genuine debate between Christians and Muslims on the Trinity will pit the teaching of the New Testament against that of the Qurʾān. Shenk does not attempt to interpret the Qurʾān and Kateregga does not try to interpret the New Testament. In that respect, they merely present their own scriptural inheritance without engaging with that of the other. Shenk seemed content to follow this procedure in order to conduct a peaceful discussion in which he was able to witness to his own faith without criticising the faith of Kateregga. How unlike the World Council of Churches discussion in which Cragg tried to get al-Fārūqī to admit that he had not interpreted the Qurʾān accurately by dismissing the possibility of the Incarnation!

The Western Theological Presentations in the Light of Muslim Responses

Keith Ward is the first example of a theologian in the West attempting to engage in dialogue with Muslims within the construction of his own theology. He had published a good deal of theological reflection before turning to producing a comparative theology in the 1990s. Ward was a noted philosophical theologian who dialogued with secular thinking, but his turn to dialoguing with the perceptions of people of other faiths as distinct from people of no faith came in his mature years, when he held a chair at Oxford University. He came to the conviction that appealing to the revelation of God as the basis for truth came up against the parallel convictions of vast populations of humanity that they possessed revelation from God, and yet that these alternative revelations contradicted one another. In the first volume of his five-part systematic theology, he put forward his methodology. "I am inclined to say that one cannot properly understand the mode of divine revelation within Christianity unless one can set it in the context of human religious activity in general, for only in its widest context can one discern the true meaning of such revelation."[16]

When he turns to Muslims in his tour of significant religious communities and examines the Qurʾān, Ward finds that the accusations made about the Trinity do not accurately reflect orthodox Christian teaching. Such Christians would not say that God is Christ or that Mary is worshipped alongside Christ, as the Qurʾān alleges. Ward's explanation for this anomaly is that Muḥammad regarded Christians as confused rather than blasphemous. Certainly, the tenor of the Qurʾānic criticisms of Christians is to get them to re-examine their beliefs until they come into conformity with the true revelation brought by Muḥammad. Ward is probably right to see the situation this way. The Qurʾān does call Christians, "People of the Book" who had in their possession the gospel of Jesus that God had sent in a previous era. Muḥammad is called by God to address Christians to submit to the necessary corrections that he sent his prophet to announce to the Christian communities of Arabia.

In this light, Ward acknowledges that presenting the Trinity to Muslims is fraught with difficulty. The Qurʾān is preoccupied with the oneness of God and forbids polytheism. The Christian response to the accusation of polytheism is, "The Christian God is not *in* a Trinity; rather, God is a Divine Triad in himself."[17] But the task of making this clear to Muslims is rather exacting, given their intense safeguarding of the unity of God. Christians must show Muslims that Jesus taught and lived out the truth that God is love in his essential nature, and that he manifested the Divine Word in such a way that he united human and divine nature in order to reconcile humans to God, and to raise humans "to participate in the Divine Life by the persuasive power of love".[18]

Ward did not engage with Muslim theologians in this dialogue with the Qurʾān, but in the second volume of his systematic theology he debates with one twentieth-century Muslim intellectual, Muhammad Iqbal. Ward sees parallels between Iqbal's understanding of the relationship of God to His creation and the Christian conception of the Trinity. He believes that there can be dialogue on these grounds for Christians who can make connections with such a Muslim perspective. Iqbal sees God as the infinite, self-unfolding source of all things, so Christians can present their belief that God is the ineffable source of all things. Iqbal's belief that God is the self of the universe in which everything is united is an opportunity for Christians to state that the Logos, as the Son of God, is the wisdom of God who unites and completes everything. Iqbal's view that God co-operates with humans to guide them to the fulness of life can be the basis for a Christian witness to God as Spirit guiding humans to that fulness of life.[19]

---

[16] Ward, *Religion and Revelation*, p. 37.
[17] Ward, *Religion and Revelation*, p. 188.
[18] Ward, *Religion and Revelation*, p. 189.
[19] Ward, *Religion and Creation*, p. 67.

If Iqbal were to have responded to Ward's dialogue with him, he might simply have said that his own presentation of the action of God in creation is far more cohesive than Ward's Trinitarian perspective. The same subject is at work in each case, but with Ward's construction, there is some doubt as to whether the Logos is equivalent to God. Iqbal may have said that Ward has to introduce the Son and the Spirit as variant partners with God the Creator in order to sustain the Trinity. Ward might have replied to Iqbal that he does not regard the Son and the Spirit as "partners" with the Creator, but as modes of the being of God Himself, who reveals Himself in these discrete ways. This latter definition of the Trinity coheres with Ward's preference for understanding the Trinity as the self-revelation of God in three modes of being, rather than understanding the Trinity as the eternal *perichoresis* of three divine centres of consciousness who reveal themselves within the creation. Towards the end of *Religion and Creation*, Ward sums up his developed view of the Trinity as "a Triad of the depth of being, the power of being, and the manifestation of being".[20] He goes on to state that, "These are not three distinct subjects of awareness, but three forms of the being of God, in each of which its whole being is expressed in a different manner".[21]

In his 2015 work, *Christ and the Cosmos*, Ward argues that the social Trinity is counterproductive for Christians who dialogue with Muslims, who see the one God with multiple attributes. "The idea of God as a sort of society is a bad idea. It is repugnant to Jews, Muslims, and many monotheists (including me)."[22] This means that Christians ought to think of God in a similar way to Muslims. "It is the same God who thinks, feels, and wills. There are not, after all, different beings who do these things."[23] Ward admits that the Christian conception of God must involve some sort of complexity within him. The Christian sense of the threefoldness of God, as He has revealed Himself as Father, Son and Holy Spirit, points to a threefoldness in the nature of God, which is not identical to the Father, Son and Holy Spirit but is enshrined in the patterns of relationship between them. There is a "threefoldness of subjectivity, creativity, and unitive love which is not strictly identical with the Trinity as it is expressed in the human world".[24] Just how humans can come to understand that threefoldness is beyond their grasp. While they can appreciate the revelation of Father, Son and Holy Spirit, humans cannot go beyond to enter into the nature of this threefold revelation. What appears to them as three individuals who relate to each other is much more likely to be "a deeper 'immanent' threefoldness of primal origin, expressed thought, and beatific love. It is not a society of three distinct individuals."[25]

Why does Ward want to hold on to the Trinity of Father, Son and Holy Spirit if ultimately God's threefold nature cannot be reduced to these scriptural notions? He finally accepts that the New Testament way of speaking about God

---

[20] Ward, *Religion and Creation*, p. 336.

[21] Ward, *Religion and Creation*, p. 336.

[22] Ward, *Christ and the Cosmos* (Cambridge: Cambridge University Press, 2015), preface, pp. x–xi.

[23] Ward, *Christ and the Cosmos*, p. 13.

[24] Ward, *Christ and the Cosmos*, p. 256.

[25] Ward, *Christ and the Cosmos*, p. 256.

is valuable, even if not conclusive. On the one hand, there are other ways of knowing God apart from being Father, Son and Holy Spirit, as Jews and Muslims testify. On the other hand, the way of knowing God as Father, Son and Holy Spirit is "a way uniquely fitted to enable human beings to find fulfilment in God".[26] In the final analysis, Ward prefers his Christian inheritance over the rigid monotheism of Jews and Muslims but works as hard as he can not to alienate them in his exposition of his Christian preferences.

In his reflections on Ward's *Religion and Revelation*, the Turkish Muslim scholar Mahmut Aydin recognises that Ward comes to the teaching of the Qurʾān from the perspective of a pluralistic theology of religions in which what people hold as sacred is a form of the revelation of God to them. Thus, Muslims receive that revelation within the Qurʾān while Christians receive that revelation within the New Testament. Any discrepancies between the scriptures are a product of different times and situations in which human beings have lived and the willingness of God to accommodate these differences. Aydin thinks this pluralistic approach is valuable since it provides a way of accepting that different scriptures are forms of the revelation of God. "Although his perception of the Qurʾān differs from orthodox, even modernist, Muslim understanding, in our opinion this should be regarded as a significant step forward towards a more positive appreciation of the Qurʾān by Christians."[27]

Hans Küng is much more critical of the Qurʾān than Keith Ward when he states, "The Qurʾān does not show the slightest comprehension of Christian dogma (the Trinity and the divinity of Jesus)."[28] He regards Muḥammad as changing from a positive view of Christians once they engaged in warfare against him. The implication is that the Prophet of Islam made no real attempt to understand Christian teaching concerning the Trinity even when he held the more positive view of Christians. Ward thinks that the Qurʾān presents a confused view of the Trinity but does not charge Muḥammad with deliberate obtuseness. Ward argues that the revelation of God found in the Qurʾān accommodates the perceptions of the people to whom it was given. In other words, Küng thinks that the Qurʾān obstructs the revelation of the Triune God, whereas Ward thinks that God has not revealed Himself in a Trinitarian form to those who received the Qurʾān.

Küng is aware of the history of Christian–Muslim relations and understands the painful task of Christians under Islamic rule to maintain that their belief in the Trinity did not contradict monotheism. However, he does not present any of the arguments of the Christian apologists who were engaged in defending monotheism within trinitarianism. The reason for this neglect is Küng's rejection of the Greek theological terminology enshrined in the creeds that those Christian Arab theologians were determined to defend. From Küng's point of view, none of these earlier theologians can be commended for their valiant efforts, since the

---

[26] Ward, *Christ and the Cosmos*, p. 261.
[27] Mahmut Aydin, *Modern Western Christian Theological Understandings of Muslims Since the Second Vatican Council* (Washington, DC: The Council for Research in Values and Philosophy, 2002), p. 163.
[28] Küng, *Islam*, p. 115.

presuppositions on which they built their arguments were faulty. His call for the ecumenical churches to leave behind the Greek language of the creeds and return to the language of the New Testament reflects the similar plea of Kenneth Cragg, who does not think there is any value in using the terminology of God as one *ousia* in three *hypostases* in dialogue with Muslims.

So, a return to New Testament terminology is essential, according to Küng. How does that help to explain the Trinity to Muslims? He takes the view that God has revealed Himself in various ways as Father, Son and Holy Spirit. His concentration on the oneness of God in parallel with Jews and Muslims means that, like Ward, he reads the New Testament as the self-revelation of the one God through Jesus Christ and the Holy Spirit. Like Ward, also he does not warm to the social portrait of the Trinity. When we encounter Jesus or the Spirit in the gospels and the apostolic letters, we encounter God at work in different forms to make Himself known among human beings. There is no presentation in the New Testament of some eternal relationship between Father, Son and Holy Spirit as three distinct persons who communicated with each other before the creation came to be. Rather, the New Testament presents "the way in which God himself has acted, spoken, made himself known and revealed himself through Jesus in the gift of his Holy Spirit to us, to our very unholy spirit and for our salvation".[29] Küng believes that this dynamic view of the self-revelation of the one God will make much more sense to Muslims than speculation about eternal relationships between the persons of the Trinity that have dogged the history of Christian theology and render almost impossible any true dialogue between monotheistic Muslims and Trinitarian Christians.

Clearly there is some gain if contemporary Christians return to the New Testament foundations of their theology. The Catholic Küng shares with the Anglican Ward very similar assumptions about how to present the Trinity to Muslims. For them, the oneness of God is central such that his threeness needs to be subsumed under that unity. Hence, their preference for a modal view of the Son and Spirit is understandable. Yet for Muslims, the status of the Son as divine is still a major obstacle to seeing him as a mode of the self-revelation of God. Jesus may have been a perfect human being, but he cannot be perfect God. If Jesus is a mode of revelation, then so are the other prophets, who equally are perfect human beings. This is precisely the teaching of the Qurʾān and this is precisely why the Qurʾān rejects the divine nature of Jesus. While Küng wants to preserve Jesus as a unique human expression of God's self-revelation, he is unwilling to see him as the eternal Son of God who existed with the Father before creation, as the Gospel of John and the letter to the Colossians present. Küng plays down the fact that talk about the eternal relationship between the Father and the Son did not arise at the time of the production of the creeds in Greek language but is embedded in the very Greek terminology of the Apostles. His attempt to make conversation with Muslims easier founders on his lack of regard for the actual teaching of the apostolic documents.

Mahmut Aydin applauds Küng for his openness to Muslims and his recognition of the Qurʾān as a revelation of God. He appreciates Küng's

---

[29] Küng, *Islam*, p. 515.

emphasis on the oneness of God as shared by both Christians and Muslims, and that Küng reserves faith in Jesus as the particularly Christian way of responding to the revelation of God without denying that Muslims respond to the revelation of God in another way. In Küng's foreword to Paul Knitter's 1995 work *One Earth Many Religions*, he states his conviction that Christians believe that Jesus is the criterion of the revelation of God. Küng argues that, "A Christian theologian, even in dialogue with followers of other religions, must defend the normativity and finality of Jesus Christ as God's revelatory event for Christians – without, however, making any arrogant claims of superiority over other religions."[30] Aydin thinks that this is a decided improvement over more traditional Christian attitudes to Islam.

> Küng reconsiders the traditional doctrines such as the Trinity and Incarnation in the light of current Christian–Muslim dialogue and new scientific developments in order to make those doctrines acceptable to Muslims … Küng himself moved from holding Jesus as the normative and final word of God not only for Christians but also others, to recognising him as God's normative and final revelation only for Christians.[31]

Aydin thinks this approach to Muslims as authentic receivers of the revelation of God makes for far better relations between Christians and Muslims.

> In the dialogue process what we need is a full commitment to our own faith and its mediator, and yet at the same time an openness toward other faiths and their mediators, in the sense of acknowledging that God has made himself known and has made salvation available through those mediators also.[32]

Miroslav Volf comes to dialogue with Muslims from his own personal background of growing up in a nation that comprised a substantial Muslim population and which descended into anarchy and civil war between Christians and Muslims in the 1990s. This motivated him to respond to the 138 Muslim scholars who issued a call to Christians to come to a common word between Christians and Muslims in 2007. This call, led by the Jordanian royal family, was motivated by the aftermath of the destruction of the Twin Towers in New York in 2001 and the war in the Middle East that ensued. Volf found himself at the heart of an intense period of dialogue from 2008 to 2010 between Christian and Muslim scholars centred around the Yale response to the Muslim call. Perhaps Volf was well placed to organise such a response.

His presentation of the Trinity to Muslims centres on denial of the Qurʾānic criticisms of threeness in God. He asks Muslims to accept that orthodox Christians do not believe that there is a trinity of God, Jesus and Mary. Yet he acknowledges that Muslims see the sonship of Jesus as implying worship of another deity. Thus, the problem of plurality in God cannot be removed by

---

[30] Aydin, *Modern Western Christian Theological Understandings of Muslims*, p. 231. Aydin quotes Küng from P. Knitter, *One Earth, Many Religions*, (Maryknoll NY: Orbis, 1995), p. ix.

[31] Aydin, *Modern Western Christian Theological Understandings of Muslims*, p. 233.

[32] Aydin, *Modern Western Christian Theological Understandings of Muslims*, p. 236–37.

Christians pointing out that Mary has never been worshipped as divine by mainstream Christians.

He appeals to the difficulty shared by Christians and Muslims of using human language to speak about God. "Our difficulties in speaking of God would not go away if God were not the Holy Trinity. All words we use of God – such as 'sustainer' and 'master' or 'gracious' and 'merciful' (Q1:1–4) are inadequate."[33] Volf tries to undercut Muslim confidence in the reliability of the Qurʾānic language by arguing that the Qurʾān itself cannot do justice to the nature of the transcendent Creator. But this argument would lead in the end to a stalemate and open the door to the secular premiss that all talk of God is really a projection of human sensibility. In fact, Volf claims that the Trinity expresses the nature of God in a far more complete way than the Qurʾānic emphasis on the unity of God. He asks, "How is God to be love before there were any creatures to love? Only if, in God's own very being, God loves and is love," and answers, "The one God is internally differentiated", and that from the "beginning" God loves "the other".[34]

By interrogating two highly influential Muslim intellectuals, Ibn Taymiyya and al-Ghazālī, Volf thinks he can spot a serious weakness in the Muslim conception of the love of God. Ibn Taymiyya argues that "God's self-love is the reason God created the world, and God's self-love is the source of all other loves".[35] Al-Ghazālī believes that, "In God's self-love, the absolute unity of all reality is affirmed as identical with the unity of God; all individuality, all multiplicity is then ultimately an illusion."[36] However, in contrast to these key Muslim thinkers, Christians affirm that human beings are not illusory products of God's self-love because they believe that God loves within the Trinity.

> Christians strenuously resist speaking about the unreality and illusoriness of creatures. As monotheists, they are able to do so coherently partly because of the doctrine of the Trinity, because they believe that the one God is internally differentiated, and that from the "beginning" God loves "the other".[37]

In other words, Volf commends the Trinity to Muslims as a meaningful way of understanding the love of God for humanity, which he does not find in Islamic thought. However, Andy Bannister thinks Volf is misguided for emphasising the love of God as a possible source of agreement between Christians and Muslims. He cites the Muslim writer Murad Hofmann, who points out,

> In the Qurʾān we are told that Allah is self-sufficient. This fundamental self-description definitely excludes that Allah is in love with his creation … Therefore it is safer and more accurate not to speak of "love" when addressing His clemency, compassion, benevolence, goodness, or mercy.[38]

---

[33] Volf, *Allah*, p. 160.
[34] Volf, *Allah*, p. 169.
[35] Volf, *Allah*, p. 167.
[36] Volf, *Allah*, p. 169.
[37] Volf, *Allah*, p. 169.
[38] Bannister, *Do Muslims and Christians Worship the Same God?* p. 64. He quotes Murad Hofmann, 'Differences Between the Muslim and the Christian Concept of Divine

One Muslim who responded to Volf in one of the dialogue sessions Volf organised was Reza Shah-Kazemi, from the Institute of Ismaili Studies in London. Shah-Kazemi agrees with Volf that language about God is limited by our human situation. While Christians and Muslims believe in the same Creator, they speak differently about him. He outlines how Christians may speak of God to Muslims.

> The Christian invitation to the Muslims might be envisaged as follows: we not only believe in the one, transcendent God as you do, but, in addition, we believe that this very God became man without sacrificing any of His transcendence; and that the miraculous nature of this incarnation, once it is accepted and empowered by faith, will allow you to see that the Trinity is in fact the least inadequate expression of the full plenitude, profound mystery, and salvific power of the divine nature.[39]

Here Shah-Kazemi does not relate to Volf's argument about the love of God expressed in the Trinitarian relations, but he does acknowledge the fact that the Trinity is predicated on the Incarnation of the Son. He then outlines how Muslims may speak of God to Christians.

> The Muslim invitation will be to add to the universal monotheistic principle, expressed by the first testimony, "no divinity but God", the specifically Islamic appeal, not to God become man, but to "the Perfect Man", this being expressed by the second testimony: "Muhammad is the Messenger of God".[40]

In other words, the Muslim reaction to Christian language about God is to fall back on the premiss that God revealed the truth about Himself via the final prophet, Muḥammad, who came to correct the Christian conception of Jesus and thus the Christian conception of the Trinity.

Another Muslim response within the network of dialogues set up by the Christian responses to the Common Word initiative demonstrates the difficulty Muslims have with the Trinity as proposed by Volf. Joseph Lumbard, who was involved with the Jordanian royal family in writing the Common Word document, and who was teaching Islamic studies at Brandeis University in the USA, asks, "What of the Word is Common?" in a collection of articles by Christians and Muslims about the Common Word document. He admits that the Qur᾽ān might be read by Muslims in the light of Christian teaching concerning the Trinity when he raises the questions "Does the Qur᾽ān criticize traditional Christian Trinitarian theology? Or could it actually be read as opposing the tritheistic misunderstandings of Christian theology that Christians themselves have opposed?"[41] Even if Muslims concede the Christian case at this point, they

---

Love', in *14th General Conference of the Royal Aal al-Bayt Institute for Islamic Thought* (Amman, 2007), pp. 1–14 (pp. 8–9).

[39] Reza Shah-Kazemi, 'Do Muslims and Christians Believe in the Same God?', in Miroslav Volf (ed.), *Do We Worship the Same God? Jews, Christians, and Muslims in Dialogue* (Grand Rapids: Eerdmans, 2012), pp. 76–147 (p. 146).

[40] Shah-Kazemi, 'Do Muslims and Christians Believe in the Same God?', p. 147.

[41] Joseph Lumbard, 'What of the Word is Common?', in Waleed El-Ansary and David K. Linnan (eds), *Muslim and Christian Understanding: Theory and Application of "A Common Word"* (New York: Palgrave Macmillan, 2010), pp. 93–109 (p. 105).

will still have basic problems with the Christian doctrine of the Trinity. He had already pointed out that,

> Muslims can only accept the efficacy of the Christian understanding of Father, Son, and Holy Spirit so long as the Father remains God as such, the one transpersonal and ineffable source of divinity, as in the opening apposition of the Nicene Creed: "I believe in one God, the Father Almighty, Maker of heaven and earth, and of all things visible and invisible." But Muslims cannot accept that the Father, Son, and Holy Spirit are all of the same essence (*homoousios*) and thus equally divine, such that what can be predicated of one can be predicated of the other.[42]

Lumbard quotes from John Meyendorff's orthodox formulation of the role of the Father as "the 'cause' (*aitia*) and the 'principle' (*arche*) of the divine nature, which is in the Son and in the Spirit".[43] Lumbard acknowledges that seeing the Father as the cause of the Son and the Spirit is a mitigating factor for Muslims in the way the Trinity is understood. But Lumbard goes on to argue that Muslims will still see the sovereignty of God as impugned by the attribution of divinity to the Son and the Spirit. "The fact that anything is seen as sharing in any way with the Ultimate Divine Principle will appear as the ultimate sin of *shirk* – associating others with God."[44] He refers to sayings of Jesus in John's gospel to illustrate the Muslim reaction to the Trinity.

> In other words, when the Trinity is presented in terms of "the Father is greater than I" (John 14:28) such that the Father is maintained as the source of all divinity, it could be understood in Islamic terms. But when presented in terms of "I and the Father are one" (John 10:30), such that "each [is] God because [they are] consubstantial," [Meyendorff, p. 183] it is more difficult to find common ground.[45]

Another contributer to the same volume, the Iranian Shiʿī scholar Seyyed Hossein Nasr, reflects on the dialogues that took place between Christians and Muslims as a result of the Common Word letter which he himself had signed.

> We have learned through our many discussions that Muslims will not be able to convince Christians to put aside the doctrine of the trinity, nor Christians persuade Muslims not to insist that God "does not beget nor is He begotten." During our gatherings, Muslims have heard Christian presentations based completely on Christocentrism, while Muslims insist on a theocentric perspective. This difference in the understanding of revelation has also made clear that a chasm separates the Islamic meaning of revelation as a universal reality stretching from Adam to the Prophet of Islam from the particularism that Christians associate with the advent of the coming of Christ, which remains for most of them a unique event in human history.[46]

Volf's desire to respond to the Common Word letter by arranging dialogues between Christians and Muslims was shared by other Christians, but the responses of Muslims demonstrates that the intense effort put out by Volf and

---

[42] Lumbard, 'What of the Word is Common?', p. 104.

[43] John Meyendorff, *Byzantine Theology: Historical Trends and Doctrinal Themes* (New York: Fordham University Press, 1974), p. 183.

[44] Lumbard, 'What of the Word is Common?', p. 104.

[45] Lumbard, 'What of the Word is Common?', p. 104.

[46] Seyyed Hossein Nasr, '"A Common Word" Initiative: *Theoria* and *Praxis*', in El-Ansary and Linnan (eds), *Muslim and Christian Understanding*, pp. 21–28 (p. 22).

others tested their knowledge of Muslim approaches to the Qur᾿ān and the long history of Muslim attitudes to Christian doctrine. Perhaps one lesson that can be learned from the dialogues is that there is no substitute for detailed study of the religious viewpoint of the other. When Christians like Volf ask Muslims to reinterpret their antipathy to the Trinity, they need to take seriously the long history of Christian–Muslim encounter. His characterisation of the Trinity as the love between the Father and the Son expressed via the Spirit falls foul of the strictures mentioned by Lumbard that the divinity of the Father cannot be shared with the other members of the Trinity. Yet for Volf the necessity of sharing the Christian belief in the love of God makes any encounter with Muslims worthwhile. For him there is little point in Christians keeping silent when they have such good news to share.

Veli-Matti Kärkkäinen follows Ward in accepting that systematic theology must include dialogue not just with Western secularism but also with global religious beliefs. He acknowledges his indebtedness to Ward's pioneering work but goes way beyond what Ward accomplished. Kärkkäinen left Finland to work in Thailand and learned to live in a non-Western culture, whereas Ward lived continuously in the UK. Kärkkäinen places each item of Christian belief in dialogue with the alternative beliefs of others and therefore produces a rich conversation between Christian faith and other convictions. His treatment of Islamic beliefs is exemplary for completeness, given that in his earlier life he was engaged with Thai Buddhism.

Kärkkäinen's presentation of the Trinity in an Islamic context recognises the Qur᾿ānic denial of threeness in God. He notes that this rejection of threeness is related to the Christian claim that Jesus is the Son of God and to the assertion that the God of the Qur᾿ān is not involved in producing offspring through relations with a woman. "A foundational reason for the strict rebuttal of the Christian doctrine of the Trinity includes the absolute exaltedness of Allah and the sheer absurdity of the idea of God having a child by a woman."[47] Therefore, a Christian presentation of the Trinity to Muslims must deal with this double rejection of plurality within God Himself and the assumption that the plurality is the result of sexual relations with a woman. While Kärkkäinen has not lived within an Islamic culture, he has drunk deeply from the wells that supply Islamic thought patterns.

He notes a further problem raised by the Qur᾿ān with respect to the Trinity: that Christians are guilty of wrongly associating Jesus with God. The sin of *shirk*, of associating the created world with God such that worship is given to creatures, is central to the teaching of the Qur᾿ān. "When the Qur᾿ān gives 'Praise to God who took not up a son' (17:111; 19:35; 19:92; 25:2), it must be noted that Christians also affirm this statement, as it is not about incarnation but rather about adoptionism."[48] Thus, Christians must point out that they agree with the Qur᾿ānic denial that God "took up a son". Kärkkäinen does not elaborate on what he would say to a Muslim to clarify this point, but he would most likely indicate that Christians along with Muslims deny that Jesus was "elevated" to a divine

[47] Kärkkäinen, *Trinity and Revelation*, p. 372.
[48] Kärkkäinen, *Trinity and Revelation*, p. 373.

status after being born as a human being. He does mention that the Incarnation is the opposite of the notion of God elevating the human Jesus to divinity. "God's gracious relation or association with humanity, the eternal Word becoming human, is not *shirk*."[49] Here he demonstrates that it is imperative for Christians to present the Trinity by means of the Incarnation. He parts company with Hans Küng, who believes that the Incarnation of the Son has to be set aside in favour of Jesus being a special manifestation of the activity of God in the world. Rather, the presentation of the eternal nature of the Son beyond time and space is crucial for Christian theology, according to Kärkkäinen. While Hans Küng thinks that Jesus as the self-revelation of God in a human being is the way to make sense of Jesus, Kärkkäinen holds that without the eternal reality of the Son there is no Trinity. In fact, Hans Küng may well fall foul of the Qur᾽ānic strictures about God elevating the human Jesus to His own divinity.

Kärkkäinen's exposition of the Trinity follows closely that of the German Lutheran Wolfhart Pannenberg, who calls the Trinity "concrete monotheism in contrast to the notions of an abstract transcendence of the one God and abstract notions of a divine unity that leaves no place for plurality".[50] Kärkkäinen does not develop his own view but feels that sitting under Pannenberg's language is sufficient. Indeed it is somewhat surprising that Kärkkäinen recommends that his readers follow the Trinitarian teaching of the Athanasian Creed rather than him developing his own presentation of the way the Father, Son and Holy Spirit are persons who are united within the Godhead, according to the Athanasian Creed, "The Godhead of the Father, of the Son, and of the Holy Spirit is all one, the glory equal, the majesty coeternal".[51] But it is precisely here that explanations of the Trinity for Muslims may get into difficulties. Given that Kärkkäinen has opted for a social Trinity of three dynamically related persons in a united Godhead, he comes up against Ward's doubts about the validity of this concept in dialogue with Jews and Muslims. Ward takes the view that only a Trinity of self-revelation will suffice. Thus, the Son and the Spirit are modes of the revelation of God. For Ward, the Spirit cannot really be conceived as a person and this is his basis for rejecting the social theory of the Trinity.

Kärkkäinen does believe that the Spirit is a personal centre of conscious thinking and willing and he goes on to dialogue with Muslims about the Spirit. But when he expounds the Qur᾽ānic references to the Spirit of God, he notes that there is little room for the Christian notion of the Holy Spirit as a manifestation of God Himself. In fact, in the later volume of his systematic theology he doubts whether Christians can find any real assistance within the Qur᾽ān for a Trinitarian view of the Spirit. Disappointingly, he does not go on to indicate how Christians should present the Holy Spirit to Muslims. Perhaps he is not so far from Ward in this respect. Ward feels that the Spirit is best articulated as a divine power or force rather than as a person who has self-consciousness. Certainly the

---

[49] Kärkkäinen, *Trinity and Revelation*, p. 374.
[50] Kärkkäinen, *Trinity and Revelation*, p. 374. He quotes Pannenberg, *Systematic Theology, vol. 1*, pp. 335–36.
[51] Kärkkäinen, *Trinity and Revelation*, p. 374. He quotes from Brannan, *Historic Creeds and Confessions*, available at www.ccel.org, p. 5.

Qur'ān supports this view of the Spirit of God. Kärkkäinen has not helped his Christian reader to overcome this problem of viewing the Spirit as merely the energy of God when in dialogue with Muslims.

Presenting the Holy Spirit to Muslims is taken on by two of the Christian theologians living in Muslim societies, Ibrahim Luqa in Egypt and Imad Shehadeh in Jordan. To such theologians we now turn to see how Christian life within Muslim culture impacts the manner and content of Christian dialogue with Muslims.

The Presentations by Christian Theologians within Islamic Nations in the Light of Muslim Responses

Ibrahim Luqa wrote his presentation of the Trinity for Muslims by leaning on earlier Arab Christian presentations and by referring to earlier Muslim responses to the Trinity. This Coptic Orthodox priest was schooled in that long tradition of Christian–Muslim engagement and represents the best of that tradition. He calls on his fellow Christians to take that tradition seriously and harness the results for twentieth-century dialogue. Two different Christian approaches to presenting the Trinity are proposed by Luqa. Firstly, he advocates the theory of ʿAmmār al-Baṣrī that Christians believe in a trinity of God who exists with two essential attributes of life and speech. Secondly, he offers the Trinitarian analogy of Yaḥya Ibn ʿAdī that the Triune God is likened to the mind of a human person in being the intelligence (*al-ʿaql*), the one who thinks (*al-ʿaqil*) and the meaning of thought (*al-mʿaqul*). He does not discriminate between these two alternative descriptions of the Trinity and clearly feels that they are both compatible with one another. They both, to be sure, emphasise that God is a unity and play down any hint of polytheism to a Muslim reader. Luqa does not develop a social theory of the Trinity. His aim is to argue that the Trinity explains the kind of unity that exists within the nature of God in such a way that Muslims will accept that Christians are monotheists. In this endeavour Luqa sits within the traditional Christian defence of the Trinity within Arab Christian culture. This explains his interpretation of the Qur'ān as not attacking an orthodox formulation of the Trinity but polytheistic views held by non-Christian groups in the seventh century.

His detailed assessment of the interpretations of Muslim commentators on the Qur'ān marks out Luqa from any of the other writers surveyed so far. Here he takes stock of how Muslim scholars read the concept of the Word and Spirit of God said to have been given to Jesus in the Qur'ān. In his attempt to argue that the Word and Spirit come from the very essence of God, he points out that all the commentators he has read fail to acknowledge this self-evident truth. When they interpret the statement that Jesus received the word of God, "Muslim commentators on the Qur'ān state that 'the word' is not from God but is from the power of the word of God."[52] When they interpret the statement that Jesus received the Spirit of God, "The commentators have erred when they have made the Spirit originate from the hidden spiritual power and not from the essence of

[52] Luqa, *Christianity in Islam*, p. 101.

God … It is certain that the Spirit is from God, or he is the Spirit of God, and like his Word, he is God."[53] Luqa has made a valuable contribution to the interrogation of Muslim scholarship on the Qur'ān, a feat not matched by any other Christian scholar who has attempted to present the Trinity to Muslims. The response of Muslims to Luqa's book was cut short when the Egyptian government banned the selling of the book in the 1960s. What had been possible under British administration was no longer acceptable under Egyptian independence and the strength of feeling in a largely Muslim nation that the Christian minority must not engage in printed criticism of Muslim beliefs.

Censorship by a Muslim government has been a feature of life for Christian minorities in most Muslim nations in the post-colonial era. Albert Walters shows how the Muslim majority in Malaysia has steadily eroded the freedom of the Christian minority to publish material deemed unacceptable to Muslims, including their Malay-language Bible referring to God as Allah. While Christians managed to argue that they should be able to continue to use that Malay Bible, the government insisted that Muslims must not be given access to it. In the Malay context, Walters points out that Christians do not have easy relations with Muslims and that the opportunity to share Christian beliefs with Muslims is difficult. His research into how lay Christians speak to Muslims about the Trinity demonstrates that they tend to rely on analogies from the created world to explain their faith in the Triune God. Thus, three various forms of water indicate that water can be found in more than one form without ceasing to be water. Walters advocates such a use of analogy from nature for his fellow Malay Christians.

He also thinks that speaking of the Trinity as a relationship of friends might be helpful in his Malay context. He appeals to Jürgen Moltmann's idea that "Trinity from below is a process of living relationships of love between friends and companions of various religious backgrounds and the three Persons of the Trinity and open to the inclusion of the world."[54] If his fellow Malay Christians could form friendships with their Muslim neighbours, that would be a living example of the good relations that inhere within the Trinity, which inspires them to reach out to Muslims in a friendly way. He argues,

> A renewed understanding of the Trinity will move Malaysian Christians away from a tendency towards self-preoccupation to one of active social involvement in the direction of a Christian community that is more human-centred and hence more God-centred as Jesus himself was.[55]

In other words, Walters advocates a lifestyle powered by the friendly relations within the Trinity rather than a proclamation governed by the revelation of the Trinity found in the New Testament or in the history of the church. Just how the members of the Trinity relate to one another is not really Walter's concern. The rather loose language of Jesus being God-centred shows that Walters does not think it necessary to develop a view of the Trinity as the eternal relations between

---

[53] Luqa, *Christianity in Islam*, p. 112.

[54] Walters, *We Believe in One God?* p. 281. He quotes from Moltmann, *The Trinity and the Kingdom of God*, pp. 174–76.

[55] Walters, *We Believe in One God?* p. 282.

Father, Son and Holy Spirit. For him, copying Jesus the man is the way to be Christian.

Walters does not stop to examine how Malay Muslims react to Christian faith in the Trinity. He interviewed Christians but not Muslims. However, it seems clear to the reader that Walters felt that Muslims were not available to speak to in his Malay situation of increasing hostility of the Muslim government towards Christians. Hence his advocacy of friendship is rather one-sided, since it might not be reciprocated by those who think of enmity rather than friendship. Naturally, the Christian belief in the Trinity is portrayed by the Malay government as hostile to the truth of the oneness of God, and as a result, every effort should be made to protect Malay Muslims from contamination by Christians who undermine the truth of the one God. How Muslims can afford to be friends with Christians in such a hostile environment is not discussed by Walters.

Imad Shehadeh set up a seminary for Evangelical Protestants in Amman, Jordan in the 1990s and was still running the school at the time of writing his large study of the Triune God, which he first published in Arabic before translating it into English. Jordan represents those Muslim majority nations that accept Christian theological institutions and, unlike Malaysia, have not exercised the same level of censorship over Christian publications. His work on the doctrine of God defines his method as comparing and contrasting what he calls "Oneness in Trinity" and "Absolute Oneness". He argues that Absolute Oneness is a belief in God found throughout the world but his actual exposition of this belief is based on Islam. Therefore, what follows in his book *God With Us and Without Us; Volumes One and Two: The Beauty and Power of Oneness in Trinity Versus Absolute Oneness*, is a systematic study of the aspects of these two rival theories.

Shehadeh accepts that belief in Absolute Oneness is partly true because it argues against multiple divine beings that many other humans believe in. So there is a shared assumption between the advocates of Oneness in Trinity and Absolute Oneness that there is in reality just one Creator of the universe and that there can be no other divinities equal to Him. However, Shehadeh argues that the holders of Oneness in Trinity think of the Creator as existing eternally in three persons who are equally God. He states his case as follows,

> Oneness in Trinity differs from Absolute Oneness in that it goes further by believing that God revealed himself as existing in three equal but distinct persons in an unending relationship. This is the nature of God eternally, that is, from eternity past to eternity future, outside of creation, with or without its presence. In this faith, God is one in a first sense and plural in a second sense. For he is one in the sense of essence or nature, without being composed of parts. But he is also three in the sense of persons. These persons are the Father, the Son and the Holy Spirit, whereby each of them is equally God, without separation or confusion, and each is distinct from the others.[56]

Shehadeh is content to put forward a social theory of the Trinity as an eternal reality rather than just the way that God has chosen to relate to creation. He

[56] Shehadeh, *God With Us*, p. 40.

evidently does not sense a need to be reticent about the eternal relations within God, as Ward does. Thus, for Shehadeh, plurality is essential to God's nature even before the creation of time and space, whereas Ward thinks that the Trinity revealed in the New Testament may only relate to God's relations with Planet Earth and not necessarily to other worlds He has created. Shehadeh reflects John of Damascus' conception of the eternal relations existing between Father, Son and Holy Spirit before the world came into being, the eternal *perichoresis* between the three persons of the Godhead. Ward worries about how such a conception of God can help in dialogue with Jews and Muslims, but Shehadeh has no such concerns. He is convinced that only the eternal nature of the relations between the three persons in the one God can do justice to the New Testament revelation.

The reason for the three persons existing within one God is based on love, according to Shehadeh. Like Volf, Shehadeh gets involved with Muslim conceptions of the love of God for His creatures. Muslims have difficulty with the idea of God loving any other than Himself. This is the fundamental weakness of Absolute Oneness. God must love Himself, as Muslim intellectuals have constantly argued. They put forward two arguments for the self-love of God. Firstly, God cannot love another eternal being because this would mean more than one God, but in the Qur'ān it is revealed that there is only one God, who has no partners. Secondly, God cannot love his creatures because in the Qur'ān it is revealed that there is nothing like God in the world He made, and therefore, God cannot depend on humans in a relationship of need or dependency. However, Shehadeh responds to these Muslim premisses with his advocacy of the reality of the love of God expressed in the eternal love of God within the three eternal persons. "If love is one of God's eternal attributes, it requires the presence of the lover and the one loved (or beloved), in addition to love itself. Simply put, how can love be active eternally without a relationship?"[57] Notice here that Shehadeh puts forward the Augustinian version of the love of God, in which the Holy Spirit is the bond of love between the Father and the Son, rather than the Damascene version that he has so far favoured. The Holy Spirit seems at this point to be relegated to "love itself" rather than to a person who loves the Father and the Son, and who is loved by the Father and the Son.

Nevertheless, Shehadeh does return to the full personality of the Holy Spirit later on when he defends the need for threeness in God. He argues that the love of God demands three persons to be complete. The love of the Father for the Son needs to be enlarged by love for the Spirit. He uses the analogy of human love. "It is necessary for the activity exchanged between two persons to encompass shared activity with a third person. For example, the love exchanged between two extends beyond the two to become a shared love between three, thereby becoming completed love."[58] Therefore, the Spirit is described at this point as the third person in the eternal divine relationship. Here the family analogy presented by David Brown when he was a missionary in Jordan is renewed by this Jordanian theologian.

[57] Shehadeh, *God With Us*, p. 108.
[58] Shehadeh, *God With Us*, p. 163.

Shehadeh applies the Trinity to the life of those who believe in the Triune God. Unlike believers in the Absolutely One God, who is so utterly transcendent that they cannot be sure of His love, believers in the One God in Trinity can be sure of His love. He argues, "The mutual indwelling of the Father and the Son without us and which is extended to believers so that it is with us expresses the deepest relationship between God and humanity and the deepest relationship between believers that begins now and continues for all eternity."[59] The vital reason for Christians to uphold the Trinity is to testify to their own experience of the love of God, which is founded on the eternal love of God that has reached out to them. Shehadeh firmly believes that this dynamic experience will have persuasive power in dialogue with upholders of Absolute Oneness.

> The appeal of this book to adherents of Absolute Oneness is that they begin the journey of trust in the perfection, equality and harmony of all God's attributes. This will make their faith grow so that they enter a personal relationship with God, and then become receptive to any revelation from God about his nature, no matter how difficult it is for them to change their thinking.[60]

However, he is not unaware of the difficulties that Muslims face in re-organising their conception of God to accommodate his Christian view. He quotes the Palestinian Muslim Isma'īl al-Fārūqī in dialogue with Kenneth Cragg who rejected Cragg's appeal for Muslims to make room for the love of God for humanity expressed in the Incarnation by saying, "God does not reveal himself to anyone. Christians talk about the revelation of God himself – by God of God – but that is the great difference ... You may not have complete transcendence and self-revelation at the same time".[61] Shehadeh interprets al-Fārūqī rejection of the belief that God has revealed Himself as the long-standing position of Islamic thought going back to the dominance of Sunni Ash`arite interpretation of the Qur'ān from the tenth century onwards. If Muslims continue to uphold this point of view, then it is impossible for human beings to depend on God's attributes. The value of dialoguing with Muslims is found precisely at this juncture, for Christians have the opportunity to show that the Triune God is dependable and trustworthy. "Oneness in Trinity declares that the attributes of action spring, not from an unpredictable will of God, but from his revealed nature, which combines all his attributes as he is in himself. This in turn leads to the possibility of depending upon and trusting the attributes of God."[62] It is a testament to Shehadeh's optimism that he founded a seminary to train leaders for the relatively small number of Evangelical Protestant churches in the Middle East and that he felt able to publish such a thorough defence of the Triune God in his Islamic milieu.

---

[59] Shehadeh, *God With Us*, p. 297.
[60] Shehadeh, *God With Us*, p. 148.
[61] Shehadeh, *God With Us*, p. 112. He quotes from Isma'īl al-Fārūqī, 'On the Nature of Islamic Da'wah', *International Review of Missions* 65 (1976), p. 405.
[62] Shehadeh, *God With Us*, p. 135.

Conclusion

This survey of Christian attempts to convey the meaning of the Trinity to Muslims has highlighted several issues in that endeavour. Firstly, there is the conviction of Middle Eastern Christians in the early period of Islamic rule that the Qurʾān supports the Trinity even while there are texts that appear to oppose tripling the one God. John of Damascus read in Q4:171 that Jesus had the Word and Spirit of God as proof that the Muslim insistence that God is one without the Trinity is to mutilate what God has joined together. His argument was followed by a significant number of Christian theologians in the Middle East, including the writer of the 'Anonymous Apology' and Timothy in the eighth century. Then in the ninth century, Abū Qurra, ʿAmmār al-Baṣrī and Peter of Bayt Raʾs all make use of John's argument about God having His Word and Spirit. Iliyyā of Nisibis in the eleventh century and Paul of Antioch in the thirteenth century have versions of the same argument.

Secondly, John's reading of Q4:171 was adopted by subsequent Christian apologists in order to argue for Qurʾānic support for the essential attributes of God being speech and life. The most influential of these writers was ʿAmmār al-Baṣrī, whose articulation of the argument was repeated by Peter of Bayt Raʾs, Iliyyā of Nisibis and Paul of Antioch. The discussion of essential attributes in God changed from the attempt by Christians to demonstrate that God did indeed have essential attributes to Muʿtazilī Muslims who said that the attributes of God were only metaphors for His reality, to attempts by Christians to demonstrate that God had only three essential attributes rather than the seven advocated by the followers of al-Ashʿarī. This change can be seen in the eleventh-century writing of Ibn al-Ṭayyib and Iliyyā of Nisibis, who both felt the need to engage with the newer reality of the ascendency of the Ashʿarite view.

Thirdly, Middle Eastern Christians were keen to point out to Muslims that the created world demonstrates that some things can be one and three at the same time in order to defend the rationality of the Trinity. These indications of Trinity in the world varied from writer to writer, but it is interesting to observe how persistent Christians were in seeking out such analogies from creation to understand the Creator as three in one, despite Muslims responding that the Qurʾān prohibits comparisons between the Creator and His work in Q42:11, "There is nothing like Him". The eighth-century 'Anonymous Apology' lists seven analogies for the Trinity.

> First: the disc, rays and heat of the sun do not imply three suns. "We do not say three suns." Second: the eye, the pupil and the light in the eye are not three eyes. Third: the soul, the body and the spirit are not three human beings. Fourth: the root, the branches and the fruit of a tree are not three trees. Fifth: the source, the river and the lake is the same water. Sixth: the human mind, the word that comes from

> the mind and the spirit that resides in the mind are all of one human being. Seventh: the mouth, the tongue and the word that is spoken all come from one person.[1]

Timothy repeats the first, third, sixth and seventh analogies. Abū Qurra introduces a new analogy when he argues that Peter, Paul and John are an analogy for the three members of the Trinity since they share the same human nature, just as the members of the Trinity share the same divine nature. But he also argues that the Father, Son and Holy Spirit are not separated or differentiated, since they would then be three divine beings rather than one divine being, so limiting the value of the analogy which clearly relies on the fact that there are three independent persons who are separated and differentiated from one another. Abū Qurra offers three further new analogies. If there are three lamps in a house, they each give light but the light is one and indivisible. When three speakers recite the same poem simultaneously, the hearer hears one poem. Three pieces of gold are just one kind of gold, not three kinds.

Abū Rā'iṭa uses Abū Qurra's analogies of the three lamps and three human beings who now are Adam, Eve and Abel, as well as the analogies of the soul, the mind and speech, and the sun, its light and heat, which were used by the 'Anonymous Apology'. ʿAmmār al-Baṣrī refers to fire and water. Just as three flames from a fire share the same perfect essence, and yet are not called three fires, and three drops of water are not called three waters, so Father, Son and Holy Spirit who share the same perfect divinity are not called three gods. He too uses the analogy of three human beings, but this time they are Abraham, Isaac and Jacob.

Peter of Bayt Ra's uses the analogy of the soul, the mind and speech, but is less concerned with adding analogies than his predecessors. Yaḥya ibn ʿAdī developed his own analogies. Rather than appealing to three human beings sharing the same human nature, he argued that one human being can be defined in more than one way. He said that just as Zayd is one subject who can be defined as living, rational and mortal, so God is one substance in three attributes, which are goodness, power and wisdom. He develops the earlier Zayd analogy into a description of different types of activity of Zayd who can be doctor, an accountant and a writer as an analogy for the relationship between the three members of the Trinity. Yaḥya changes tack again in introducing a new analogy for the three attributes of God as intellect, the intelligent one and intellection. Here he promotes the idea of three essential components of the nature of the human mind as a way of understanding the essential components of the mind of God.

Ibn al-Ṭayyib alters Yaḥya's analogy of intellect, the intelligent one and intellection to the idea that the divine essence has the attributes of knowledge, knowing and of being known, but does not appeal to any other analogies. Iliyyā of Nisibis uses the analogies of the sun and the human soul to argue that just as the essence of the human soul and its speech and life are one human soul and the essence of the sun and its heat and light are one sun, so the essence of God and His Word and Spirit are one God. Paul of Antioch refers to the analogies of the human soul, fire and the sun to argue that when we speak about the mind, speech

---

[1] Gibson, *A Treatise*, p. 76.

and life of a human being, it does not involve three human beings and when we speak about the flame, heat and light of a fire, we do not involve three fires, and when we speak about the disk, light and heat of the sun, we do not involve three suns. This summary of the appeal to analogies for threeness to co-exist with oneness in the history of Middle Eastern Christian attempts to defend the oneness of God in the Trinity shows how central such analogies were to all of the writers cited.

The modern period of global Christian–Muslim interaction has shown both continuity and discontinuity with the earlier Middle Eastern period. Continuity with the three aspects surveyed above can be seen in several modern writers. Firstly, there is one theologian who finds the Trinity supported by Q4:171. Ibrahim Luqa follows the Middle Eastern Christian tradition of reading Q4:171 as defining God in Trinity. He indicates that God is the one who exists in life and speech, which are not created but are eternal within him. But Luqa is unique among the writers surveyed and this may be a result of his being embedded in Egyptian Christian culture as a Coptic Orthodox priest. Western Christian reticence with interpreting Q4:171 to undergird the Trinity is expressed by Veli-Matti Kärkkäinen who, having examined Q4:171, notices that the Word of God cannot be aligned with the divine Logos, because the word is spoken by God into Mary's ear and causes the birth of Jesus in her pure womb. Since the message of Q4:171 is located within a section that exhorts people to give up saying that God is three, Kärkkäinen argues that Christians should not link the "word of God" here with divinity.

Secondly, the discussion of essential attributes in God arising from the Word and Spirit in Q4:171 is continued by Luqa, who repeats the presentation of ʿAmmār al-Baṣrī that God has two essential attributes of speech and life, demonstrating the lasting impact of the ninth-century Basran theologian on twentieth-century Coptic Christianity. Here again, Luqa is unique among the modern theologians. The interaction of the eleventh-century theologians with the Ashʿarite view that God has seven essential attributes is echoed in the writing of Ibrahim Luqa as well as Imad Shehadeh. Luqa seeks to restrict the essential attributes to two rather than seven, while Shehadeh says that all of God's attributes are essential to Him rather than just some of them. Shehadeh believes that the key to understanding the attributes of God lies in seeing the love of God as central to all of them, and the love of God is expressed by the three persons, Father, Son and Holy Spirit, who from all eternity have related to one another in a relationship of love and who relate to creation by means of that love.

Thirdly, the appeal to analogies within the created world for oneness in threeness is continued by some modern writers. Pfander asks his Muslim reader to consider that the unity of things can be found in their triplicity. He repeats the early use of the analogies from fire and the human being. Heat, light and combustion are different from one another, yet when combined form only one fire. A human consists of body, soul and spirit, yet he is not three men and his body, soul and spirt do not conflict with the oneness of his personality. He then adds a new analogy from the discoveries of modern science that a single ray of sunlight consists of the three primary colours, red, green and blue, yet its unity is not destroyed by this plurality.

David Brown repeats the analogy of the human being as threefold. A man is neither simply his body, nor his mind, nor his spirit, but a unity of these three exceedingly complex elements, which are normally integrated together so that he lives and acts as a single person. He adds the analogy of a family of one man, one woman and so many children, who are in a living relationship with each other. They depend on one another physically, emotionally, intellectually and spiritually, and so are united together. This analogy supports Brown's social view of the Trinity. A solitary God would have had no activity beyond the contemplation of Himself, but a Triune God is active in the love expressed by the three centres of personal consciousness within the divine being.

David Shenk also uses the analogy of the human personality of mind, body and spirit. He argues that we make things with our hands, we think through problems with our mind and our spirit is expressed through our personality, yet these three dimensions of our selfhood are the one person whom we are.

Ibrahim Luqa refers to the analogy of fire. Burning, heat and light are one fire. Just as fire is one substance in three properties, so God is one substance in three properties. He also uses Yaḥya ibn ʿAdī's analogy of the human mind to point out that the intelligence (*ʿaql*), the one who thinks (*ʿāqil*) and the meaning of thought (*maʿqūl*) are one in God.

Albert Walters advocates the analogy of water found in three different forms as source, wellspring and living water to depict the Trinity. He also appeals to friendship between people as an analogy for the Trinity. Since God is friendly and hospitable, then there must exist such a relationship within the Godhead.

Imad Shehadeh has the analogy of loving relationships between three human beings. Just as the love exchanged between two human beings extends beyond the two to become a shared love between three, so the exchanged love between the Father, Son and Holy Spirit completes their relationship as one God.

However, there is a marked tendency in the modern period for Christians to ignore Middle Eastern approaches. This is partly to do with a feeling of unease with the impact of Greek philosophy on the Christian tradition. The Anglican Kenneth Cragg and the Catholic Hans Küng both argue that modern Christians should leave aside the fixed Greek tradition of the credal formulations in favour of a return to the more fluid, dynamic language found in the apostolic writings of Paul and John. They plead for greater freedom for modern Christians to adopt that New Testament language to make communication with Muslims more possible with a much simpler conception of the Trinity. Cragg even believes that Muslims will sort out the reality of the Trinity once they understand the Incarnation as a dynamic interaction between God and Jesus, with the Spirit being that dynamic interaction.

Western Christians generally have not felt comfortable with the Eastern concept of the Trinity in terms of the co-inherence of the three members of the Trinity, as expressed most clearly by John of Damascus. They have largely been influenced by Augustine's idea that there is co-inherence between the Father and the Son, but the Spirit is seen as the love bond between them, as can be seen in Cragg's approach. Keith Ward has written much to dispute the Eastern social Trinity, believing that holding to three centres of consciousness is likely to make dialogue with Muslims even more difficult for Christians. He prefers to assert the unity of God by describing the Father, Son and Holy Spirit as aspects of the work of the one God in relation to the creation. He believes that the reformed Protestant Karl Barth and the Catholic Jesuit Karl Rahner both are right to speak of the revelation of the one God in three modes of activity. Still, there are modern Christians who have sided with the Eastern approach. The Anglican David Brown eloquently presents the Trinity as a divine family of Father, Son and Holy Spirit, who each are centres of consciousness and who each contribute to the reality of God, just as members of a family do. The Jordanian Evangelical Imad Shehadah also commends the richness of the three members of the Trinity interacting with each other for the sake of humanity over against the blandness of the Muslim conception of a totally transcendent God who does not interact with humans.

Modern global Christians do not naturally see the members of the Trinity as attributes of God, and therefore it is no surprise that the preoccupation of Eastern Christians with arguing for God to have essential attributes is missing from Western Christian presentations of the Trinity for Muslims. Mark Swanson, an American Lutheran theologian who was teaching in the Evangelical Seminary in Cairo in 1991, notes the continuing use of the traditional understanding of the Trinity as one God with three essential attributes among Egyptian Copts but also that more Western influenced Egyptian Christians had questioned whether such a view truly reflects New Testament teaching.[2] He adjudicates this debate by accepting that there is an apologetic utility to the appeal to essential attributes. "The attribute apology, being relatively easy to grasp and to explain will no doubt remain popular among Christians as long as they are called upon to account for their faith in the Trinity, and to defend themselves against the charge of *shirk*."[3] In a 2005 article written for American Christians after moving to Luther Seminary in St Paul, Minnesota, Swanson cautiously suggests that much can be learned from Abū Qurra and Abū Rāʾiṭa in their attempts to defend Christians from the charge of *shirk* made by Muslims against them. He summarises their importance for twenty-first century Christians.

> How should Christians talk to Muslims specifically about the doctrine of the Trinity? A first answer must be: only after *listening* to Muslims, whose critique of Christian God-talk frequently hits the mark and should be welcomed as a call to clarity and reform in thought and practice. A second answer is suggested by the examples given above: Christians will speak most effectively when they do so in ways that reflect appreciation of issues creating lively discussion within the Muslim community itself.[4]

Thus, modern Christians need to deal with Muslim preconceptions when presenting the Trinity to them and Abū Qurra and Abū Rāʾiṭa offer sound advice about how to go about this task.

---

[2] See Mark N. Swanson, 'Are Hypostases Attributes? An Investigation Into the Modern Egyptian Appropriation of the Medieval Arabic Apologetic Heritage', *Parole de l'Orient* 16 (1990–1991), pp. 239–250.

[3] Swanson, 'Are Hypostases Attributes?', p. 249.

[4] Mark N. Swanson, 'The Trinity in Christian–Muslim Conversation', *Dialog: A Journal of Theology* 44 (2005), pp. 256–63 (pp. 261–62).

There are two other voices making the same appeal. The Anglican priest Michael Ipgrave was the inter faith relations adviser to the Archbishop's Council of the Church of England and executive secretary of the Ecumenical Churches' Commission for Inter Faith Relations at the time of the publication of his Durham University PhD thesis in 2003 entitled *Trinity and Inter Faith Dialogue: Plenitude and Plurality*.[5] He advocates that Christians should present the Trinity to Muslims in terms of the divine attributes accepted by Muslims. He believes that the early debates among Muslims concerning the attributes of God should be entered into by modern Christians because these discussions are still central to Islamic communities.

> The attributes in Islam are directly associated with the divine personality, as they are those features of divinity which enable the establishment of relationship between God and His creatures. Indeed, the importance of this enablement was one of the factors that led the *mutakallimun* to insist on the distinction of the attributes from the divine essence. Otherwise, for example, instead of praying to the person of God as the knowing One the Muslim would be praying to that aspect of personality – knowledge – which enabled God to be the knowing One.[6]

Given that Muslims in the twenty-first century still talk about the attributes of God, then Christians should not avoid such debate but willingly engage in it. He suggests that "Such a dialogue would be built on the insight that God's very accessibility, his susceptibility to predication and to devotion, raises the possibility of some measure of inchoate plurality within the divine plenitude."[7]

Of course, it depends on which Muslims are in the conversation. Ipgrave does not distinguish between Sunni Muslims, who uphold the seven essential attributes of God over against the many more non-essential attributes, and Shiʿī Muslims, who continue to maintain the Muʿtazilī doctrine that the attributes are only metaphors for the reality of God that transcends any description. However, the context of dialogue in England is generally with Sunni Muslims, so Ipgrave's suggestion is related to the actual situation of English Christians.

The other voice is the American Evangelical Joseph Cumming, who was working with Miroslav Volf at Yale University. He has also encouraged Christians to present the Trinity by dialoguing with Sunni Muslims over the seven essential attributes of God. Like Swanson, he wants contemporary Christians to look back to the Middle Eastern debates between Christians and Muslims over the essential attributes of God to gain insight into how Muslims approach the description of God in terms of plurality.[8] He says to Christians, "There is a huge amount of common ground between Muslims and Christians on the fundamental issues at stake in the *ṣifāt* and in the Trinity – far more common ground than is generally supposed by either Muslims or Christians."[9]

---

[5] See Michael Ipgrave, *Trinity and Inter Faith Dialogue: Plenitude and Plurality* (Bern: Peter Lang, 2003).

[6] Ipgrave, *Trinity and Inter Faith Dialogue*, p. 373.

[7] Ipgrave, *Trinity and Inter Faith Dialogue*, p. 375.

[8] See Joseph Cumming, 'ṣifāt al-dhāt in al-Ashʿārī's Doctrine of God and Possible Christian Parallels', in E. Reisacher (ed.), *Toward Respectful Understanding and Witness Among Muslims* (Pasadena, CA: William Carey Library, 2012), pp. 111–45.

[9] Cumming, 'ṣifāt al-dhāt in al-Ashʿārī's Doctrine of God', p. 143.

Another emphasis in modern Western Christianity is the notion that the love of God is central to the Trinity. This had led some Christian theologians to make a sharp distinction between Christianity and Islam, so that presenting the Trinity to Muslims is akin to demonstrating that in Islam God is not defined by love. The British Evangelical Michael Reeves wrote a book on the Trinity in 2012 in which he contrasts the Biblical truth of the Triune God with the Islamic insistence on the unity of God. He notices "How the Qur'ān explicitly and sharply distinguishes Allah from the God described by Jesus".[10] After quoting Q4:171 and Q112 he argues that,

> Allah is a single-person God. In no sense is he a Father ("he begets not"), and in no sense does he have a Son ("nor is he begotten"). He is one person, and not three. Allah, then, is an utterly different sort of being to the God who is Father, Son and Spirit. And it is not just incompatibly different numbers we are dealing with here: that difference, as we will see, is going to mean that Allah exists and functions in a completely different way from the Father, Son and Spirit.[11]

The New Testament shows how the Triune God operates. At the baptism of Jesus, "The Father declares his love for his Son, and his pleasure in him, and he does so *as the Spirit rests on Jesus*. For the way the Father makes known his love is precisely through giving his Spirit."[12] The Spirit is not an impersonal force because,

> He speaks and sends (Acts 13:2, 4); he chooses (Acts 20:28), teaches (John 14:26), gives (Isaiah 63:14); he can be lied to and tested (Acts 5:3, 9); he can be resisted (Acts 7:51), grieved (Isaiah 63:10; Ephesians 4:30) and blasphemed (Matthew 12:31). In every way he is presented alongside the Father and the Son as a real person.[13]

The correct reading of such texts must mean that the Spirit is a person and therefore the Trinity is a relationship between three persons. Reeves concludes, "We are dealing with three real and distinct persons, the Father, the Son and the Spirit. And they must be real persons: there could be no true love between them if they were, say, just different aspects of one single divine personality."[14] For him, the New Testament evidence supports the social theory of the Trinity and those Christians who begin with the one God and define the Son and the Spirit as ways that God has revealed Himself are undermining scriptural teaching.

Reeves is convinced that the Bible reveals God to be relational, in that He loves others. Firstly, the Father loves His Son and shows that He loves human beings whom He has created. "God the Father is a God who delights to have another beside him (his eternal Son). He is a God who thinks that is good. And thus he is a God who can declare his creation good. If he had been eternally alone, preoccupied only with himself, it is hard to believe he could do that."[15]

---

[10] Michael Reeves, *Delighting in the Trinity: An Introduction to the Christian Faith* (IVP: Downers Grove, IL, 2012), p. 17.
[11] Reeves, *Delighting in the Trinity*, pp. 17–18.
[12] Reeves, *Delighting in the Trinity*, p. 29.
[13] Reeves, *Delighting in the Trinity*, p. 32.
[14] Reeves, *Delighting in the Trinity*, p. 32.
[15] Reeves, *Delighting in the Trinity*, p. 52.

But Muslims cannot agree with this definition of God as love. Reeves quotes al-Ghazālī, "God does indeed love them [people], but in reality He loves nothing other than Himself, in the sense that He is the totality [of being], and there is nothing in being apart from Him," and comments,

> Because Allah really "loves nothing other than Himself," he does not really turn outward to express his love to others. Thus there can be no reason why anything else should exist. Really, therefore, "there is nothing in being apart from Him." Of course, the Qur'an speaks of Allah's love and of creation, but it is hard to see quite how those things can be. The universe, in Islamic thought, must have only a shadowy, uncertain existence.[16]

It is interesting to observe that this introduction to the Trinity should be written with Islam in mind, and that Reeves should have taken the trouble to read the Qur'ān and al-Ghazālī. But his conclusion is that the message of the Trinity is completely at odds with the message of Islam and that it is best to declare the wonder of the love of God even if Muslims cannot accept this.

Another example of this trend is Gerald Bray, who was research professor of divinity at Beeson Divinity School and an ordained Church of England minister when he produced a one-volume systematic theology in 2012 entitled *God is Love: A Biblical and Systematic Theology*. In a section considering the relationship of other religions to Christianity, he regards Islam as "a regression from the saving message of Jesus Christ to something altogether more limited. It is a religion of justice rather than of love, of fate rather than of forgiveness and restoration to new life."[17] The denial of the Trinity in Islam results in a view of God that is beyond the reach of human beings. "Shorn of such doctrines as the Trinity and the divinity of Christ, Islam can justly claim to offer its followers a simpler form of monotheism than Christianity does, but the price it has paid for this is the loss of any personal relationship with God."[18] Thus, the task of Christians is to witness to the Trinity rather than to attempt to argue for the Trinity in terms Muslims understand.

> Islam means submission to an all-powerful and hidden deity, not fellowship with the Father, Son, and Holy Spirit in the inner life of God. Or to put it a different way, Muslims can never see themselves as anything more than servants of God, whereas Christians affirm that we are his children, a difference of status that makes all the difference in the world.[19]

Similar sentiments are seen in Andy Bannister's 2021 book *Do Muslims and Christians Worship the Same God?* Bannister has a PhD in Islamic studies from the London School of Theology on the way that the oral environment of seventh-century Arabia had left its mark on the text of the Qur'ān. Eleven years of encounters with Muslims in London led him to the conclusion "that Christianity

---

[16] Reeves, *Delighting in the Trinity*, p. 52. He quotes from Abu Hamid al-Ghazālī, *The Revival of Religious Studies*, Reza Shah-Kazemi (trans.), (Louisville: Fons Vitae, 2002), 6:36.

[17] Gerald Bray, *God is Love: A Biblical and Systematic Theology* (Wheaton Illinois: Crossway, 2012), p. 433.

[18] Bray, *God is Love*, p. 433.

[19] Bray, *God is Love*, p. 461.

was true – uniquely, exclusively true – and Islam was not merely wholly different, but also *false*."[20] His thorough study of the Qurʾān resulted in his belief that the descriptions of God found there are significantly different from those found in the Bible. The descriptions of God that are common to the Bible and the Qurʾān are outweighed by the descriptions that are not similar. "It is perfectly possible for Muslims and Christians to agree entirely that God *exists* – even to agree on some of God's functions (creating, ruling, judging). But that's not enough; rather, we must ask about the *identity* of the god that Muslims and Christians believe in and see how well the descriptions line up."[21] Bannister chooses five characteristics that are central to the identity of the God of the Bible and compares these with the portrayal of Allah in the Qurʾān.

Firstly, the God of the Bible is relational but the God of the Qurʾān is transcendent. Isaiah 57:15 has God saying, "I live in a high and holy place, but also with the one who is contrite and lowly in spirit", and Revelation 21:1 states, "Behold the dwelling of God is with humanity, and he will take up residence with them, and they will be his people and God himself will be with them". Bannister concludes, "The biblical theme of God's relationality appears at the *beginning* of history, at creation; it appears in the *middle* of biblical history, in the person of Jesus; and it also appears at the *end* of history, in the Bible's highly relational language of what our eternal future will be like."[22] He contrasts this relationality of God in the Bible with the utter transcendence of God in the Qurʾān, which says more than fifty times that "Allah is over all things", and quotes the British Muslim Shabbir Akhtar, who compares the Islamic view of God with the Christian one. "Muslims do not see God as their father … Men are servants of a just master; they cannot, in orthodox Islam, typically attain any greater degree of intimacy with their creator."[23]

Secondly, the God of the Bible can be known but the God of the Qurʾān can be known about, although not known in a relationship. In Exodus 3:14, God reveals His identity at the burning bush to Moses, "I am who I am", making Himself known by His personal name, and in Jeremiah 24:7, God says to Israel, "I will give to them a heart to know me, that I am Yahweh, and they will be my people, and I will be their God, for they will return to me with the whole of their heart." John 14:6-9 has Jesus saying, "I am the way, the truth and the life. No one comes to the Father except through me. If you really knew me, you would know the Father as well. From now on, you do know him and have seen him."[24] However, when the Qurʾān relates the story of Moses at the burning bush in Q. 20:10-16, God calls Himself "Your Lord". Bannister uses this to argue that "The Qurʾān takes the famous biblical story of Moses and the burning bush and removes from it the tender scene where God reveals his own, personal name".[25]

---

[20] Bannister, *Do Muslims and Christians Worship the Same God?*, p. 13.
[21] Bannister, *Do Muslims and Christians Worship the Same God?* p. 48.
[22] Bannister, *Do Muslims and Christians Worship the Same God?* p. 50.
[23] Bannister, *Do Muslims and Christians Worship the Same God?* p. 51. He quotes from Shabbir Akhtar, *A Faith for All Seasons: Islam and the Challenge of the Modern World* (Chicago, IL: Ivan R. Dee, 1990), p. 180.
[24] Bannister, *Do Muslims and Christians Worship the Same God?* p. 56.
[25] Bannister, *Do Muslims and Christians Worship the Same God?* p. 57.

As for Jesus, "The Qur᾽ān takes the person of Jesus (the ultimate example of God's making Himself known in the Bible) and downgrades him to being just another messenger in Q4:171."[26] Bannister concludes, "For the Qur᾽ān, one can know *about* Allah and know that Allah has sent prophets and messengers (such as Jesus) so that human beings might be without excuse. But when it comes to Allah revealing *himself*, that is a line that the Qur᾽ān steadfastly refuses to cross," and quotes the Palestinian Muslim Isma᾽il al-Fārūqī, "Allah does not reveal Himself to anyone in any way. Allah reveals only his will … that is the greatest difference between Christianity and Islam."[27]

Thirdly, the God of the Bible is holy in moral perfection but the God of the Qur᾽ān is holy because he is all-powerful, not because he is morally perfect. Bannister quotes Habakkuk 1:12-13, "O Yahweh my God, my holy one. Your eyes are too pure to see evil, and you are not able to look at wrongdoing," and Matthew 5:48 where Jesus says, "Be perfect, as your heavenly Father is perfect." He points out that the Qur᾽ān calls Allah "holy" three times in Q59:23, 2:30 and 62:1, and comments, "It is not because he is too holy to look on sin that Allah judges, but because he is all-powerful," quoting Q27:78, "Surely your Lord will decide between them by his judgment. He is the Mighty, the Knowing."[28] Bannister argues that the God of the Qur᾽ān does not judge humans on the basis of his moral purity, as is testified in the Bible. "When Allah does judge, he does so not out of his character as holy and pure, nor out of any kind of faithfulness to promises or covenants he has made with humanity, but purely arbitrarily, out of his will."[29]

Fourthly, the God of the Bible is love but the God of the Qur᾽ān acts in mercy. Bannister appeals to the statement "His love endures forever", repeated twenty-six times in Psalm 136. He quotes God saying in Jeremiah 31:3, "I have loved you with an everlasting love; I have drawn you with loving-kindness", and then the description in John 3:16, and 1 John 4:16, that "God is love". He concludes, "Love is not something God *does*; love is something God *is*. This gives Christians tremendous confidence in their ability to trust God, knowing that the heart of his identity is love."[30] Bannister believes that the love of God is central to the New Testament revelation of the Trinity of Father, Son and Holy Spirit. He argues, "If God was not triune but single and solitary, it would not be possible for him to be loving without first creating something to love," and quotes the British Evangelical theologian Michael Reeves, who believes that the Father, Son and Holy Spirit represent "a God who is not essentially lonely, but who has been loving for all eternity as the Father has loved the Son in the Spirit. Loving others is not a strange or novel thing for this God at all; it is at the root of who

[26] Bannister, *Do Muslims and Christians Worship the Same God?* p. 58.

[27] Bannister, *Do Muslims and Christians Worship the Same God?* p. 58. He quotes from Isma᾽il al-Fārūqī, 'On the Nature of Islamic Da῾wah', *Proceedings of the Chambésy Dialogue Consultation* (Leicester: Islamic Foundation, 1982), pp. 47–48.

[28] Bannister, *Do Muslims and Christians Worship the Same God?* p. 60.

[29] Bannister, *Do Muslims and Christians Worship the Same God?* pp. 60–61.

[30] Bannister, *Do Muslims and Christians Worship the Same God?* p. 62.

he is."[31] When it comes to the Qur'ān, Bannister says that "The Qur'ān is very reticent about talking of Allah and love. Twenty-three times Allah is described as not loving unbelievers. Nineteen times Allah is said to love those who obey him," and quotes the Muslim scholar Daud Rahbar, "There is not a single verse in the Qur'ān that speaks of God's unconditional love for mankind."[32] Despite this, the Yale Christian theologian Miroslav Volf has argued, according to Bannister, that "The mercy of God is effectively the same as his love."[33] But this cannot be defended from a Muslim interpretation of the Qur'ān, which is represented by Murad Hofmann when he writes, "In the Qur'ān we are told that Allah is self-sufficient. This fundamental self-description definitely excludes that Allah is in love with his creation … therefore it is safer and more accurate not to speak of 'love' when addressing His clemency, compassion, benevolence, goodness, or mercy".[34]

Fifthly, the God of the Bible has suffered but the God of the Qur'ān does not suffer. Bannister quotes Genesis 6:6, "Yahweh regretted that he had made humankind on the earth, and he was grieved in his heart," and Hosea 11:1-2, 8, "When Israel was a child, I loved him, and out of Egypt I called my son. But the more I called Israel, the further they went from me … How can I give you up, Ephraim? How can I hand you over, Israel? My heart is changed within me; all my compassion is aroused." Paul describes divine suffering in Philippians 2:6-11, and Bannister quotes the Anglican New Testament scholar Richard Bauckham, "Jesus' humiliation belongs to the identity of God as truly as his exaltation does. The identity of God – who God is – is revealed as much in self-abasement and service as it is in exaltation and rule. The God who is high can also be low, because God is God not in seeking his own advantage but in self-giving."[35]

Bannister turns to the Qur'ān and finds, "As one reads the Qur'ān, it is certainly clear that human sinfulness and disobedience is a problem, that Allah gets angry about sin, but nowhere is there any hint of sadness or grief."[36] He holds that the difference between the Bible and the Qur'ān at this point is down to the concept of humans being made in the image of God.

> That human beings bear the image of God is not some peripheral theological idea; it is absolutely central to the Bible's understanding of who human beings are and it

---

[31] Bannister, *Do Muslims and Christians Worship the Same God?* p. 62. He quotes from Reeves, *Delighting in the Trinity*, pp. 40–41.

[32] Bannister, *Do Muslims and Christians Worship the Same God?* p. 63. He quotes from Daud Rahbar, *God of Justice: A Study in the Ethical Doctrine of the Qur'ān* (Leiden: Brill, 1960), p. 225.

[33] Bannister, *Do Muslims and Christians Worship the Same God?* p. 64. He refers to Volf, *Allah*, pp. 153–56.

[34] Bannister, *Do Muslims and Christians Worship the Same God?* p. 64. He quotes from Hofmann, 'Differences Between the Muslim and the Christian Concept of Divine Love', pp. 8–9.

[35] Bannister, *Do Muslims and Christians Worship the Same God?* pp. 65–67. He quotes from Richard Bauckham, *God Crucified: Monotheism and Christology in the New Testament* (Carlisle: Paternoster Press, 1998), p. 61.

[36] Bannister, *Do Muslims and Christians Worship the Same God?* p. 68.

> flows very naturally out of the Bible's understanding of who God is. Not least, it suggests that because we have been made in the image of a God who is relational and personal, we too are relational and personal.[37]

He then quotes Colossians 1:15, "The Son is the image of the invisible God" and argues, "In other words, says the Bible, if you want to understand why human beings are the way they are – personal, relational, creative, moral and so forth – you must look to the God whose image they bear. And if you want to understand what that image looks like in all its fullness, look to Jesus."[38] This Biblical teaching is in stark contrast, according to Bannister, to Qur'ānic teaching, which emphasises that nothing can be compared to God. In the final analysis, "Islamic theology has always been very clear that Allah is utterly other; no human being, neither individual nor corporately, could represent him."[39]

The view that love is central to the Trinity is shared by some of the theologians surveyed in this book. David Brown articulated the same emphasis on love in 1969 when he stated,

> A solitary centre of personal consciousness would have had no activity beyond the contemplation of himself and this, we imagine, would have been barren and fruitless. The divine being, however, conceived in terms of the Divine Trinity, would have found the fullest and most fruitful of activity in the mutual and ever-loving relationships of the three centres of personal consciousness within the divine being.[40]

David Shenk in 1980 expressed similar views. "How does one express the awareness that God loves totally, that the very essence of God is love, that even within God Himself there is an ongoing, eternal fellowship of self-giving love, that the very unity of God is bound up in His eternal self-giving love"?[41] Miroslav Volf in 2011 describes the Trinity as a relationship of love.

> The one God is internally differentiated, and from the "beginning" God loves 'the other' ... Moreover, the kind of love that is at the foundation of all reality, then, is not love that ultimately redounds to itself. Instead, it is a love that gives to the other as well as receives from the other. From this standpoint, God's creating to benefit creatures is exactly what God's love does – it gives to the other for the other's sake, and not merely for one's own sake.[42]

Imad Shehadeh likewise regards the mutual love of the members of the Trinity as the central motif. "The eternal relationship between the Father and the Son is characterized by a horizontal equally reciprocal relationship in love, knowledge, indwelling, glorifying and the association of the Holy Spirit with all the attributes active between them".[43] This reciprocal love is then poured out on human beings. "It is astonishing that the mutual indwelling of the persons of the Trinity extends

---

[37] Bannister, *Do Muslims and Christians Worship the Same God?* p. 81.
[38] Bannister, *Do Muslims and Christians Worship the Same God?* p. 82.
[39] Bannister, *Do Muslims and Christians Worship the Same God?* p. 84.
[40] Brown, *The Divine Trinity*, p. 80.
[41] Luqa, *Islam and Christianity*, p. 86.
[42] Volf, *Allah*, p. 169.
[43] Shehadeh, *God With Us*, p. 257.

to believers. So the Father, Son and Holy Spirit dwell within believers, and believers are in the Father and the Son."[44]

The reaction of Muslims to the Trinity has not changed much between the two periods. Muslims have rejected the Christian reading of the Son and the Spirit in Q4:171. They have questioned the handling of the Word and Spirit from God in Jesus in Q4:171 to mark essential attributes in God. Either attributes of speech and life are thought to be metaphors for God's essential being, or they are simply two of seven attributes that are essential to God's being. Christian attempts to find analogies for threeness within oneness in the created world have been rejected by Muslims as inappropriate for the transcendent majesty of God, who is beyond compare. Above all, Muslims sense that Christians wish to enlarge the oneness of God by adding two individuals, Jesus and the Holy Spirit. Yet the necessity for Christians to explain their belief in the Trinity will never diminish and they will continue to find ways to present that belief in terms that Muslims can understand, even if they think that Christians are misguided. For Christians, the love of God is seen in the reciprocal relationships between the Father, Son and Holy Spirit, who each express that love to human beings as the overwhelming grace of the one Creator of everything.

---

[44] Shehadeh, *God With Us*, p. 296.

Bibliography

ʿAbduh, Muhammad, *Risalat al-Tawhid*, *The Theology of Unity*, Ishaq Musaʿad and Kenneth Cragg (trans.), (London: George Allen and Unwin, 1966).

Abū Qurra, Theodore, 'Treatise on the Trinity', in Constantin Bacha (ed.), *Les Oeuvres Arabes de Théodore Aboucara* (Beyrouth: Maṭbaʿat al-Fawāʾid, 1904), 23–47.

Abū Rāʾiṭa, Ḥabīb Ibn Khidma, 'Reply to the Melkites on the Union (of the Divine and Human in Christ)', in Georg Graf (ed.), *Die Schriften des Jacobiten Ḥabīb Ibn Ḫidma Abū Rāʾiṭa*, CSCO 130 (Louvain: L. Durbecq, 1951), 65–72.

Abū Rāʾiṭa, Ḥabīb Ibn Khidma, 'The First Letter on the Holy Trinity', in Sandra T. Keating (ed. and trans.), *Defending the 'People of Truth' in the Early Islamic Period: The Christian Apologies of Abū Rāʾiṭa* (Leiden: Brill, 2006), 164–215.

Akhtar, Shabbir, *A Faith for All Seasons: Islam and the Challenge of the Modern World* (Chicago, IL: Ivan R. Dee, 1990).

ʿAmmār al-Baṣrī, 'Book of the Proof Concerning the Course of the Divine Economy', in Michel Hayek (ed.), *ʿAmmār al-Baṣrī: Apologie et Controverses* (Beyrouth: Dar el-Machreq, 1977), 19–90.

ʿAmmār al-Baṣrī, 'Book of Questions and Answers', in Michel Hayek (ed.), *ʿAmmār al-Baṣrī: Apologie et Controverses* (Beyrouth: Dar el-Machreq, 1977), 93–265.

Aquinas, Thomas, *Summa Contra Gentiles*, *vol. 1*, AC Pegis (trans.), (Notre Dame IN: Notre Dame University Press, 1975).

Aquinas, Thomas, *Summa Contra Gentiles*, *vol. 4*, CJ O'Neil (trans.), (Notre Dame IN: Notre Dame University Press, 1975).

Aristotle, *Metaphysics, Books I–IX, vol. 17*, Hugh Tredennick (trans.), (London: Heinemann, 1933).

Aristotle, *The Categories, vol. 1*, Harold P. Cooke and Hugh Tredennick (eds and (trans), (London: Heinemann, 1983).

Augustine, *The Trinity*, Edmund Hill (trans.), (Brooklyn: New City Press, 1991).

Awad, Najib George, *Orthodoxy in Arabic Terms*: *A Study of Theodore Abu Qurrah's Theology in its Islamic Context* (Berlin: De Gruyter, 2015).

Aydin, Mahmut, *Modern Western Christian Theological Understandings of Muslims Since the Second Vatican Council* (Washington, DC: The Council for Research in Values and Philosophy, 2002).

Bannister, Andy, *Do Muslims and Christians Worship the Same God?* (London: IVP, 2021).

Al-Bāqillānī, Abū Bakr, 'Refutation of the Christians in the Book of Introduction', in David Thomas (ed. and trans.), *Christian Doctrines in Islamic Theology* (Leiden: Brill, 2008), 144–203.

Basetti-Sani, Giulio, 'For a Dialogue Between Christians and Muslims', *Muslim World* 57 (1967), 186–96.

Basetti-Sani, Giulio, *The Koran in the Light of Christ* (Chicago: Franciscan Herald Press, 1977).

Bauckham, Richard, *God Crucified: Monotheism and Christology in the New Testament* (Carlisle: Paternoster Press, 1998).

Beaumont, Mark, *Christology in Dialogue with Muslims: A Critical Analysis of Christian Presentations of Christ for Muslims from the Ninth and Twentieth Centuries* (Oxford: Regnum, 2005).

Beaumont, Mark, 'Speaking of the Triune God: Christian Defence of the Trinity in the Early Islamic Period', *Transformation* 29 (2012), 111–27.

Beaumont, Mark, 'Debating the Concept of God', in Douglas Pratt and Charles Tieszen (eds), *Christian–Muslim Relations*; *A Bibliographical History, vol. 15*: *Thematic Essays (600–1600)* (Leiden: Brill, 2020), 99–112.

Beaumont, Mark, *The Theology of ʿAmmār al-Baṣrī: Commending Christianity Within Islamic Culture* (Piscataway, NJ: Gorgias Press, 2021).

Beaumont, Mark, *ʿAmmār al-Baṣrī's Arabic Apologetics: The Book of the Proof Concerning the Course of the Divine Economy and the Book of Questions and Answers* (Piscataway, NJ: Gorgias Press, 2022).

Bell, Joseph N., *Love Theory in Later Hanbalite Islam* (Albany: State University of New York Press, 1979).

Bennett, Clinton, 'The Legacy of Karl Gottlieb Pfander', *International Bulletin of Missionary Research* 20 (1996), 76–81.

Bennett, Clinton, *Understanding Christian–Muslim Relations* (New York: Continuum, 2008).

Bettenson, Henry (trans.), *The Early Christian Fathers* (Oxford: Oxford University Press, 1969).

Bettenson, Henry (trans.), *The Later Christian Fathers* (Oxford: Oxford University Press, 1970).

Bidawid, Raphaël J. (ed. and (trans., *Les Lettres du Patriarche Nestorien Timothée I* (Rome: Testi e Studi, 1956).

Boff, Leonardo, *Trinity and Society* (Maryknoll, NY: Orbis, 1988).

Brannan, Rick (ed.), *Historic Creeds and Confessions*, available at www.ccel.org.

Bray, Gerald, *God is Love: A Biblical and Systematic Theology* (Wheaton Illinois: Crossway, 2012).

Brown, David, *The Divine Trinity* (London: Sheldon Press, 1969).

Brunner, Emil, *Revelation and Reason* (London: SCM Press, 1947).

Bualwan, Kamal, 'Yaḥya ibn ʿAdī's conception of "the One"', *Parole de l'Orient* 28 (2003), 485–95.

Cheikho, HPJ, *Dialectique du Langage sur Dieu: Lettre de Timothee I (728–823) à Serge* (Rome: Pontificum Institutum Studiorum Orientalium, 1983).

Cragg, Kenneth, *The Call of the Minaret* (New York: Oxford University Press, 1956).

Cragg, Kenneth, *Jesus and the Muslim*: *An Exploration* (London: George Allen & Unwin, 1985).

Cumming, Joseph, 'ṣifāt al-dhāt in al-Ashʿarī's Doctrine of God and Possible Christian Parallels', in Evelyne A. Reisacher (ed.), *Toward Respectful Understanding and Witness Among Muslims* (Pasadena, CA: William Carey Library, 2012), 111–45.

Cunningham, David, 'Developing Alternative Trinitarian Formulas', *Anglican Theological Review* 80 (1998), 8–29.

Al-Dimashqī, Ibn Abī Ṭālib al-Anṣārī, 'Response to the Letter from the People of Cyprus', in Rifaat Ebied and David Thomas (eds and trans), *The Letter from the People of Cyprus and Ibn Abī Ṭālib al-Dimashqī's Response* (Leiden: Brill, 2005), 150–497.

Dodge, Bayard (trans.), *The Fihrist of al-Nadīm: A Tenth-Century Survey of Muslim Culture, vol. 1* (New York: Columbia University Press, 1970).

Ebied Rifaat and David Thomas, *The Letter from the People of Cyprus and Ibn Abī Ṭālib al-Dimashqī's Response* (Leiden: Brill, 2005).

Esack, Farid, *Qurʾan Liberation & Pluralism: An Islamic Perspective of Interreligious Solidarity Against Oppression* (Oxford: Oneworld, 1997).

Al-Fārūqī, Ismaʿīl, 'On the Nature of Islamic Daʿwah', *International Review of Missions* 65 (1976), 391–409.

Al-Fārūqī, Ismaʿīl, 'On the Nature of Islamic Daʿwah', *Proceedings of the Chambésy Dialogue Consultation* (Leicester: Islamic Foundation, 1982).

Faultless, Julian, 'Ibn al-Ṭayyib', in David Thomas and Alex Mallett (eds), *Christian–Muslim Relations: A Bibliographical History, vol.* 2 (Leiden: Brill, 2011), 667–97.

Frank, Richard M., *Beings and Their Attributes: The Teaching of the Basrian School of the Muʿtazila in the Classical Period* (Albany NY: State University of New York Press, 1978).

Al-Ghazālī, Abū Ḥāmid, in Reza Shah-Kazemi (trans.),*The Revival of Religious Sciences* (Louisville: Fons Vitae, 2002).

Gibson, Margaret D. (ed. and trans.), *A Treatise on the Triune Nature of God* (London: Cambridge University Press, 1899).

Glei, Reinhold F., 'The Heresy of the Ishmaelites', in David Thomas and Barbara Roggema (eds), *Christian–Muslim Relations: A Bibliographical History, vol. 1* (Leiden: Brill, 2009), 297–301.

Graf, Georg, *Geschichte der Christlichen Arabischen Literatur*, vol. 2 (Vatican City: Biblioteca Apostolica Vaticana, 1944–1953).

Griffith, Sidney H., 'Ḥabīb ibn Ḫidmah Abū Rāʾiṭah, a Christian *mutakallim* of the First Abbasid Century', *Oriens Christianus* 64 (1980), 161–201.

Griffith, Sidney H., 'The Concept of *Al-Uqnūm* in ʿAmmār al-Baṣrī's Apology for the Doctrine of the Trinity', in Samir K. Samir (ed.), *Actes du Premier Congrès International d'Études Arabes Chrétiennes* (Rome: Pontificum Institutum Studiorum Orientalium, 1982), 169–90.

Griffith, Sidney H., 'ʿAmmār al-Baṣrī's *Kitāb al-Burhān:* Christian Kalām in the First Abbasid Century', *Le Museon* 96 (1983), 145–81.

Griffith, Sidney H. 'The Monks of Palestine and the Growth of Christian Literature in Arabic', *The Muslim World* 78 (1988), 1–28.

Griffith, Sidney H., *The Church in the Shadow of the Mosque* (Princeton: Princeton University Press, 2008).

Griffith, Sidney H., 'Paul of Antioch', in Samuel Noble and Alexander Treiger (eds), *The Orthodox Church in the Arab World 700–1700* (DeKalb: Northern Illinois University Press, 2014), 216–35.

Gunton, Colin, *The One, the Three and the Many* (Cambridge: Cambridge University Press, 1993).

Haddad, Rachid, *La Trinité Divine Chez les Théologiens Arabes 750–1050* (Paris: Beauchesne, 1985).

Haddad, Wadi Z., 'A Tenth-Century Speculative Theologian's Refutation of the Basic Doctrines of Christianity: Al-Baqillani (d. AD 1013)', in Yvonne Yazbeck Haddad and Wadi Z. Haddad (eds), *Christian–Muslim Encounters* (Gainsville: University of Florida Press, 1995), 82–94.

Hodgson, Leonard, *The Doctrine of the Trinity* (London: Nisbet, 1943).

Hofmann, Murad W., 'Differences Between the Muslim and the Christian Concept of Divine Love', in *14th General Conference of the Royal Aal al-Bayt Institute for Islamic Thought* (Amman, 2007), 1–14.

Husseini, Sara L., *Early Christian–Muslim Debate on the Unity of God: Three Christian Scholars and their Engagement with Islamic Thought* (Leiden: Brill, 2014).

Ibn ʿAdī, Yaḥya, 'Treatise Explaining in Which Respect it is Valid for the Christians to Say that the Creator is One Substance and Three Hypostases', in Augustin Périer (ed.), *Maqālāt li-Yaḥya ibn ʿAdī. Petits Traités Apologétiques de Yaḥya ibn ʿAdī* (Paris: J. Gabalda, 1920), 44–62.

Ibn ʿAdī, Yaḥya, 'Treatise Concerning the Rightness of the Christian Belief that the Creator is One Substance and Three Attributes', in Louis Cheikho (ed.), *Vingt Traités Théologique d'Auteurs Arabes Chrétiens (IX au XIIIe Siècle)* (Beirut: Imprimerie Catholique, 1920), 70–74.

Ibn ʿAdī, Yaḥya, 'Treatise Showing the Errors of Abū Yūsuf Yaʿqub ibn Ishaq al-Kindī's Refutation of the Christians', in Augustin Périer (ed.), 'Un Traité de Yaḥya ibn ʿAdī: Défense du Dogme de la Trinité Contre les Objections d'al-Kindi', *Revue de L'Orient Chrétien* 22 (1920–1921), 3–12.

Ibn ʿAdī, Yaḥya, 'Treatise on the Unity of God According to the Teaching of the Christians', in Samir K. Samir (ed.), *Le Traité de l-Unité de Yaḥya ibn ʿAdī (893–974)* (Jounieh: Patrimoine Arabe Chrétien 2, 1980).

Ibn Taymiyya, Taqī al-Dīn Aḥmad, 'A Sound Reply to the One who Changed the Religion of the Messiah', in Thomas F. Michel (trans.), *A Muslim Theologian's Response to Christianity* (New York: Caravan Books, 1984).

Ibn al-Ṭayyib, Abū al-Faraj ʿAbd Allāh, 'The Third Treatise on the Trinity', Michael F. Kuhn (trans.), in Michael F. Kuhn, *God is One: A Christian Defence of Divine Unity in the Muslim Golden Age* (Carlisle: Langham, 2019), 238–61.

Ibn al-Ṭayyib, Abū al-Faraj ʿAbd Allāh, 'The Second Treatise on the Trinity', Michael F. Kuhn (trans.), in Ayman S. Ibrahim (ed.), *Medieval Encounters: Arabic-Speaking Christians and Islam* (Piscataway, NJ: Gorgias Press, 2022), 440–48.

Iliyyā of Nisibis, 'Session 1', in Samir K. Samir (ed.), 'Entretien d'Elie de Nisibe avec le vizir Ibn ʿAli al-Maghribi sur l'unité et la Trinité', *Islamochristiana* 5 (1979), 31–117.

Iliyyā of Nisibis, 'Treatise on Kiyān', in Samir K. Samir (ed.), 'Un traité nouveau d'Elie dec Nisibe sur le sens des mots Kiyan et Ilah', *Parole de l'Orient* 14 (1987), 109–53.

Ipgrave, Michael, *Trinity and Inter Faith Dialogue: Plenitude and Plurality* (Bern: Peter Lang, 2003).

Iqbal, Muhammad, *The Reconstruction of Religious Thought in Islam* (Oxford: Oxford University Press, 1934).

John of Damascus, 'The Heresy of the Ishmaelites', Daniel J. Sahas (trans.), in Daniel S. Sahas, *John of Damascus on Islam* (Leiden: Brill, 1972), 132–41.

John of Damascus, *On the Orthodox Faith*, Norman Russell (trans.), (New York: St Vladimir's Seminary Press, 2022).

Kärkkäinen, Veli-Matti, *A Constructive Christian Theology for the Pluralistic World, vol. 1. Christ and Reconciliation* (Grand Rapids: Eerdmans, 2013).

Kärkkäinen, Veli-Matti, *A Constructive Christian Theology for the Pluralistic World, vol. 2. Trinity and Revelation* (Grand Rapids: Eerdmans, 2014).

Kärkkäinen, Veli-Matti, *A Constructive Christian Theology for the Pluralistic World, vol 4. Spirit and Salvation* (Grand Rapids: Eerdmans, 2016).

Kateregga, Badru D. and David W. Shenk, *Islam and Christianity: A Muslim and a Christian in Dialogue* (Nairobi: Uzima Press, 1980).

Knitter, Paul, *One Earth, Many Religions* (Maryknoll NY: Orbis, 1995).

Kuhn, Michael F., *God is One: A Christian Defence of Divine Unity in the Muslim Golden Age* (Carlisle: Langham, 2019).

Kuhn, Michael F., 'Abū al-Faraj ʿAbd Allāh ibn al-Ṭayyib (d. 1043): A Scholar-Priest Explains the Trinitarian Persons', in Ayman S. Ibrahim (ed.), *Medieval Encounters: Arabic-Speaking Christians and Islam* (Piscataway, NJ: Gorgias Press, 2022) 415–52.

Küng, Hans, *Global Responsibility: In Search of a New World Ethic* (New York: Continuum, 1993).

Küng, Hans, *Islam: Past, Present and Future* (Oxford: Oneworld, 2007).

Lamoreaux, John, *Theodore Abu Qurrah* (Provo, Utah: Brigham Young University Press, 2005).

Llull, Ramon, 'The Book of the Gentile and the Three Wise Men', in A. Bonner (trans.), *Selected Works of Ramon Llull (1232–1316), vol. 1* (Princeton: Princeton University Press, 1985).

Lumbard, Joseph, 'What of the Word is Common?', in Waleed El-Ansary and David K. Linnan (eds), *Muslim and Christian Understanding: Theory and Application of "A Common Word"* (New York: Palgrave Macmillan, 2010), 93–109.

Luqa, Ibrahim, *Christianity in Islam* (Rikon: The Good Way, no date).

Madelung, Wilfred, *Der Imām al-Qāsim ibn Ibrāhīm und die Glaubenslehre der Zaidlten* (Berlin: De Gruyter, 1965).

Makhlouf, Avril M., 'The Trinitarian Doctrine of Yaḥya ibn ʿAdī: An Appraisal', *Parole de l'Orient* 10 (1981–1982), 37–50.

Massignon, Louis, *Les Trois Prieres d'Abraham* (Tours: Arrault imprimeur, 1935).

Matthews, Walter R., *God in Christian Experience* (London: Nisbet, 1930).

Mawdudi, Sayyid Abul Aʿla, in Zafar Ishaq Ansari (trans.),*Towards Understanding the Qurʾan, vol. 1* (Leicester: The Islamic Foundation, 1988–1989).
Meyendorff, John, *Byzantine Theology: Historical Trends and Doctrinal Themes* (New York: Fordham University Press, 1974).
Mingana, Alphonse, 'The Apology of Timothy the Patriarch Before the Caliph Mahdi', *Woodbrooke Studies II* (1928), 1–162.
Moltmann, Jürgen, *The Trinity and the Kingdom of God* (London: SCM, 1981).
Al-Nāshiʾ al-Akbar, 'Refutation of the Christians', in David Thomas (ed. and trans.), *Christian Doctrines in Islamic Theology* (Leiden: Brill, 2008), 36–77.
Nasr, Seyyed Hossein, '"A Common Word" Initiative: *Theoria* and *Praxis*', in Waleed El-Ansary and David K. Linnan (eds), *Muslim and Christian Understanding*: *Theory and Application of "A Common Word"* (New York: Palgrave Macmillan, 2010), 21–28.
Pannenberg, Wolfhart, *Systematic Theology, vol. 1* (Grand Rapids: Eerdmans, 1992).
Paul of Antioch, 'Letter to a Muslim Friend', in Rifaat Ebied and David Thomas (eds and trans), *Muslim–Christian Polemic During the Crusades* (Leiden: Brill, 2005), 54–147.
Paul of Antioch, 'Letter to a Muslim Friend', Sidney H. Griffith (trans.), in Samuel Noble and Alexander Treiger (eds), *The Orthodox Church in the Arab World 700–1700* (DeKalb: Northern Illinois University Press, 2014), 219–34.
Périer Augustin (trans.), 'Un traité de Yahya ben ʿAdi, défense du dogme de la trinité contre les objections d'al-Kindi', *ROC* 22 (1920–1922), 13–21.
Peter of Bayt Raʾs, 'Book of the Proof', in Pierre Cachia (ed.), *Eutychius of Alexandria*: *The Book of the Demonstration*, CSCO 192 (Louvain: L. Durbecq, 1960).
Pfander, Karl G., *Miftahuʾl-asrar – the Key of Mysteries: A treatise on the Doctrine of the Trinity in Unity*, W. St Clair Tisdall (trans.), (London: Christian Literature Society for India, 1912).
Platti, Emilio, 'Yaḥya ibn ʿAdī', in David Thomas and Alex Mallett (eds), *Christian–Muslim Relations*: *A Bibliographical History, vol. 2* (Leiden: Brill, 2011), 390–438.
Powell, Avril, *Muslims & Missionaries in Pre-Mutiny India* (Richmond: Curzon Press, 1993).
Putman, Hans, *L'Église sous Timothée I: 780–832* (Beirut: Dar el-Machreq, 1975), appendix, 7–51.
Al-Qāsim ibn Ibrāhīm, 'Refutation of the Christians', in I. di Matteo (ed.), 'Confutazione contro I Cristiani dello zaydati al-Qāsim b. Ibrāhīm', *Rivista degli Studi Orientali* 9 (1921–1922), 301–64.
Rahbar, Daud, *God of Justice: A Study in the Ethical Doctrine of the Qurʾan* (Leiden: Brill, 1960).
Rahman, Fazlur, *Islam* (London: Weidenfeld and Nicolson, 1966).
Rahner, Karl, *The Trinity* (New York: Seabury Press, 1974).
al-Rāzī, Fakhr al-Dīn, *The Large Commentary on the Qurʾān (Al-Tafsīr al-Kabīr*) (Beirut: 1978).

Reeves, Michael, *Delighting in the Trinity: An Introduction to the Christian Faith* (Downers Grove, IL: IVP, 2012).

Ridgeon, Lloyd VJ., *Crescents on the Cross* (Oxford: Oxford University Press, 2001).

Rissanen, Seppo, *Theological Encounter of Oriental Christians with Islam During Early Abbasid Rule* (Åbo: Åbo Akademi University Press, 1993).

Roggema, Barbara, 'The Disputation Between a Monk of Bēt Ḥālē and an Arab Notable', in David Thomas and Barbara Roggema (eds), *Christian–Muslim Relations: A Bibliographical History, vol. I* (Leiden: Brill, 2009), 268–73.

Samir K. Samir, 'The Earliest Arab Apology for Christianity (c. 750)', in Samir K. Samir and Jorgen S. Nielsen (eds), *Christian Arabic Apologetics During the Abbasid Period (750–1258)* (Leiden: Brill, 1994), 57–116.

Schirrmacher, Christine, 'The Agra Debates of 1854', *The Bulletin of the Henry Martyn Institute of Islamic Studies* 13 (1994), 74–84.

Shah-Kazemi, Reza, 'Do Muslims and Christians Believe in the Same God?', in Miroslav Volf (ed.), *Do We Worship the Same God? Jews, Christians, and Muslims in Dialogue* (Grand Rapids: Eerdmans, 2012), 76–147.

Shehadeh, Imad N., *God With Us and Without Us; Volumes One and Two: The Beauty and Power of Oneness in Trinity Versus Absolute Oneness* (Langham: Carlisle, 2020).

Swanson, Mark N., 'Are Hypostases Attributes? An Investigation into the Modern Egyptian Appropriation of the Medieval Arabic Apologetic Heritage', *Parole de l'Orient* 16 (1990–1991), 239–50.

Swanson, Mark N., 'Some Considerations for the Dating of *fī tatlīt allāh al-wāhid* (Sinai Ar. 154) and *al-gāmiʿ wugūh al-īmān* (London, British Library op. 4950)', *Parole de L'Orient* (1993), 118–41.

Swanson, Mark N., 'The Trinity in Christian–Muslim Conversation', *Dialog: A Journal of Theology* 44 (2005), 256–63.

Swanson, Mark N., 'Peter of Bayt Raʾs', in David Thomas and Barbara Roggema (eds), *Christian–Muslim Relations: A Bibliographical History, vol. 1* (Leiden: Brill, 2009), 902–06.

Swanson, Mark N., 'An Apology for the Christian Faith', in Samuel Noble and Alexander Treiger (eds), *The Orthodox Church in the Arab World* (DeKalb, IL: Northern Illinois University Press, 2014), 40–59.

Thomas, David, 'The Doctrine of the Trinity in the Early Abbasid Period', in Lloyd Ridgeon (ed.), *Islamic Interpretations of Christianity* (London: Routledge, 2001), 79–95.

Thomas, David, 'Paul of Antioch's *Letter to a Muslim Friend* and*The Letter from Cyprus*', in David Thomas (ed.), *Syrian Christians under Islam: The First Thousand Years* (Leiden: Brill, 2001), 195–214.

Tolan, John, 'Liber de Veritate Catholicae Fidei Contra Errores Infidelium qui Dicitur Summa Contra Gentiles', in David Thomas and Alex Mallett (eds), *Christian–Muslim Relations: A Bibliographical History, vol. 4* (Leiden: Brill, 2012), 523–27.

Volf, Miroslav, *Exclusion & Embrace: A Theological Exploration of Identity, Otherness, and Reconciliation* (Nashville: Abingdon Press, 1996).

Volf, Miroslav, *Allah: A Christian Response* (New York: HarperOne, 2011).

Walters, Albert S., *We Believe in One God? Reflections on the Trinity in the Malaysian Context* (Delhi: ISPCK, 2002).

Ward, Keith, *Religion and Revelation: A Theology of Revelation in the World's Religions* (Oxford: Clarendon Press, 1994).

Ward, Keith, *Religion and Creation* (Oxford: Clarendon Press, 1996).

Ward, Keith, *Christ and the Cosmos* (Cambridge: Cambridge University Press, 2015).

Al-Warrāq, Abū ʿĪsā, 'Refutation of the Trinity: The First Part of the Refutation of the Three Christian Sects', in David Thomas (ed. and trans.), *Anti-Christian Polemic in Early Islam* (Cambridge: Cambridge University Press, 1992), 66–181.

Watt, W. Montgomery (trans.), *Eutychius of Alexandria: The Book of the Demonstration*, CSCO 193 (Louvain: L. Durbecq, 1960).

Williams, Rowan, 'A Common Word for the Common Good', letter written 14/07/2008, accessed at acommonword.com.

General Index